# How to Cook

*—over 200 essential recipes to feed yourself,*
*your friends & family*

Annie Bell trained as a chef before becoming the cookery writer for *Vogue*, and then food writer on the *Independent*. She has been principal cookery writer on the *Mail on Sunday's YOU Magazine* for over 15 years. In this, her latest volume, she has gathered together her core repertoire of recipes to hand down to her children. Annie Bell's previous cookbooks include the *Gorgeous* series, *Soup Glorious Soup*, *The Camping Cookbook*, *The Picnic Cookbook*, *Annie Bell's Baking Bible* and *Low Carb Revolution*.

All the recipes have been tested in a fan oven.

All measurements given as spoons are rounded, which is how the ingredient is likely to naturally settle on the spoon. Level or heaped will be specified.

Salt means Maldon flakes, unless it says 'fine'.

Pepper means freshly ground black peppercorns.

Start to Finish Times: These are designed to give you some idea of what time you need to start cooking. None of the recipes involve more than about 20 minutes preparation time.

# How to Cook
*—over 200 essential recipes to feed yourself,*
*your friends & family*

Annie Bell

Photography by Nassima Rothacker

# Contents

# Introduction
## —*today a novice,*
## *tomorrow a cook*

This book has been gently simmering away on the back burner for many years. Ever since I had children really. Knowing that the time would come when they took their first faltering steps into a kitchen, possibly on going to college, before becoming more engrossed in cooking for themselves and their families. That time has come, and so this book is a watershed for me. But it's also a book for my generation.

The bookshelves in our house are positively groaning under the weight of the cookery books they hold, and yet I have lost count of the number of times that someone will have turned to them in need – for a recipe for spaghetti puttanesca, to check the cooking time for roast lamb, to find out the secret ingredients for a glaze for chicken teriyaki, or a sleepy early-morning reminder of a pancake batter – and suddenly felt let down. Plenty of recipes for asparagus bavarois with chanterelles and spit-roast suckling pig, but what about the essentials?

So to kick off this book, I make no apologies for the fact that I have filled it with simple recipes or ones that are familiar favourites. That is the aim. I feel passionately about the need for a cookbook such as this, at a time when, if statistics are to be believed, fewer and fewer people know how to cook. This book has to do with recipes that you are likely to cook day-in, day-out, and as such the real need is for the best possible version, one that has been thoroughly tested and pared down to those steps that are absolutely essential in order to get good results. There are suggestions for how to vary them, and with time you are bound to have your own ideas on this score. My hope is that you will take the recipes and make them your own.

The kind of food that you will relish cooking in the long-term will be just as personal as the music you listen to, the clothes you wear and the books that capture your imagination. So it matters that you learn to cook your way – in your own time and at your own pace – and finish your dishes in a way that reflects who you are. No one recipe will ever turn out exactly the same at the hands of different cooks, and nor should it. That is the artisanal sleight of hand we seek when out shopping for ingredients. We should value it just as much in our own endeavours. So please don't look at the photographs here as the ultimate, where yours is somehow lesser if it is different.

But what if you have never cooked before, ever? Mum makes the toast, you eat it. Everyone's been there at some point. Watching someone crack an egg for the first time, I cannot but help feel that gauche hesitance as they furtively give it a knock against the side of the bowl, almost scared of what might happen. Learning how to cook is on a par with learning how to drive. At first you consciously think through every single move from flicking the indicator to applying the brake or changing gear. And then, after a while, it becomes so second nature that if you had to stop and analyse what order you did everything in, you would probably stall the car.

And there are plenty of other firsts – from grinding pepper to seasoning a dish with salt, turning on a gas ring, chopping an onion, or peeling garlic cloves. But there is a real pleasure in acquiring this multitude of tiny skills. This book is not about mastering complicated techniques, it's more about learning how to feel at ease with the many small processes that together add up to being a cook.

It also helps enormously to understand why you are performing any particular task in the way that is suggested. Recipes are very good at telling you what to do, without necessarily explaining the reason. Why do you season a chicken before it is roasted rather than after? Why do you kick off a vinaigrette with a teaspoon of Dijon mustard, or add a little oil to the pan when frying with butter? Why do you smack cucumbers for a Korean salad? Why do you get better crackling if you cut the rind off the meat and roast it separately? Answer all these questions, and you are well on your way to becoming a cook. The key to independence is understanding as well as doing. Hence the footnotes or KNACKS below the recipes, designed to give you that extra bit of information.

None of us carries an encyclopedic knowledge of cooking temperatures and times – there is always a need to look these things up – but life in the kitchen becomes ever more fluid as your confidence and independence grows. If you understand the core steps of pot-roasting a chicken, making a frittata, or mixing a dressing (actually we still look that one up in our house), cooking soon becomes a pleasure.

My own cookery journey goes from childhood Rock Cakes, gleaned from what is now a kitsch period-piece, Paul Hamlyn's *Cookery in Colour*, on to working my way through Jane Grigson's classics and Margaret Costa's *Four Seasons Cookery Book* in my twenties. And then, via the occasional stint as a chef, to today, when I still get the same frisson from trying to cook a dish in a new and different way to how I did it all those years ago. Cooking is a journey.

The collection of recipes that follows seeks to take you on a tour through all the classical or great marriages of ingredients. I personally don't believe that you can mix the flavour palates and types of dishes particular to different cultures with any great abandon. I can think of a handful of chefs who do this with real panache, but they are the exception. For the most part it simply muddies the landscape. Soy sauce in Italian food? Olive oil in Japanese? Ravioli with a curry? Not for me. If I am going to combine pork with apple and I want a third partner, it is unlikely to be miso and more likely mustard, because these ingredients share a geographical heritage and somehow work together. Flavour combinations are to do with lateral thinking. If you have a particular ingredient to hand and you want to marry it with another, the best way forward is to start by asking yourself where it derives from and what else comes from that area. If you base dishes on this time-honoured alchemy, you will never go far wrong.

Just because food is familiar isn't to say we cannot enjoy it in a way that is up-to-date and fashionable. So often it is how we serve food that dates it more than the dish itself – start googling the decades and all will become clear, from the presentation and table decorations to the choice of plates, cutlery and glasses. I relish the way that eating has become much more relaxed in recent years, which tallies with my own love of rusticity, or food that is spontaneous, messy and carefree. I enjoy being able to eat with my fingers, to wipe a plate clean with whatever salad or vegetables have been placed centrally on the table. In fact, in our house at suppertime, everything is plonked on the table – on a trivet if it is searing hot, usually in the pan in which it has cooked – and everyone is free to get in there and combine the dishes in the way they want. So everything in this book is about big sharing bowls and plates.

And lastly an introduction to the cast you are likely to encounter in the pages that follow, as my pleasure in cooking lies with having someone to eat and share it with, which I couldn't be doing without my husband Jonnie and son Louis. The recipes are infused with their love of comforting home-cooked classics. They are my toughest critics, and any new dish placed on the table is closely scrutinised as we discuss if it could have been done differently, or improved. And then there is Rothko, our lovely disabled son, who can't cook but loves eating, and has great taste.

—*Annie Bell*

# Capsule Kitchen

Whenever anyone visits us for the first time, their reaction when they see my kitchen is invariably 'you cook in that?' Well, yes, I do. It may well be on the micro side but it never feels small to me, being one end of a conservatory gives the illusion of space. I have always been completely happy cooking in galley kitchens, where nothing is further away than a yoga plunge, compared to my farmhouse kitchen in France where I manage my twenty-minute daily walk simply in the throes of unstacking the dishwasher.

Some of the best fun is to be had in cooking in challenging circumstances, and I look back fondly to the one-ring Baby Belling in our garret flat just after leaving university when I cooked much more ambitiously than I do today. Big kitchens don't necessarily make for better food. And as with travelling, there is a certain relief to be told it's hand luggage only. You pack what you actually need. It is surprising just how little it takes to cook, both in terms of space and equipment.

I am forever advising people who want to learn to cook, to go and do a *stage* in a professional kitchen. Even if you never get any further than peeling potatoes, the discipline of working in a tiny space will remain with you all your life. You have your board, a large one, on which you do pretty much everything, with a small amount of space around. Making a mess is a luxury you can't afford – if you don't clear up and wipe down after one task there is no room to start the next one. It is a tardis-like operation.

### Getting organised

A recipe, essentially, is a map designed to get you from A to B without losing you along the way. The quality of the recipe is clearly important, and that's my job, but equally as driver you need to read it through from start to finish before setting off. One of the keys to success in cooking is organisation – making sure that you have everything you need prepared and ready for the moment it will be used. If, say, you are halfway through frying some vegetables for a dish when suddenly you are told to add a teaspoon each of finely chopped garlic, chilli and ginger, and you haven't prepared them, you stand to burn the vegetables while doing so.

In an ideal world, a kitchen counter should look like one of those studio images on *Masterchef*, lots of little pots and bowls neatly arranged in front of you at the ready. This is exactly how restaurants operate. And clearing up as you go along is also really, really important. I still get the equivalent of bad hair days when I'm cooking, when I can't face the kitchen sink until it is piled so high with pots and pans waiting to be washed that I no longer have anything to cook in. And then I try to rope Jonnie in to help, but this isn't a practice I'm recommending.

# Cooking in the Oven

One of the great differences between home and restaurant cooking lies in our use of the oven. As home cooks we have a huge advantage here. Cooking on a hob may be speedy, but it calls for careful monitoring and attention as well as skill. But pop something into the oven and you can wander off and do something else. So you will find in the recipes that follow, there is a LOT of use of your oven. In fact, if I can possibly transpose a dish from stove-top to oven (e.g. when cooking sausages, risottos or stews, etc.) I will do.

### Fan, electric or gas?

I swear by a fan oven for achieving consistently great results. They are especially good for roasting potatoes, veggies and meat, anything where you want the dish to colour and caramelise. If you are using an electric or gas oven, you may find the temperature will differ slightly from that suggested depending on the brand.

### Preheating the oven and positioning the shelves

The average oven will take around 15 minutes to heat up. Always place the oven shelf in the medium position if you are cooking just one item. If using two shelves, position them about a quarter of the way from the top and the bottom. And never cook on the oven floor, which will only ever result in tears – it is usually one of the heating elements.

*A note of caution:* When opening the oven door to remove anything, stand well back or you may end up with singed eyebrows. Vegetables, in particular, can let out a large cloud of very hot steam, but even dry air can burn.

### Slow-cooking

If a stew or roast takes longer than 2 hours to cook, it falls into the 'slow-cooked' category. This usually involves a low temperature, and is most easily achieved in the oven. Cooking for an extended period on the hob can be very hit and miss. If the heat is that bit too high it will result in the fat from the meat boiling into the juices, whereas at the correct temperature it should settle on the surface ready to be spooned off at the end, making for a lighter and cleaner gravy. There is also less risk of the dish drying out.

### Grilling

With the advent of ridged griddles, most of us use our overhead grills less. But they are a great way of colouring a gratin, or any dish topped with cheese or breadcrumbs. Otherwise contact grilling on a griddle (or a large dry frying pan), is the best route to ensuring that meat, fish and veggies turn golden on the outside while remaining tender and succulent within.

# Cooking on the Hob

### Boiling

Always place small pans over a small ring, otherwise you will end up burning the food in the corners without heating the middle. Bring liquids to the boil over a medium-high heat, but then turn it down to a simmer.

### Frying

Aside from when you are cooking chopped veggies, when it is easiest to heat the oil in the pan before adding the vegetables, frequently the best route when frying larger items such as steaks or chops is to brush the food with oil beforehand, to avoid spattering everything in sight with a fine mist. There is no need for frying to be a greasy process.

*Meat* – fatty meats such as lamb and pork, bacon too, will fry or colour in their own fat, there is no need to add any more. When frying duck breasts, start with the fatty side and drain off the fat as it renders. Lean meats such as chicken and beef benefit from an initial brushing of oil.

*Vegetables* – with the exception of aubergine, which is best brushed with oil beforehand and then seared, here you need to add a tablespoon or two of oil to the pan before adding the vegetables.

*Eggs* – don't overdo the oil here, a teaspoon or two should do it.

*Fish* – fatty fish such as salmon should fry in the rendered fat, but other types are best brushed with oil first and then seared.

---

### Hob Temperature Guide

Give frying pans and saucepans a few minutes to reach the suggested temperature, and 4–5 minutes for cast-iron griddles and casseroles.

*Very low heat* – place the pan on the smallest ring on the lowest heat.

*Low heat* – either place the pan on the smallest ring over a medium-low heat, or on a large ring over a low heat.

*Medium heat* – either place the pan on the smallest ring over a medium-high heat, or over a medium heat on a large ring.

*Medium-high heat* – place the pan on the smallest ring over a high heat, or over a medium-high heat on a large ring.

*High heat* – set the pan over the highest heat the size will allow. If cooking on gas, don't let the flames come up the sides.

---

# Essential Kit

## Utensils

A big jug or pot beside the stove is an ideal way of storing all the utensils you might require during the throes of using the hob. A good starter kit should include:

*Wooden spoons* – for just about everything. They will stand in for a spatula to turn food you are frying, and they won't scratch non-stick.

*Big stainless-steel spoons* – for stirring thick food such as mash or chilli.

*Potato masher* – for pressing the water out of drained vegetables such as spinach, and puréeing certain soups. In fact, a potato masher is useful for all manner of things, bar mashing potatoes when I prefer to use a mouli-legumes.

*Slotted spoon* – for removing vegetables from boiling water, as well as poached eggs and quail's eggs.

*Spatulas* – for loosening and turning food. A metal one is best for the griddle, and a non-stick one for non-stick pans.

*Ladle* – for soups and liquids.

## Pots & Pans

*Non-stick frying pan* – 24cm is a good medium-large size, ideal for frittatas, omelettes and pancakes. A heatproof or detachable handle will allow for it being transferred to the oven.

*4–5 saucepans* – ranging in size from 16–24cm. Stainless steel with a heavy-duty base should see you through a lifetime.

*Non-stick wok* – one with a flat base, and sloping sides. Alternatively you can use a large non-stick frying pan, in which case the best ones, ironically, are the least expensive. It is that cheap-as-chips flimsy non-stick pan in the supermarket, guaranteed to burn anything like a chop or chicken fillet, that will do the best job of stir-frying vegetables quickly. Being thin, the heat reaches the food rapidly – but since you are stir-frying, there is no chance of it burning.

*Cast-iron lidded casserole* – a 30cm oval casserole is a great all-rounder, and the ideal shape for pot-roasting chicken.

*Roasting pans* – a minimum of two cast-iron roasting pans, e.g. 25cm and 38cm, which will also double for pies.

*Non-stick baking sheets* – a couple of these.

*Mixing bowls* – it is hard to have enough of these in a range of sizes. Both ceramic and stainless steel are ideal.

*For stockists, see page 312.*

# Essential Kit

## Key Kit

*Chopping board* – a large wooden board (e.g. 60 x 45cm) will allow you to have multiple stages of a recipe on the go at the same time.

*Knives* – the absolute essentials are a 16cm cook's knife for chopping and working with large cuts of meat or vegetables, a small 12cm paring knife for garlic and other small veggies, and a 14cm serrated knife for tomatoes and anything else likely to be slippery or tricky. A serrated bread knife (e.g. 25cm) is also a must-have.

*Pestle and mortar* – for grinding small quantities of spices.

*Rolling pin* – as well as rolling pastry, this is great for battering butterflied chicken fillets or anything else that needs flattening out.

*Measuring jugs* – a couple of 500ml jugs have multiple uses.

*Electronic scales* – accuracy is everything.

*Timers* – look for one that counts in seconds as well as minutes, and that goes up to 99 or multiple hours as opposed to one or two. A four-way timer is ideal, so much easier than having two or three on the go that hide themselves behind a bag of flour or under a tea-towel.

*Mouli-legumes* – the key to perfect mashed potato, but failing that a potato ricer will perform the same function, albeit slowly.

*Peppermill* – a traditional wooden peppermill is an old friend in the kitchen, but it doesn't need to be larger than 15–18cm tall.

## Gizmos & Gadgets

*Potato peeler* – the classic Rex peeler can't be beaten. I like to have a couple on the go, either to rope in assistance or in case one breaks.

*Magic whisk* – great for making mayonnaise, emulsifying salad dressings and teasing the lumps out of sauces.

*Lemon squeezer* – go for something basic that drains into a cup or pot.

*Zester* – to remove fine strands of lemon, orange or lime zest, leaving behind the bitter pith.

*Garlic press* – the handiest presses come with a removable grid that can be taken out and cleaned with ease.

*Olive pitter* – great for cherries as well as olives.

*Graters* – a traditional box grater that stands on the board is by far the easiest to use and comes with multiple options. A small nutmeg grater is also a good friend.

*Meat thermometer* – for testing the inner temperature of joints of meat (see page 111).

*Pastry brush* – for brushing aubergine and ingredients to be seared, as well as for pastry.

*For stockists, see page 312.*

# Food Processor

I am in awe of this small machine that can carry out pretty much any arduous aspect of cooking with speed and efficiency. Unless you are regularly catering for 6–8 and above, a compact model will do nicely. You don't want a bowl that swamps the ingredients.

The main blade will finely chop and blend. It does a brilliant job of making pastry, reducing the butter to fine crumbs in seconds. Of various attachments, the most useful are the fine and coarse graters, a spiked Parmesan grater, and a slicer for potatoes, carrots and other hard veggies to be layered and baked or eaten raw. The dough blade, too, is good for pizzas. The feeder tube, when marked with measurements, is brilliant for small quantities of liquid up to about 250ml.

Food processors are incredibly easy to use: 'on' and 'off' is about as complicated as it gets, with a 'pulse' button for brief bursts of action. With some preparations, it is a good idea to scrape the bowl down now and again to ensure the ingredients are evenly blended. A mini bowl is great for small quantities.

# Blender

Essential for soups and smoothies where you want a completely smooth texture. The more advanced models also come with an ice-crushing feature which is brilliant for slushies and whizzy ice-creams made using frozen fruit and cream. Never fill the blender beyond halfway – soups especially may spill out from the lid.

# Electric Whisk

In addition to whisking egg whites, you can use this instead of an orbital mixer to incorporate air into cake mixtures.

# Electric Coffee Grinder

Even if you don't grind your own coffee, it's worth having one of these for grinding spices and small quantities of nuts.

# Essential Techniques

## How to Chop an Onion or Shallot

For the novice, a serrated knife is indispensable, for gripping the onion or shallot.

First slice off the top and bottom, and then cut through the skin and outer layer and peel this off. Halve the onion downwards, and place each half flat on the board.

*Sliced* – cut across into half moons.

*Chopped* – slice from the top to the base, at 3–4mm intervals for finely chopped, or approx. 1cm intervals for coarsely chopped. Cut across the slices into dice.

## How to Prepare Chillies

It is the seeds in a chilli that contain the heat; I usually remove them. I prefer medium to very hot chillies, which can be difficult to control. Size is the best indicator of heat, the smaller the fiercer. A heaped teaspoon of finely chopped flesh will provide a noticeable warmth in most recipes. I rarely go hotter, however you can always pep a dish up with the addition of some cayenne pepper.

## How to Skin Tomatoes

Bring a medium-sized pan of water to the boil and fill a large bowl with cold water. Cut out a cone from the top of each tomato and remove the core. Plunge into boiling water for about 20 seconds (if the tomatoes are ripe you may see the skin split, which indicates they are ready), and then into cold water. Slip off the skins.

## How to Zest a Lemon (or other Citrus Fruit)

It is the essential oil in the exterior of the fruit we are after. There are three options here, depending on whether you are going to eat the zest, for instance when flavouring a cake, or simply use it to scent a stew, custard or soup – when it will be removed before eating.

*Finely grated* – for cakes, biscuits, puddings and salad dressings. Either use a fine grater or remove the zest in strands using a zester and finely chop them by hand.

*Coarsely grated* – for risottos, pasta dishes, or where the zest is likely to be cooked. Use a zester to remove fine strands; these will soften during the cooking process.

*Strips of peel* – for sauces, soups, custard or stews. Remove long strips with a potato peeler and discard them at the end.

# Essential Techniques

## How to Season

Delicately crushing a pinch of Maldon sea salt flakes between your fingers, and the accompanying rustle, is as satisfying as twisting the knob on a Peugeot peppermill and the scent of freshly ground black corns.

As to when to salt food – *before, during* or *after* cooking, you will find passionate advocates of each. Personally, I always season poultry, meat and fish well before roasting, but frequently at the end when frying vegetables as it draws out the moisture. Using this osmotic effect to your advantage, you can season and set aside cucumber, carrot, fennel or celeriac, and by drawing out the juices the texture will be softened. Note that tossed salads should only be seasoned *at the very last minute* otherwise they will collapse. Saying that, every recipe that follows will tell you exactly when to salt.

I like to have two types of salt to hand, a coarse sea salt (the slightly wet French *sel gris* is lovely stuff) in a salt pig beside the stove for pans of boiling water. And then a Maldon for everything else, to which I am so addicted I even take it to France; *fleur de sel* pales by comparison. As to flavoured and other types, these can be fun, play around at barbecue time.

## Stock Cubes & Powders

I always keep chicken, beef, fish and vegetable stock cubes or powder in the drawer. The only caveat is to be wary of hidden salt and to season the dish very lightly at the end. In the case of soup, make up the stock to half the strength. Marigold Swiss vegetable bouillon is a classic. For homemade chicken and vegetable stock recipes, see page 24.

*Piment d'Espelette* – this elusive chilli powder is governed by strict export controls, but most good delis in France (including some supermarkets) should offer it up. It has a gentle warmth, balanced by a delicate sweetness. I use it liberally to season almost everything and keep it alongside the peppermill and sea salt. It oxidises quickly, however, so once open I'd recommend storing the jar in the freezer and only keeping out enough for a couple of weeks.

# Shopping Tips – Small Words, Big Difference

*Aged balsamic* – some balsamic is little better than cordial. Buy a good one with a bit of age; you only ever use it sparingly.

*Artisanal* – this indicates the product has either been made by hand or on a small scale.

*Bronze die* – for pasta produced in a traditional fashion. This offers a richer texture and, being slightly rougher, holds the sauce better.

*Extra virgin* – keep an inexpensive extra virgin for cooking, and a better regional oil for use in salads or to serve raw; fine aromas will be driven off by heat. I favour Sicilian and Umbrian oils.

*Free range* – if chicken or pork doesn't advertise this, assume it isn't. This is the very least you want, not only for your bird or pig but for your table too. The difference in quality of both flavour and texture is considerable.

*Full fat* – beware low-fat products, dairy especially, which rarely offer the same experience and are frequently saltier. Equally be wary of reduced-fat meat, which generally cooks to a dry and tough finish.

*Golden caster* – my sugar of default, it dissolves with ease and combines gracefully with other ingredients. For any quantity go for 'golden' (unrefined) sugar, which has the best flavour, unless the recipe states 'white' caster sugar (which is generally used for cosmetic reasons).

*Mature* – this can mean a more pronounced flavour, and generally indicates a better product. Time costs money.

*No added* – caution here, it doesn't necessarily mean the product is natural, so always read the small print.

*No artificial* – as above.

*Organic* – produced without pesticides, chemical fertilisers or other artificial chemicals. Certainly purer and better for the environment, but may or may not be a better quality. I always specify organic eggs if the yolks remain runny, as the incidence of salmonella is fractional.

*Outdoor reared* – usually advertises well-reared pork, again you want to know your pig has had a happy life.

*Pole and line caught* – this mark indicates small-scale fishing.

*Unfiltered* – filtering removes a lot of the goodness in oils, and vinegars too, especially cider vinegar, where the 'mother' has all sorts of beneficial health benefits. So it's a positive little word to look out for.

*Unsalted butter* – salted butter burns more readily than unsalted, but it is lovely for flavouring potatoes and veggies, or spreading on a warm scone or pancake. Unsalted is the one you will be relying on for cooking with.

# Essential Techniques – Pastry

## Shortcrust Pastry

Makes **400g** / Start to Finish **1 h**

If you think of shortcrust pastry in terms of being a biscuit, its potential soon becomes clear. Instead of being a tough, dry container for a filling that gets left at the side of the plate, when it is homemade with the right amount of butter (for which, read 'a lot'), it resonates with the creamy luxury of its flavour and melts in your mouth. While I will not nag you to make your own bread, I will definitely nag you to make your own pastry.

plain flour – 225g, plus extra for dusting
sea salt – pinch
unsalted butter – 150g, chilled and diced
medium egg – 1, separated
cold water – approx. 1 tablespoon

**Make the pastry**
Place the **flour** and **salt** in the bowl of a food processor, add the **butter** and reduce to fine crumbs. Add the **egg yolk** (reserving the white for baking blind) and then, with the motor running, trickle in just enough **cold water** for the dough to cling together into lumps. Transfer the mixture to a large bowl and bring together into a flattened patty using your hands.

**Rest the pastry** *
Wrap the pastry in clingfilm and chill for at least 1 hour. (It will keep well in the fridge for up to a couple of days. It also freezes well, so you may like to make a second batch while you are at it.)

The knack
* **Why rest the pastry?** Resting the pastry in the fridge allows the gluten in the flour to relax, making it easier to roll out.

## Sweet Shortcrust Pastry

Makes **800g** / Start to Finish **2 h**

A benchmark for good sweet pastry is whether you would choose to nibble on it as a biscuit. If it is only palatable when it is smothered in custard, it has failed the audition – anything tastes great smothered in custard. This method results in crispy but firm pastry that is easy to work with and holds its shape.

softened unsalted butter – 150g
golden caster sugar – 150g
medium eggs – 2
plain flour – 400g, sifted
ground almonds – 50g *

**Make the pastry**
Cream the **butter** and **sugar** in a food processor. Incorporate the **eggs**, gradually add the **flour** and ground **almonds** and bring the dough together into a flattened patty using your hands.

**Rest the pastry**
Wrap the pastry in clingfilm and chill for at least 2 hours. (It will keep well in the fridge for up to a couple of days.)

The knack
* **Why ground almonds?** These account for the delicate, crisp bite, but if you are catering for the nut-sensitive then feel free to replace with plain flour instead.

# How to Line a Tart Case

(Shortcrust pastry only)

Choose a tart tin with a removable base, approx. 24cm in diameter for this quantity of pastry, and at least 4cm deep. Beware those with shallow sides since the pastry will shrink slightly as it cooks.

### Roll out the pastry

Lightly dust your worksurface with flour and gently knead the pastry until it is pliable enough to roll out. Using a rolling pin, roll out the pastry to form a circle large enough to fit your tin, approx. 3mm thick. I find the best method is to roll away from you in one direction, rotate the dough by 90° and then roll again – this way it should stay nice and round.

### Line the tin

Carefully transfer the pastry to the tart tin; I find it helps to partially wrap it around the rolling pin. It is quite a durable pastry and shouldn't tear or collapse. Gently ease the pastry into the sides of the tin with your fingertips, and then trim off the overhanging pastry with a knife. Reserve the trimmings to patch the pastry case after it is baked.

# How to Bake Blind

(Shortcrust pastry only)

The trick to avoid uncooked or stodgy pastry is to bake the pastry case 'blind', until it just starts to colour, before filling it.

### Preheat the oven and prepare the pastry base

Preheat the oven to 180°C fan/200°C electric/ gas 6. Prick the base all over with a fork and line it with a sheet of foil, tucking it over the sides to secure the pastry to the tin. Fill the centre with baking beans or a dried pulse such as chickpeas, which will stop the pastry bubbling up.

### Bake the case

Bake the case for 15 minutes, and then remove it from the oven. Carefully take out the foil and baking beans. (These can be reused again, just wrap them up in the foil and keep them for the next time.)

### Build up the sides if necessary

If any of the sides have shrunk more than they should, use a little of the reserved pastry to patch them. Remember the tart can only be filled as far as the lowest point of the sides, so it is important to build them up if necessary.

### Glaze the base and return to the oven *

Brush the base and sides of the case with beaten egg white, return to the oven and bake for a further 10 minutes until lightly coloured.

The knack

\* **Why glaze the base?** Brushing the cooked pastry case with beaten egg white helps seal the pastry, preventing the filling from soaking in.

# Freezer & Storecupboard Essentials

## Chicken Stock

Start to Finish **1 h 15 m**

Hope over reality leads me to turn the proceeds of every roast chicken or guinea fowl into stock. And it does have so many uses, not just for soups, but pots of lightly braised veg, gravy, sauces, a *soupçon*, anywhere basically where that little bit of character over and above water is called for. If you don't have space in your freezer, homemade chicken stock will keep for several days in the fridge. If after a few days you find that it is still sitting there, simply bring it to the boil in order to kill off any bacteria that might otherwise lead it to spoil, and then return it to the fridge for another few days.

cooked chicken carcass – 1
dry white wine – small glass
Maldon sea salt – 1 teaspoon

**Bring the carcass slowly to the boil**
Place the **chicken carcass** in a saucepan that will hold it snugly, add the **wine** and cover with water by 2cm. A great deal of the art lies in bringing it to the boil. It is fine to do this over a high heat, however make sure you reduce it to low before it comes to a rolling boil otherwise you risk a cloudy, for which read greasy, stock.

**Simmer and finish**
Having brought it to an imperceptible simmer, with just a few small bubbles rising, skim off any foam on the surface. Add the **salt** and simmer for at least 1 hour, longer if you prefer. Strain the stock and taste. If it seems at all thin, pour it back into the pan and cook at a rolling boil to reduce by up to half its volume to concentrate the flavour. Leave to cool, then cover and chill. A jellied stock is always a good sign that you have a good rich broth. Either way, skim off any fat from the surface before using it.

## Vegetable Stock

Start to Finish **30 m**

Don't get too strung up about the mix of veggies except to bear in mind that ones such as fennel and celery taste stronger than carrot or leek; cabbages too are likely to overwhelm more delicate flavours.

mixed vegetables (e.g. carrot, leek, celery, onion, fennel, swede, celeriac, tomato) – approx. 1kg (prepared weight), diced
garlic cloves – 2, peeled and finely chopped
dry white wine – small glass
thyme – few sprigs
sea salt, black pepper

**How to make vegetable stock**
Place **all the ingredients** in a large saucepan, and cover with water by about 3cm. Bring to the boil, and simmer over a low heat for 15 minutes. Strain, reserving the stock, and then set aside to cool. Cover and chill until required. This freezes well.

**The knack**

**Veggie mash:** To make the stock seem less of an extravagance, the strained veggies can be puréed with butter, cream, a few herbs and some seasoning, and served up as a side dish.

# All-round Tomato Sauce

Makes **approx. 800ml** / Start to Finish **1 h 40 m**

A box of slightly mushy or over-ripe tomatoes in a market or greengrocer are just the ticket here. But, failing that, cherry tomatoes have the most intense flavour and sweetness and would be a good everyday option.

This is a great sauce, either for pouring over a pile of pasta with some grated Parmesan, or you could stir some other goodies into it or use it as a passata.

cherry tomatoes – 1.35kg, halved

Maldon sea salt – 1 heaped teaspoon

caster sugar – 1 level teaspoon

unsalted butter – 100g

extra virgin olive oil – 4 tablespoons

### Stew the tomatoes

Place the **tomatoes** in a medium-sized saucepan, cover with a lid and cook over a low heat for 20–30 minutes or until they collapse, stirring them occasionally.

### Sieve the tomatoes and simmer the sauce

Pass the cooked tomatoes through a sieve, using the back of a ladle to help, or through a mouli-legumes and return to the pan, washing it out if necessary. Add **all the remaining ingredients** and simmer very gently, uncovered, for 60 minutes or until the sauce has thickened to a thin pouring consistency.

### Store the sauce

Leave the sauce to cool before transferring it to a bowl or container. This freezes well.

# Tomato Chutney

Makes **3 x 500ml jars** / Start to Finish **3 h 30 m**

There is nothing to be ashamed about in being a one-chutney wonder. That is all you need, a good basic that you can adapt.

eating apples – 500g, cored, but not peeled, and chopped into 5mm dice

beefsteak tomatoes – 1.3kg, skinned (see page 18) and chopped

red onions – 700g, peeled and finely chopped

cider vinegar – 500ml

garlic cloves – 4, peeled and finely chopped

fresh root ginger – 1 tablespoon, finely chopped

raisins – 400g

soft brown sugar – 450g

cayenne pepper – ½ teaspoon

cinnamon stick – 1 x 7cm

Maldon sea salt – 1 tablespoon

### How to make tomato chutney

Place **all the ingredients** in your largest pan and bring to the boil. Simmer over a low heat for 3–3 ½ hours, stirring occasionally, but more frequently towards the end to prevent sticking. The time the chutney will take to cook will depend on the size of the pan, the heat and the water content of the vegetables. Don't worry about paying too much attention at the beginning, but keep a watchful eye towards the end – by which time there should be a small amount of sticky syrup floating on the surface. To check for a set, spread 2 tablespoons of the chutney onto a cold plate, leave it to cool for a few minutes, and then judge whether it is the right consistency.

Once the chutney is cooked, discard the cinnamon stick and spoon into warm sterilised jars. Fasten the lids and set aside to cool.

# Breakfast

*I*

# Essential Eggs

## Boiled Eggs

Start to Finish **8–14 m**

The route to ridicule: 'The guy couldn't boil an egg.' Another way of saying he couldn't find his way out of a paper bag. But what happens if you really CAN'T boil an egg? The suggestion is you can't cook at all. My method scarcely involves instruction. Why try and complicate something this easy?

### How to boil an egg

Bring a pan of water to the boil, a small pan for up to about 3 eggs, and medium for 4–6. Lower the eggs carefully into the boiling water with a spoon, rather than dropping them, otherwise they might crack on hitting the bottom. Start your timer immediately and cook as follows:

*Perfect dippy egg:* 5 minutes – the yolk will be runny in the centre, with the thinnest layer of set but creamy yolk at the edge. Get in there with buttered toast fingers or asparagus spears.

*Lightly boiled*: 7 minutes – the yolk will have just set while remaining creamy. Great in salads.

*Fully boiled*: 9 minutes – the yolk will be well on its way to being powdery, with just a hint of firm but creamy yolk. Great for egg mayonnaise, when they are mashed, or 'mimosa' where you coarsely grate the peeled eggs, or finely chop them and scatter them over cooked veggies, salads and seafood. *

*Quail's eggs:* 3 minutes – the yolks will be slightly wet in the centre. Serve with a bowl of salt for dipping, and perhaps some radishes.

### The knack

\* **If serving cold:** Transfer the cooked eggs to a bowl of cold water to cool before peeling.

## Poached Eggs

Serves **2** / Start to Finish **15 m**

My family's favourite pan is a battered aluminium egg poacher that looks as though it survived WWI, with four neat cups, one for each egg. I cannot tell you quite how much this appals me, given that in my eyes the real thing should be cooked freeform in a pan of simmering water. However, since one of my own favourite pieces of kit is an egg squarer (bought from Macey's in San Francisco while watching the Galloping Gourmet demonstrate many years ago), I guess I shouldn't carp. In truth the 'real' method of poaching an egg is no harder than cooking an egg in a pan, a pod or whatever else presents itself as a handy gadget for the task. And it's good to know you don't have to store yet another one-task pan.

white wine vinegar – good slug

large eggs – 2

### How to poach an egg

Fill your largest saucepan three-quarters full with water, bring it to the boil and add the **vinegar**. Turn the heat down and keep the water at a trembling simmer throughout. *

Break the first **egg** into a teacup. Using a large spoon, gently stir the water into a whirlpool and drop in the egg. Repeat with the second egg. The eggs will immediately sink to the bottom of the pan, leaving strands of white floating, and then after about 2 minutes they will rise to the surface. Cook for a further 2 minutes, and then remove using a slotted spoon. Drain thoroughly, trimming off the tendrils of white against the side of the saucepan.

### The knack

\* **Don't let the water boil** while the eggs are poaching or the whites will disintegrate.

# Fried Eggs

Serves **2** / Start to Finish **5 m**

In addition to breakfast, fried eggs are also great for Sunday night suppers. An *uitsmijter* (pronounced ausmeiter), a staple in cafés in Amsterdam, is a Bell family tradition – courtesy of a Dutch uncle on Jonnie's side. Essentially a fried egg sandwich, it makes the perfect end-of-weekend light meal, readily transported to laps in front of the telly. Our favourite combination is thick buttered toast with roast ham and an egg fried sunny-side up, but you could include cheese as well if you wish – a few slivers of Edam work a treat, in which case leave the egg on the runny side and pop under the grill until the cheese melts. I have been asked to pass on from Louis that they are great with Jerk barbecue sauce.

groundnut or vegetable oil – 2 teaspoons
medium or large eggs – 2
sea salt, black pepper

**How to fry an egg**
Heat a large non-stick frying pan over a medium-high heat and add the **oil**, tipping to coat the base. Carefully break in up to 2 **eggs** and season with **salt and pepper**. *

Fry for about 2 minutes or until the undersides are golden and the edges are lacy and crisp. Very carefully turn the eggs over with a spatula and cook the yolk-side for about 10 seconds until the surface is just set. Slip the eggs out of the pan onto a plate, turning them the right way up.

**The knack**

* **Cracking the eggs:** Unless you are very dexterous, it does take a few attempts to master this one, so make sure that you allow for a few breakages – either when cracking the egg into the pan or when turning – and don't beat yourself up or lose heart.

# Scrambled Eggs

Serves **2** / Start to Finish **10 m**

Properly made scrambled eggs are almost like a sauce, at least that's how I tend to think of them. This leads me to thoughts of how to serve them – crispy bacon (heaven), fried mushrooms, smoked salmon – and I'm dreaming of someone bringing me breakfast in bed.

medium or large eggs – 3
medium or large egg yolks – 2 *
whole milk – splash
sea salt, black pepper
unsalted butter – knob

**How to scramble eggs**
Whisk the **eggs** and **egg yolks** in a bowl with the **milk** and some **seasoning**. Pour into a small non-stick saucepan and add a knob of **butter**.

Place the pan over a low heat and after a couple minutes, once they've begun to warm up, stir constantly with a wooden spoon, covering the base of the saucepan. The eggs will begin to thicken. Once they reach the consistency of custard, remove the pan from the heat. Continue to stir the eggs off the heat until they are thick and creamy, without being set. If necessary, pop the pan back on the heat momentarily to thicken them a little bit more, and so on, until you achieve the right consistency. With no time to waste, divide between two plates and serve straight away.

**The knack**

* **Why egg yolks?** Instead of lacing my scrambled eggs with loads of cream and butter, I prefer to add extra egg yolks that serve the same purpose.

# Smoked Salmon & Lemon Frittata

Serves **4** / Start to Finish **15 m**

Unlike a French omelette, a frittata is as much about the filling as the eggs. This one is laden with smoked salmon and mascarpone and flavoured with lemon zest. They make a rustic statement.

medium eggs – 6

lemon juice – 1 tablespoon

lemon zest – ½ teaspoon, finely grated

flat-leaf parsley – 3 tablespoons, coarsely chopped

black pepper

sliced smoked salmon – 150g, cut into strips 2cm wide

extra virgin olive oil – 1 tablespoon

mascarpone or quark – 2 tablespoons

**Whisk the eggs**
Whisk the **eggs** with the **lemon juice, zest, parsley** and a little **black pepper** in a large bowl. Fold in the **smoked salmon**, separating out the strips.

**Fry the frittata**
Preheat a 24cm non-stick frying pan with a heatproof handle over a medium heat for several minutes, and at the same time preheat the grill to high. Add the **olive oil** to the frying pan, tip in the omelette mixture and cook for 3 minutes.

**Finish under the grill**
Dot the **mascarpone** or **quark** over the surface, and place the pan under the grill for a further 3–4 minutes or until the frittata is golden and puffed in the centre. Serve hot or at room temperature.

**Variation**

**Crab Frittata:** Omit the smoked salmon and fold 150g crabmeat (preferably a mixture of white and brown meat) into the whisked mixture.

# Best Ever Omelette

Serves **1\*** / Start to Finish **10 m**

This whisked omelette guarantees great results, unlike a traditional rolled omelette, which despite its reputation for speed and ease is the hardest of egg dishes to get right. You only have to dine your way around Normandy on an omelette and a glass of cider, as I frequently do, to know the extremes between good and bad. Eggs set hard with heat which is why an omelette is usually cooked *baveuse* to leave it alluringly wet in the middle. Here the foam provides that succulence, with a gorgeous golden buttery crust on the outside.

medium eggs – 2
sea salt, black pepper
unsalted butter – 20g

### Variations

**Herb Omelette:** Fold 1 tablespoon finely chopped herbs into the whisked egg mixture – chives, parsley or *fines herbes* (2 teaspoons parsley, 1 teaspoon each chives and chervil, and ½ teaspoon tarragon).

**Cheese Omelette:** Scatter over and lightly fold 20g freshly grated Parmesan or 25g finely grated Gruyère or Emmental into the whisked egg mixture.

**Heat the pan**
Heat a 24cm non-stick frying pan over a medium-low heat for 4–5 minutes until it is a nice, even temperature.

**Whisk the eggs**
Meanwhile break the **eggs** into a large bowl and season with a little **salt and pepper**. Using an electric whisk at high speed, whisk the eggs for 3 minutes until they are very thick, pale and moussey, and several times the volume.

**Melt the butter and add the omelette mixture**
Remove the pan from the heat, add the **butter** and swirl it around until it has completely melted. Return the pan to the heat, tip in the egg mixture and level the surface using a spoon.

**Fry the omelette**
Cook the omelette for approx. 4 minutes, until the underside is deep gold and lacy if you carefully lift the edge with a palette knife or spatula. The uncooked surface should feel warm to the touch.

**Dish up**
Loosen the omelette around the sides using a palette knife and carefully fold in half. Slide onto a plate – the mousse should ooze from the inside – and eat without delay while it is still fluffy.

*Serving suggestion*
— Serve with a slice of smoked salmon, Parma or honey-roast ham.

**Omelette**

**The knack**

\* **Scaling up:** If cooking for more than one person, then you will need one pan per omelette. Alternatively try the souffléed omelette on page 32, which serves 2.

# Deluxe Souffléed Omelette

Serves **2** / Start to Finish **15 m**

This lavish recipe is based on the famed omelettes of La Mère Poulard in Mont St-Michel, a destination that sadly these days is Normandy's Disneyland, although the restaurant does still make a fab omelette. It makes for a theatrical spectacle, where the omelettes are whisked and cooked on an open fire. Eggs and butter alone? So they claim, but I'm not sure I believe them. We find a little *je ne sais quoi* in the way of Parmesan helps that golden crust along nicely.

This is a sturdier omelette than the whisked version on page 31, meaning it should remain fluffy and souffléed for that much longer.

medium eggs – 4, separated *
sea salt, black pepper
Parmesan – 40g, freshly grated
lightly salted butter – 40g

**Heat the pan**
Heat a 25–26cm non-stick frying pan over a medium-low heat for 4–5 minutes until it is a nice, even temperature.

**Whisk the eggs and make up the omelette mixture**
Meanwhile place the **egg whites** in a bowl and whisk until they form stiff peaks, using an electric whisk. Whisk the **egg yolks** in a separate large bowl with a pinch of **salt** and a grinding of **black pepper** – there is no need to wash out the whisk, providing you whisk the whites first. Spoon half of the egg whites on top of the yolks and fold over using a large spoon until blended. Repeat with the remaining half, and finally fold in the **Parmesan**.

**Melt the butter and cook the omelette**
Remove the pan from the heat, add the **butter** and swirl it around until it has completely melted. Return the pan to the heat, tip in the egg mixture and level the surface using a spoon.

**Fry the omelette**
Cook the omelette for 4–6 minutes until the underside is deep gold and lacy if you carefully lift the edge with a palette knife or spatula. The uncooked surface should feel warm if you touch it with the back of your finger.

**Dish up**
Loosen the omelette around the sides using a palette knife, carefully fold in half and slide onto a plate.

The knack

* **To separate an egg:** Give the egg a gentle but masterful tap against the side of a bowl to crack the shell, before easing the halves apart, facing upwards to contain the egg. Now play pass the parcel with the yolk from one half to the other, allowing the white to trickle into the bowl below.

# Essential Fry-ups

## Golden Sausages

Serves **4** / Start to Finish **1 h**

Baking sausages in the oven rather than frying them gets my vote every time, a surefire route to evenly bronzed and caramelised bangers, with no risk of them burning before they are done, and without that fine mist of fat that coats everything in the kitchen in sight.

vegetable oil

sausages (e.g. bangers, cocktail sausages or chipolatas) – 450–500g

**Arrange the sausages in a roasting pan**
Preheat the oven to 190°C fan/210°C electric/gas 7 and brush a roasting pan with **vegetable oil** to stop the sausages from sticking. Lay out the **sausages** in a single layer, without touching, so that they colour evenly.

**Bake the sausages**
Bake the sausages for 35–50 minutes until evenly golden, turning them with a spatula halfway through. The cooking time will depend slightly on the style of sausage and also the casing, so keep a watchful eye. Smaller sausages will cook faster than larger ones.

*Serving suggestions*
— Think beyond bacon and eggs, and serve with roasted veg or lots of chilli-fried onions.
— Serve as the 'dog' of your choice in warm buns: Mexican with lettuce, tomato salsa and guacamole (see page 52); BLT with bacon, lettuce and tomato; 4th July with bacon and coleslaw (see page 138); Sloppy Joe with chilli, grated Cheddar and chopped onions.

## Crispy Bacon

Serves **4** / Start to Finish **10 m**

Choices, choices, and the first one is smoked or unsmoked, purely a case of preference. Smoked is that much more robust and I am inclined to unsmoked, especially if it is in advance of lunch. The real importance is that the bacon is 'dry-cured'. Poorly produced, for which read 'cheap', bacon tends to carry a lot of water that oozes out as the bacon cooks, preventing it from colouring, and it also lacks flavour. The thin layers of fat in streaky bacon ensure it cooks to an even crisp gold, whereas back bacon is more likely to dry out. The edges might turn crisp, but the lean meat in the centre rarely colours without turning tough. I tend to serve streaky in sandwiches and save back bacon for Pasta Carbonara where I don't want a fatty cut.

rindless streaky bacon – 250g

*Baking in the oven:* Preheat the oven to 190°C fan/210°C electric/gas 6½. Lay the **bacon** rashers out in a single layer in a roasting pan. Don't worry if they overlap slightly, they will shrink considerably on cooking. Bake for 15 minutes, and then turn and cook for a further 5 minutes until golden and crisp.
*Grilling:* Preheat the grill to high. Lay the rashers out without touching in the base of a roasting pan, or on a rack. (You might like to line it with foil first, which saves on the washing up, but be careful not to place it too close to the heat to avoid flare-ups.) Grill the first side until golden, and then turn and cook on the other side.

*Serving suggestions*
— Serve in a white roll with tomato ketchup or chilli jam for the ultimate bacon sandwich.
— Serve in a torpedo roll with cold roast chicken, avocado and mayonnaise.

# Mushroom Fry-up

Serves **2–3** / Start to Finish **20 m**

You can use this recipe as a catch all – be it the reward after a morning's gathering or the result of a trip to a farmer's market, this should do you proud.

unsalted butter – 25g

extra virgin olive oil – 2 tablespoons

shallots – 2, peeled and finely chopped

mixed mushrooms – 400g, torn or sliced as necessary

sea salt, black pepper

flat-leaf parsley – 2 tablespoons, coarsely chopped

### Variations

**Creamy Mushrooms:** For a slightly richer take on the above, return all the cooked mushrooms to the pan, add a squeeze of lemon juice and 100ml double cream and cook until the sauce thickens. Finally stir in the parsley.

**Mushroom Pasta Sauce:** Cook as for Creamy Mushrooms (above), but leave out the parsley and stir in 1–2 tablespoons grated Parmesan instead.

### Fry the mushrooms

Heat half the **butter** and half the **olive oil** in a large non-stick frying pan over a high heat. Add half the **shallot** and cook briefly until translucent. Throw in half the **mushrooms**, without overcrowding the pan to avoid stewing, and fry for about 3 minutes, stirring occasionally until golden. If any liquid is given out, continue to fry until the mixture is dry and coloured. Remove the cooked mushrooms to a serving bowl and cover with foil to keep warm while you fry the remainder in the same way. To serve, season the mushrooms with **salt and pepper** and stir in the **parsley**.

*Serving suggestions*
— Serve on toasted brioche with a poached egg on top.
— Pile on top of scrambled eggs.
— Serve on grilled chicken or steak.
— Pile on top of baked potatoes.

# Oven Brunch Tomatoes

Serves **6** / Start to Finish **25 m**

These oven-baked tomatoes have a delicate, buttery crust, spiced with French mustard and Parmesan cheese.

white bread – 100g (trimmed weight), crusts removed

unsalted butter – 100g, diced

Dijon mustard – 1 teaspoon

sea salt, black pepper

large tomatoes – 6 (approx. 125g each), halved horizontally

Parmesan – 20g, freshly grated

**Prepare the tomatoes**
Preheat the oven to 220°C fan/240°C electric/gas 9. Whizz the **bread** to crumbs in a food processor. Add the **butter**, **mustard** and a little **seasoning** and blend to a smooth paste. Spread a generous heaped teaspoon of the mixture onto each **tomato** half, mounding it in the centre. Arrange in a single layer in a large roasting pan and dust the tops with **Parmesan**. (These can be prepared the night beforehand, in which case cover and chill.)

**Cook the tomatoes**
Bake the tomatoes in the oven for 10 minutes, and then finish off under a hot grill until golden on top.

## Variations

**Plain Grilled Tomatoes:** Preheat the grill to low. Place the halved tomatoes cut-side up on the rack of a grill tray. Season with salt and pepper and dot each one with a little knob of unsalted butter. Grill for approx. 15 minutes, until the tomatoes soften, and then increase the heat to medium-high and cook for a further 5–10 minutes until golden.

**Tomatoes with a Herb Crust:** Blend together equal quantities of white breadcrumbs, grated Gruyère and unsalted butter. Flavour with the herbs of your choice and season the mixture with salt and pepper. Spread onto the halved tomatoes and grill under a low heat for about 20 minutes.

### The knack

**How to make breadcrumbs:** Ideally use bread that is at least one day old, several even. A country-style or open-textured bread will give a rustic crumb that is great for scattering over dishes to be baked. The quickest way to make breadcrumbs is to remove the crusts, tear up the bread and whizz it to crumbs in a food processor. Any leftover crumbs can be successfully frozen in a small plastic bag and used from frozen if you wish.

# Out-of-Bed Chocolate Muffins

Makes **6** / Start to Finish **35–40 m**

Over the years I have kept a scrapbook containing all of my son Louis' notes and scribbles – from pictures of Thomas the Tank Engine and Mr Men to hobbits, warriors and the teenage notes of today, which I find left on the keyboard of my computer on an almost nightly basis. 'DO NOT set the alarm, lure me out of bed with food around 11.30', reads one. 'Wake me up with muffins', reads another.

In fact they all, coincidentally, seem to involve breakfast, so muffins are a good starting point. In pursuit of the perfect flavour, having suggested a selection of ones containing fruit, these were dismissed out of hand in favour of chocolate chip ones: 'Milk chocolate, but not just chips on the top, you need to put them all the way through.' Here you have it.

whole milk – 100ml

groundnut oil – 75ml *

medium egg – 1

vanilla extract or bean paste – 1 teaspoon

plain flour – 100g

cocoa powder – 25g

baking powder – 1 heaped teaspoon

light muscovado sugar – 90g

fine sea salt – generous pinch

milk chocolate chips – 75g **

icing sugar, for dusting (optional)

you will need a muffin tray and 6 paper cases

**Preheat the oven and prepare a muffin tray**
Preheat the oven to 180°C fan/200°C electric/gas 6, and line the muffin tray with 6 paper cases.

**Prepare the wet and dry mixtures**
Whisk the **milk, groundnut oil, egg** and **vanilla** together in a large bowl. Sift the **flour, cocoa** and **baking powder** in a separate large bowl, and then stir in the **sugar** and **salt**.

**Combine the mixtures**
Tip the wet ingredients into the dry ones and stir loosely to blend, there should be no traces of flour, but the mixture should appear wet and lumpy. Fold in three-quarters of the **chocolate chips**.

**Fill the cases and bake the muffins**
Fill the paper cases by about half. Scatter over the remaining chocolate chips, and bake for 20–25 minutes or until risen and crusty. Tuck in as soon as they are cool enough to handle, dusting with **icing sugar** if you wish. (They will keep well overnight, loosely covered with clingfilm.)

The knack

\* **For nut-allergy sufferers:** Substitute rapeseed oil for the groundnut.

\*\* **Milk v. dark chocolate:** Such is the overkill of ever-darker chocolates, it is no surprise to find a backlash among the next generation, who would no more include it in muffins than be seen walking down the street with their parents. 'Dark chocolate belongs with Stilton.' Positively vicious. But don't let this stop you using dark chocolate chips or chunks if that is your preference. White chocolate, too, is a possible. If the slightly toasty appearance of those on top is likely to bother you, then fold them all into the mix.

# Scotch Pancakes

Serves **3–4** / Makes **12** / Start to Finish **15 m**

If pancakes call for a modest sleight of hand, Scotch pancakes require none at all. Their relative thickness ensures that turning them without mishap is a promise. These are great served hot or cold on a school morning, spread with Nutella and carried out of the door to be eaten on the journey.

self-raising flour – 125g

golden caster sugar – 50g

fine sea salt – pinch

medium egg – 1

whole milk – 150ml

unsalted butter – 30g, melted

**To serve**

unsalted or salted butter

jam, honey, maple syrup or Nutella

**Make the pancake mixture**
Place the **flour**, **sugar** and **salt** in a medium-sized bowl. Break in the **egg**, and then whisk in the **milk** in two goes. Stir in the **melted butter**.

**Preheat the pan and fry the pancakes**
Heat a large non-stick frying pan over a medium-low heat for several minutes. Drop tablespoons of the batter into the pan and fry for about 1 minute until the top starts to pit with bubbles. Turn using a palette knife or spatula and cook the underside for a further 30–45 seconds until it puffs up. Dish up with **butter**, **jam**, **honey**, **maple syrup** or **Nutella**.

**Variation**

**Blueberry Pancakes (Serves 4–5 / Makes 16):** Stir 100g blueberries into the finished batter. Evenly space the berries out when dropping the mixture into the pan. Serve drizzled with syrup and scattered with more blueberries, stacking them high if you wish.

# Pancakes

Serves **2–3** / Makes **8** / Start to Finish **20 m**

Pancakes instantly spell party time. It might be eight o'clock in the morning, but the sound and smell of pancakes frying – along with the friendly clatter of a table being laid with all the extras – is immediately celebratory.

A rule of thumb when making pancakes in my house is to chuck number one in the bin. Russians have a lovely description for this when making blinis, it is the *blin*. Don't be deterred if it takes a couple before you get into your stride.

plain flour – 125g
golden caster sugar – 1 heaped teaspoon
fine sea salt – pinch
medium eggs – 2
whole milk – 300ml
unsalted butter – 20g, melted

## To serve

lemon wedges and caster sugar
jam, honey, maple syrup, Nutella or fresh berries

## Variation

**Double quantity (Serves 4–6 / Makes 16):** Use 250g plain flour, 1 tablespoon caster sugar, 3 large eggs and 2 egg yolks, 600ml milk and 40g unsalted butter.

### Prepare the batter *

*By machine:* Place **all the ingredients** except the melted butter in a blender and whizz until smooth. Give the sides and bottom of the blender a stir to make sure there's no flour clinging, and whizz again. Transfer the batter to a bowl and stir in the **melted butter**.

*By hand:* Place the **flour, sugar** and **salt** in a large bowl, add the **eggs** and mix to a lumpy wet paste using a spoon. Whisk in the **milk**, a little to begin with to smooth out the lumps, and then in bolder streams once you have a creamy batter. Finally stir in the **melted butter**.

### Preheat the pan and fry the pancakes **

Preheat a non-stick frying pan with an 18cm base (i.e. a 24cm pan) over a medium-high heat for several minutes. Ladle in just enough batter to coat the base, tipping it to allow it to run evenly over the surface. Cook for 30 seconds until the top is dry and lacy at the edges and the bottom is golden and lacy underneath. Loosen the edges using a palette knife or spatula (non-stick for a non-stick pan), slip this underneath and flip the pancake over. Give it another 30 seconds on the other side and then slide onto a plate. Cook the remainder in the same way.

### Dish up

You can either dish up the pancakes as they are cooked, or pile them up on a plate and cover with foil to keep warm. Accompany with **lemon wedges** and **sugar** or the **extras** of your choice. (Leftovers will keep well for several days in the fridge, covered with clingfilm. To reheat, fry briefly on each side in a dry frying pan.)

The knack

\* **The batter can be made well in advance,** in which case add the melted butter just before frying. If making the batter the night before, cover the bowl with clingfilm and store in the fridge until needed.

\*\* **How hot should the pan be?** A lively heat somewhere between medium and hot should ensure the mixture 'sings' as it hits the pan. Too hot and the pancakes will dry out and singe, too cool and they won't turn golden and lacy.

# Cherry Hazelnut Granola

Makes approx. **600g** / Start to Finish **1 h**

Much like making flapjacks, and just as easy. This quantity of granola will last for weeks. As well as serving it with fruit and yogurt for breakfast, it also makes for great grazing by the handful, without the guilt of a biscuit but with all the allure. Feel free to play about with the formula, including different syrups, nuts or dried fruit, just make sure you keep the quantities the same.

**For the syrup**

agave syrup – 125g

runny honey – 25g

light muscovado sugar – 50g

vegetable oil – 2 tablespoons

ground cinnamon – 1 teaspoon

vanilla bean paste – 1 teaspoon

**For the granola mix**

jumbo oats – 250g

hazelnuts – 75g, halved or coarsely chopped

sesame seeds – 25g

desiccated coconut – 25g

dried cherries or berries – 100g

you will need a 38 x 25cm roasting pan

**Preheat the oven**
Preheat the oven to 130°C fan/150°C electric/gas 2.

**Combine and bake the ingredients**
Blend **all the ingredients for the syrup** in a large bowl until amalgamated. Add the **oats, hazelnuts** and **sesame seeds** and stir to coat. Spread the mixture in a thin layer over the base of a large roasting pan and roast for 45 minutes until lightly toasted, stirring every 15 minutes. Scatter the **coconut** over the top and stir in after 30 minutes.

**Finish and store the granola**
Remove the granola from the oven and mix in the **dried cherries** or **berries**. Set aside to cool before storing in a sealed plastic bag or container.

# Blackberry & Pear Granola Sundae

Serves **4** / Start to Finish **10 m**

These sundaes make a glam good-for-you breakfast, but equally a lovely mid-morning or teatime treat. Blackberries and pear have an autumnal feel, however you could vary the fruit throughout the year.

blackberries – 400g

runny honey – 2 tablespoons

Greek yogurt – 400g

granola – 100g (see opposite)

small Comice pear – 1, peeled, quartered, cored and thinly sliced across

**Make the blackberry purée**
Purée half the **blackberries** with the **honey** in a blender, and pass through a sieve into a medium-sized bowl. Fold in the remaining blackberries.

**Assemble the sundae**
Give the **Greek yogurt** a stir, and place a heaped tablespoon in the base of 4 glasses – if you're making these to take to work you could use clip-top jars. Scatter a level tablespoon of **granola** over the yogurt, and then arrange a few slices of **pear** followed by a tablespoon of the blackberry mixture on top. Repeat the layering process, finishing with a spoonful of the crunchy granola.

## Variation

**Fruit Compote (Serves 6):** *I frequently eat chilled fruit compote scattered with berries for breakfast. Lovely with some quark too. This makes a large quantity to last you the week.*

**Either** Bramley cooking apples – 900g, peeled and cored

**Or** plums, apricots or peaches in season – 800g, halved and stoned

lemon – 2 wide strips of zest

water – 50ml

golden caster sugar – approx. 50g

Place the fruit in a medium-sized saucepan with the lemon zest and water. Bring the liquid to the boil, and then cover and simmer over a low heat for 25–30 minutes, stirring every 10 minutes until the fruit collapses into a purée. (For a smooth purée, liquidise the fruit in a blender and then press through a sieve into a bowl.) Sweeten with sugar to taste, set aside to cool and then cover and chill.

# Orange & Papaya Smoothie

Makes **2** / Start to Finish **5 m**

Smoothies can be whizzed up on a rushed school day morning, which is probably why they have become a regular in our house. This version is a great use for papaya, which can be on the bland side – until, that is, you marry it with a little citrus.

banana – 1, peeled and cut into chunks

papaya – ½ (seeds and skin discarded), cut into chunks

smooth orange or blood orange juice – 300ml

**To serve**

Greek yogurt – 2 teaspoons

passion fruit – 1, halved and seeds scooped out

**Whizz**
Place the **banana**, **papaya** and **orange juice** in a blender and liquidise until smooth. Divide between 2 glasses and top with a dollop of **yogurt** and a sprinkling of **passion fruit seeds**.

# Blueberry & Banana Smoothie

Makes **2** / Start to Finish **5 m**

You can make this smoothie using whichever berries are in season – raspberries, strawberries, blueberries, blackberries – the choice is yours.

quark – 2 heaped tablespoons

smooth orange juice – 200ml

blueberries – 150g

small bananas – 2, peeled and cut into chunks

**Whizz**
Place **all the ingredients** in a blender and liquidise until smooth. Divide between two highball glasses.

**The knack**

**Getting the balance right:** The ideal smoothie is an all-in-one. Both of these have a gorgeously thick and creamy texture, courtesy of the quark or yogurt, which tempers the acidity of the fruit.

# Cheese, Snacks & Savoury Tarts

2

# Essential Snacks

## Garlic Bread

Serves **4** / Start to Finish **30 m**

This version is buttery and crisp and laced with herbs, although you can still make a decent basic in their absence.

softened salted butter (e.g. Breton or Norman) – 50g

soft herbs (a mixture of parsley, chives, chervil, coriander or tarragon) – 6 tablespoons, chopped

garlic clove – 1, peeled and crushed

small baguette – 1

**Preheat the oven and prepare the garlic butter**
Preheat the oven to 180°C fan/200°C electric/gas 6. In a medium-sized bowl, blend the **butter** with the **herbs** and **garlic**.

**Butter the bread**
Either thickly slice the **baguette**, leaving the pieces attached at the base, and generously spread either side of each slice with garlic butter (my preferred route) OR slit the loaf in half lengthways and spread top and bottom. Wrap in foil. (The garlic bread can be prepared to this point in advance, in which case transfer it to the fridge for up to 1 day.)

**Bake in the oven**
Bake in the oven for 15 minutes, and then open up the foil and cook for a further 5 minutes to crisp the crust.

---

The knack
**Reviving a baguette:** A standard baguette is a one-day wonder, but you can bring it back to life the day after by very briefly running the length under the cold tap and baking it for 10 minutes at 170°C fan/190°C electric/gas 5.

## Bruschetta

Serves **1** / Start to Finish **5 m**

A glam name for a bit of toast. However, even at its most minimal drizzled with extra virgin olive oil and swiped with a garlic clove, bruschetta has rustic swag. A delight on its own, it updates pretty much any stew or roast in lieu of potatoes, as well as being a springboard for all sorts of on-toast scenarios.

coarse-textured white bread (e.g. sourdough or pain de campagne) – 1 thick slice *

garlic clove – 1, peeled

extra virgin olive oil *

**How to make bruschetta**
Toast the **bread** and give it a few half-hearted swipes with a **garlic clove** – be very pathetic about this, a hint of garlic is fine but nothing too boisterous. Place the toast on a plate and coat with a slug or two of **olive oil**.

*Serving suggestions*
Pile one or more of the following onto your bruschettas:
— finely chopped very ripe fresh tomatoes
— roast peppers (see page 246)
— griddled courgettes (see page 250)
— torn chunks of buffalo mozzarella
— thinly sliced Parma ham or salami

---

The knack
**\* Which olive oil?** This is a great opportunity to show off a really good olive oil. If you ever visit any of the mills in Italy, this is exactly how the very new and pungent oil is likely to be tasted and enjoyed.

# Croque Monsieur

Serves **2** / Start to Finish **20 m**

Such is the ubiquity of electric sandwich toasters these days, my frying pan method of making a toastie is inclined to attract snarky comments such as 'What on earth are you doing, mum?' Answer: 'Making a Croque Monsieur the proper way.' And with its irresistibly buttery, golden crisp exterior, there is no comparison.

softened unsalted butter, for spreading

coarse-textured white bread (e.g. pain de campagne) – 4 slices, approx. 1cm thick

Gruyère – 200g, thinly sliced

honey-roast ham – 2–4 slices

Dijon mustard, for spreading

**Assemble the sandwiches**
**Butter** the **bread** on both sides. Cover two of the slices with a layer of **Gruyère**, then a slice of **ham**, smear over some **mustard** and cover with another layer of Gruyère. Close the sandwiches with the top layers of bread. (They can be prepared to this point in advance, in which case wrap them in foil and transfer them to the fridge for up to 1 day.)

**Fry the sandwiches**
Ideally cook the two Croque Monsieur in non-stick frying pans, though ordinary ones will do. Heat two frying pans over a high heat for several minutes, or one large one if it can hold both sandwiches. Place the sandwiches in the pans, turn the heat down to medium-low and cook for 4–5 minutes on each side until golden on the outside and oozing melted cheese.

**Dish up**
Cut the toasted sandwiches into four and arrange with the cut edges showing.

# Rarebits

Serves **6** / Start to Finish **15 m**

Having been raised on a slice of toast topped with a slice of Cheddar and chucked under the grill, Rarebits lie at the luxury end of the market in my eyes. Altogether more *soigné*, you can dish these up on pretty much any occasion as a hand-me-round or eat before lunch or dinner. They are also great with soups. But otherwise just having a bowl of the ready-made rarebit mixture in the fridge answers any number of snack attacks.

day-old white bread – 6 slices

**For the rarebit mixture**

day-old white bread – 30g (excluding crusts)

mature Cheddar – 250g, cut into chunks

unsalted butter – 30g

stout (e.g. Guinness) – 3 tablespoons

Dijon mustard – 1 teaspoon

Worcestershire sauce – 1 teaspoon

medium organic egg – 1

**Make the rarebit mix**
Place the **bread for the rarebit mixture** in the bowl of a food processor and whizz to crumbs. Add **all the remaining ingredients for the rarebit mixture** and blend to a paste. (You can make the rarebit mix well in advance, in which case transfer it to a bowl, cover with clingfilm and chill in the fridge for several days.)

**Grill the rarebits**
Preheat the grill to medium. Toast the slices of **bread** and cut into triangles or smaller pieces, leaving the crusts on. Thickly spread with the rarebit mixture and arrange on a grill tray. Grill for 5–7 minutes until golden brown on top.

# Camembert Fondue

Serves **6** / Start to Finish **35 m**

Box-baked Camembert is the cutting-edge solution to a fondue. Well actually it's been around for years, but still seems endlessly stylish and minimal if the alternative is a spirit burner filled with meths, which is enough to put anyone off what they are eating. I frequently dish this up at the end of dinner in lieu of a cheeseboard. That bit more decadent, it is also a little more theatrical than passing round a board of crackers.

Camembert – 2 x 250g whole cheeses (in wooden boxes)

Calvados – approx. 1 tablespoon (optional)

**Prepare the cheese for the oven and bake it**

Preheat the oven to 150°C fan/170°C electric/gas 3½. Remove any waxed paper surrounding the **Camembert**, and place them back in their wooden boxes. If baking with Calvados, cut out a 4–5cm circle of rind in the top of each and carefully lift this off. Spoon out a tablespoon of the cheese, making a shallow trough, and fill with ½ tablespoon **Calvados** in each. Replace the rind lid, tie a piece of string around the sides of each box and bake for 25 minutes. Carefully peel back the rind to serve.

*Serving suggestion*

— Dish up with crisp endive leaves, celery sticks and shell-on walnuts. Or trickle the melted cheese over thick slices of toasted sourdough, drizzled with walnut oil, or croûtons (see page 168), and top with Parma ham.

### Variation

**Varying the cheese:** You could also make this using Livarot (1 x 500g), baking it for 40 minutes. Livarot, along with Camembert and Pont L'Evêque, is one of the cornerstone cheeses of Normandy, named after the village. Like the great Epoisses, it is more bark than bite, washed with salty water and turned during the maturing process, its unctuous and creamy curd is surprisingly gentle.

# Cheese & Pesto Pastry Straws

Makes **20–25** / Start to Finish **40 m**

Everyone loves a good cheese straw – it's the crispy edges of toasted cheese that have us coming back for more, and here I have added an extra dimension with a little pesto. It was my sister-in-law Jasmine who noticed this gap in the original manuscript, so to all the Endres, and in particular my lovely godson Milo.

groundnut or vegetable oil,
for greasing

flour, for dusting

block of puff pastry (preferably all-butter) – 225g

pesto sauce – 2 tablespoons (see page 190)

Parmesan – 25g, freshly grated *

Gruyère – 25g, grated

1 egg yolk blended with 1 tablespoon milk to form an eggwash

**Make the straws**
Preheat the oven to 180°C fan/200°C electric/gas 5 and lightly **oil** two baking sheets. Dust your worksurface with **flour** and roll out the **pastry** to form a large rectangle approx. 30 x 50cm, and approx. 1mm thick. Turn the pastry so the long side is facing you and trim the edges to neaten them. Spread the **pesto** in a thin layer over the top half, leaving a 1cm border top and bottom. Combine the **Parmesan** and **Gruyère** in a bowl and scatter evenly over the pesto. Brush the 1cm border with the **eggwash**, and then carefully bring the lower half of the pastry over the cheese and pesto topping to form a sandwich. Using a rolling pin, lightly roll the pastry all over to compress the cheese and seal the edges. Cut the filled pastry into 1cm straws, discarding the ragged end slices.

**Twist the straws and bake**
Holding one end in either hand, twist each straw to give you about five turns, and lay 2cm apart on the prepared baking sheets. Make sure you press the ends down firmly onto the baking sheet before you bake the cheese straws or they will unravel as they cook. Bake for 12–15 minutes until an even golden brown. The bottom tray may take a few minutes longer than the top.

**Loosen and store the straws**
Remove the cheese straws from the oven and immediately loosen them with a palette knife while they are still hot – any that break are cook's tips. Serve warm or just cooled; they look pretty in tall glass tumblers.

These can be stored for several days in an airtight container. Reheat in a moderate oven (150°C fan/170°C electric/gas 3 ½) for 5 minutes.

The knack

\* **How to grate Parmesan:** For any amount of grated Parmesan, the spiked grating attachment on a food processor will make light work of the task. I usually grate a whole wedge, even when I only require a fraction, given how well it keeps in the fridge. If however, you are doing it by hand, in the name of ease I would use a very fine grater rather than the spikes, and settle for something a little coarser.

**Cheese Straws**

# Nachos with Melted Cheese, Tomato Salsa & Guacamole

Serves **4** / Start to Finish **Salsa 1 h 15 m** / Guacamole 10 m / Nachos 10 m

The popularity of this line-up makes it a must for the repertoire, and when it raises its game it is worthy of our adulation. Great for those home-cinema evenings – put on a film, black out the windows, turn out the lights, nachos at the ready.

**For the nachos**

tortilla chips – 100g

Emmental – 100g, grated

**For the tomato salsa**

ripe tomatoes – 500g, skinned and deseeded (see page 18)

flat-leaf parsley or coriander – 2 tablespoons, finely chopped

extra virgin olive oil – 1 tablespoon

lemon juice – 1 tablespoon

chilli sauce (e.g. Maggi's Extra Hot) – 1 tablespoon

shallot – 1 heaped tablespoon, finely chopped

sea salt

**For the guacamole**

avocados – 2

red onion – 1 level tablespoon, coarsely chopped

medium-hot red chilli – ½ teaspoon, diced

coriander – 1 tablespoon, coarsely chopped

lime or lemon juice – 1 tablespoon

extra virgin olive oil – 1 tablespoon

sea salt

### Make the tomato salsa

Finely chop the flesh of the **tomatoes** and combine in a large bowl with the **rest of the ingredients for the salsa**. Tip into a sieve, set over a bowl to collect the juices, and chill for at least an hour or overnight. (The tomato salsa should keep well for 24 hours in the fridge; drain off any liquid that collects in the base of the bowl before serving.)

### Make the guacamole

Halve the **avocados,** twist to separate and remove the stones. Scoop the flesh into the bowl of a food processor. Add **all the remaining ingredients for the guacamole** and reduce to a coarse purée. Transfer to a serving bowl, cover with clingfilm and chill for up to half a day.

### Heat the tortilla chips with the cheese

Preheat the oven to 160°C fan/180°C electric/gas 4. Arrange the **tortilla chips** in a crowded single layer in a roasting pan, scatter over the grated **Emmental** and bake in the oven for 5–7 minutes until the cheese is gooey and melted. Scoop into a serving bowl or onto plates, and dish up straight away with tomato salsa and guacamole.

*Serving suggestion*

— Just before serving, drizzle the guacamole with extra virgin olive oil and dust with paprika, cayenne pepper or cumin.

# Cherry Tomato & Parmesan Tarts

Serves **6** / Start to Finish **40 m**

Anything that looks like a pizza is bound to get hoovered up, and these small puff-pastry tarts are a family favourite on picnics. A good choice whenever you are asked to bring along a tray of something, cut into quarters and halves for handing round.

block of puff pastry (preferably all-butter) – 300g

plain flour, for dusting

Dijon mustard, for spreading

cherry tomatoes – 300g, halved

medium egg yolk – 1

water – 1 tablespoon

sea salt, black pepper

Parmesan – 30g, finely shaved

extra virgin olive oil

**Variation**

**Varying the topping:** Use this recipe as a basic and vary the topping with anything you might find in the local pizza parlour (see page 62).

**Prepare the tart bases**

Preheat the oven to 200°C fan/220°C electric/gas 7. Divide the **pastry** into two equal blocks and dust your worksurface lightly with **flour**. Using a rolling pin, roll out each pastry block to form a large rectangle, approx. 3mm thick. Cut out 6 x 12cm circles using a bowl or plate as a guide and arrange on a couple of baking sheets.

**Assemble the tarts and bake**

Spread a thin layer of **Dijon mustard** over each pastry circle, to within about 2cm of the rim, and then scatter the **tomatoes** over the top. Blend the **egg yolk** with the **water** and brush all over the pastry border. Season the tomatoes with **salt and pepper**, dot with a few slivers of **Parmesan** and drizzle with a little **olive oil**. Bake in the oven for 15–20 minutes until golden and risen.

# Gooey Spinach & Gruyère Tart

Serves **6** / Start to Finish **2 h** (+ making the pastry)

This spinach tart comes next on the list after the classic Quiche Lorraine on the following page for having a texture to die for. I find the combination of melted cheese and spinach is positively exquisite, with or without the pastry.

shortcrust pastry (see page 22) – 400g, chilled

plain flour, for dusting

### For the filling

spinach – 800g, washed

whipping cream – 300ml

medium eggs – 3

sea salt, black pepper

freshly grated nutmeg

Gruyère – 200g, grated

cherry tomatoes – 120g, halved

groundnut or vegetable oil

you will need a tart tin, 24cm in diameter and 4cm deep

**Prepare the pastry case**
Preheat the oven to 180°C fan/200°C electric/gas 6 and place a baking sheet inside to heat up. (This should help the pastry base to crisp.) Roll out the **pastry** on a lightly **floured** worksurface and use to line a 24cm tart tin (see page 23 for instructions). Prick the base all over with a fork, line with foil, fill with baking beans and bake blind (see page 23). Set aside to cool.

**Cook the spinach**
You will probably need to cook this quantity of **spinach** in two pans, or in two batches. Place in a large saucepan with just the water that clings to the leaves, cover with a lid and steam over a medium heat for approx. 10 minutes or until the spinach collapses, stirring halfway through.

**Drain the spinach \***
Drain into a sieve and press out as much liquid as possible using a large spoon. Either set aside to cool and drain, or don some rubber gloves and squeeze handfuls of the spinach between your hands to extract every last trace of moisture. Place the spinach on a board and roughly slice it.

**Make the filling**
Whisk the **cream**, **eggs**, some **salt and pepper** and a little grated **nutmeg** in a bowl. Stir in the spinach, making sure it is evenly distributed, and then half the **grated cheese**.

**Fill the tart**
Transfer the mixture to the tart case and smooth the surface. Toss the **cherry tomatoes** in a bowl with just enough **oil** to coat them and a little seasoning. Scatter these over the surface of the tart and press them into the filling to level them with the spinach. Sprinkle over the remaining cheese, mainly towards the centre.

**Bake the tart**
Bake for 35–45 minutes until golden and fully set. Remove from the oven and leave to cool for 10–20 minutes before removing the collar. While this is best eaten hot or warm from the oven, it does reheat successfully (see page 56).

### The knack

**\* Draining the spinach:** Success here depends on squeezing out every last drop of liquid from the cooked spinach, otherwise the custard filling won't set properly. So keep squeezing and squeezing until you have a solid mass.

# Quiche Lorraine

Serves **6** / Start to Finish **2 h** (+ making the pastry)

I don't want to mislead you into thinking a Quiche Lorraine is one to knock up mid-week after work, but it remains one of the best party pieces – for lunch when you have friends staying, as the lead into dinner or served in delicate slivers to pass around with a drink. It has a nonchalant old-world glamour, a dish that's earned its stripes over the years. I never tire of pulling one of these puffed, golden tarts out of the oven, with its wobbly lightly set custard and tantalising aroma of bacon, toasted cheese and buttery pastry. This version is nothing like those rubbery, ready-made quiches.

shortcrust pastry (see page 22) – 400g, chilled

plain flour, for dusting

### For the filling

smoked lardons – 250g (or dry-cured rindless streaky bacon, cut into 1cm dice)

Gruyère – 175g, grated

whipping cream – 300ml

whole milk – 150ml

medium eggs – 3

medium egg yolk – 1

Dijon mustard – 1 teaspoon

grainy mustard – 1 teaspoon

black pepper

you will need a tart tin, 24cm in diameter and 4cm deep

**Prepare the pastry case**
Preheat the oven to 180°C fan/200°C electric/gas 6 and place a baking sheet inside to heat up. (This should help the pastry base to crisp.) Roll out the **pastry** on a lightly **floured** worksurface and use to line a 24cm tart tin (see page 23 for instructions). Prick the base all over with a fork, line with foil, fill with baking beans and bake blind (see page 23). Set aside to cool.

**Fry the lardons**
Separate out the **lardons**, place them in a large non-stick frying pan and cook over a very low heat until the fat begins to render. Turn up the heat to medium and cook, stirring frequently, until the bacon starts to colour and crisp. Scatter over the base of the tart case.

**Make the filling**
Combine half the **grated cheese** in a bowl with the **remaining ingredients for the filling** and whisk together until combined. The bacon and cheese are quite salty already, so you shouldn't need any extra, simply pepper.

**Fill the tart and bake**
Pour the custard into the tart case and scatter the remaining cheese over the surface. Carefully transfer the quiche onto the hot baking sheet in the oven and bake for about 35 minutes until golden and puffy. It may appear to wobble when moved from side to side but should be fully set. Remove the tart from the oven and leave to cool for 10–20 minutes to give the filling time to settle before removing the collar. While it is best eaten hot from the oven, this can also be eaten at room temperature or chilled. To reheat, wrap in foil and pop into a moderate oven (180°C fan/200°C electric/gas 6) for approx. 20 minutes.

*Serving suggestion*
— Being rich and very salty, it's hard to find a more apt aside than a big bowl of crispy salad leaves licked with a tart mustardy vinaigrette (see page 258), which will cut through its excess.

# Beetroot & Goat's Cheese Tray Tart

Serves **4–6** / Start to Finish **1 h 10 m**

This big puff pastry tart has pissaladière-like appeal with its base of silky onions. Perfect for handing round as an appetiser or eating with a green salad.

extra virgin olive oil – 5 tablespoons

large onions – 4, peeled, halved and thinly sliced

sea salt, black pepper

cooked beetroot (unvinegared) – 200g, thinly sliced into rounds

balsamic vinegar – 1 tablespoon

ready-rolled puff pastry (preferably all-butter) – 1 x 320g sheet, approx. 25 x 35cm

1 egg yolk blended with 1 tablespoon milk to form an eggwash

young soft goat's cheese – 100g, broken into 1–2cm pieces

lemon thyme leaves – 1 tablespoon

**Fry the onions and prepare the beetroot**
Heat 2 tablespoons **olive oil** in a large saucepan over a medium-low heat and fry the **onions** for about 20 minutes until syrupy and lightly golden, stirring frequently especially towards the end. Season with **salt and pepper**. Meanwhile toss the **beetroot** in a medium-sized bowl with 1 tablespoon oil, the **vinegar** and some seasoning.

**Assemble the tart**
Preheat the oven to 190°C fan/210°C electric/gas 6½. Unroll the **pastry** onto a baking sheet, and cut off a small 1cm triangle from each corner. Brush all around the outside with the **eggwash**, and then fold in a 1cm border all round to create a little lip. Brush again with eggwash. Pile the cooked onions in the centre and spread out in an even layer, making sure they don't extend over the lip. Arrange the beetroot slices over the surface, followed by the **goat's cheese** and **thyme**. Drizzle with the remaining 2 tablespoons olive oil.

**Bake the tart**
Bake in the oven for 25 minutes until golden and crusty. Serve about 15 minutes out of the oven, or at room temperature.

# Pizza Dough

Serves **2** / Makes **500g** / Start to Finish **1–2 h**

Both my children have been raised on the occasional after-school convenience of shop-bought pizzas, and I would hate to have been without them. However, I do balk at their lengthy shelf-life, which makes them far from fresh. So now the boys are big enough to help, we've turned Saturday lunchtimes into a family affair. Even better, it's a father and son affair. In fact this could be the recipe that tempts a reluctant cook into the kitchen.

strong white bread flour – 300g, plus extra for dusting

dried yeast – ½ teaspoon

caster sugar – ½ teaspoon

Maldon sea salt – 1 teaspoon

extra virgin olive oil – 1 tablespoon

hand-hot water – approx. 175ml

**Make the dough**

*By machine:* A food processor is the lazy pizza-lover's route to bread dough, however you could also use an orbital mixer. Set up the machine with the dough blade. Place **all the dry ingredients** and the **olive oil** in the bowl. Keeping the motor running throughout, slowly add the **water**, stopping when the mixture starts to clump – you might not need all of it. Whizz for a further 4–5 minutes to knead the dough.

*By hand:* Place **all the dry ingredients** in a large bowl with the **olive oil**. Gradually add the **water** and bring the dough together with your hand. The amount of water is for guidance only. If you add too much, simply sprinkle on some more flour until you have a workable dough again. Dust your worksurface lightly with flour, turn out the dough and knead until smooth and elastic, approx. 8–10 minutes.

**Leave the dough to rise \***

Place the dough in a lightly floured bowl and slash a cross on the surface to facilitate its rising. Loosely cover with a plastic bag or a clean tea towel and set aside in a warm place such as an airing cupboard to rise for 1–2 hours.

The knack

\* **Making the dough in advance?** I find a long, slow rising gives the dough a better flavour. Simply whizz up the dough the night before and set it aside in the fridge to chill overnight. Remove it from the fridge the following morning and leave it to rise slowly at room temperature until needed.

# Four Cheese Pizza

Serves **2** / Makes **2** / Start to Finish **30 m** (+ making the dough)

A Four Cheese Pizza is a Marguerita with lots of gooey add-ons, surely born from the decision of whether to have mozzarella, Gorgonzola, Parmesan or ricotta on top. Simple solution.

pizza dough – 500g (see page 61)
plain flour, for dusting

**For the tomato sauce**
passata rustica – 6 tablespoons
extra virgin olive oil – 1 tablespoon
sea salt, black pepper

**For the topping**
mozzarella – 100g, torn into pieces
Gorgonzola – 50g, cut into 1cm dice
ricotta – 50g
Parmesan – 50g, thinly sliced
rocket, to serve

you will need a pizza stone (or baking sheet) and a pizza paddle (or second baking sheet)

**Variation**
**Varying the topping:** Lay out any number of the following ingredients as a pizza bar, mixing and matching as you wish, using the tomato sauce as a base:
sliced or diced mozzarella or goat's cheese
strips of ham or pepperoni
pitted green or black olives
thinly sliced artichokes in oil
strips of roast pepper (see page 246)
sliced button mushrooms, coated in olive oil
drizzle of pesto sauce (see page 190)

**Preheat a baking sheet or pizza stone \***
Preheat the oven to 230°C fan/250°C electric/gas 9. Place a baking sheet or pizza stone inside the oven and preheat for 15–20 minutes.

**Punch down and knead the dough**
Punch down the **dough** with your fist, turn it out onto a lightly **floured** worksurface and knead for a minute or two until smooth. Divide the dough into two equal pieces and shape into balls. Using a rolling pin, roll one ball into a circle about 30cm in diameter. I find it easiest to part roll and part pull the dough into shape, holding the edge nearest me steady on the worksurface with my hand while rolling the opposite edge. Don't worry if it's a bit skewed, all the more artisanal.

**Transfer the pizza base to a baking sheet or pizza paddle \*\***
Dust a second baking sheet, or pizza paddle, liberally with flour and place the rolled dough on top. It is a good idea at this point to try to slide the pizza off, to check that it's not sticking, before you load it up. For a spongier pizza, you can rest the rolled pizza base for 20 minutes in a warm place before dressing.

**Top the pizza**
To make the tomato sauce, blend the **passata** and **olive oil** with some **seasoning** in a small bowl. Top the pizza with half the tomato sauce, spreading it to within a couple of centimetres of the rim using the back of a spoon or palette knife. Arrange half the **mozzarella** and half the **Gorgonzola** over the surface, dot with half the **ricotta** and scatter over half the **Parmesan** slivers.

**Bake the pizza**
Slide the pizza from the floured baking sheet or paddle onto the sheet or stone in the oven. The best way to do this is to place it right at the back of the tray or stone and give the paddle a sharp jolt forward. Bake for 8–10 minutes or until the underside is golden in patches and the edges are starting to bubble up and colour unevenly. I only have one pizza stone so I usually put one pizza in to bake and assemble the next one while the first pizza is cooking. Scatter over some **rocket** to serve.

### The knack

\* **A pizza stone** mimics the floor of a traditional bread oven. The key here is to make sure you preheat it for at least 15 minutes beforehand.

\*\* **A pizza paddle** is essential if you plan to use a pizza stone. The ones intended to service your local Pizza Express will be the size of a spade, however a short-handled one will still ensure your pizza glides onto the stone in one easy piece.

# Soup

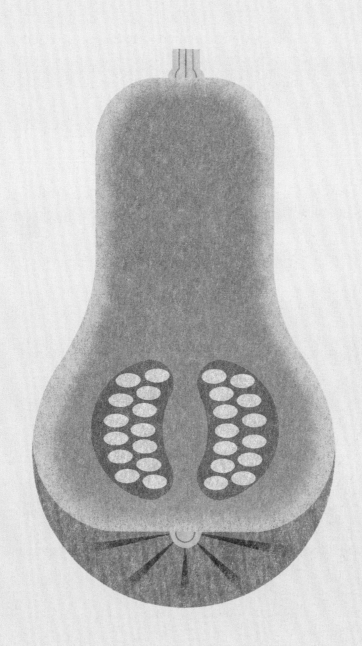

3

# Roast Tomato & Basil Soup

Serves **4** / Start to Finish **30 m**

A really vibrant tomato soup that is so much more dynamic for the tomatoes having been roasted in a very hot oven. As well as serving it steaming hot, like gazpacho this is perfect supped ice-cool on a very hot day.

medium tomatoes (preferably on the vine) – 1.5kg

extra virgin olive oil – 6 tablespoons, plus extra to serve

sea salt, black pepper

caster sugar – ½ teaspoon

basil leaves – approx. 8 large, plus a few tiny leaves to garnish

**Roast the tomatoes**
Preheat the oven to 220°C fan/240°C electric/gas 9. Arrange the **tomatoes** in a single layer in a large roasting pan. Drizzle over 3 tablespoons **olive oil** and roast for 20 minutes. Set aside until cool enough to handle.

**Liquidise the tomatoes and finish the soup**
Pinch the tomatoes off the vines using a fork and discard the stalks. Tip into a blender, along with their roasting juices, and add a good dose of **salt**, some **black pepper**, the **sugar**, large **basil leaves** and 3 tablespoons olive oil. Liquidise until smooth, then pass through a sieve into a saucepan.
To serve, reheat gently over a low heat, ladle into bowls and drizzle each one with olive oil. Garnish with a couple of small basil leaves.

# Roast Beetroot & Lemon Soup

Serves **4** / Start to Finish **50 m**

The sheer simplicity of this soup makes it true to the vegetable, whether you serve it hot or chilled. There is never any need to peel beetroots for roasting, the skin gives them a rustic edge and provides an earthy savour too.

medium raw beetroot – 1kg, washed but not peeled

extra virgin olive oil – 3 tablespoons

sea salt, black pepper

water – 800ml

lemon zest – 1 strip, removed with a potato peeler

lemon juice – 1 tablespoon

**To serve**
crème fraîche
watercress, coarsely chopped

**Roast the beetroot**
Preheat the oven to 220°C fan/240°C electric/gas 9. Without peeling the **beetroots**, trim the tops and bottoms of shoots and roots, and then quarter or cut them into wedges. Arrange in a large roasting pan, pour over the **olive oil** and season with **salt and pepper.** Roast for 40 minutes until tender, stirring halfway through.

**Liquidise the soup in batches**
Tip the cooked beetroots, along with any roasting juices, into a blender and purée with the **water**, the **lemon zest and juice**, and plenty of seasoning. Pass through a sieve into a saucepan and reheat gently over a low heat. Ladle into bowls and serve with a spoonful of **crème fraîche** and lots of chopped **watercress**.

# Allotment Reward Soup

Serves **6** / Start to Finish **25 m**

A *Potage Bonne Femme* ('Good Housewife Soup', don't be put off) is one of the most soothing home-cooked soups. Carrots, leeks and potatoes are also the comfort in an Irish stew, but without any meat this recipe is light and nourishing. The pinnacle here has to be veggies freshly pulled from the soil, and also a good homemade stock.

carrots – 300g, trimmed, peeled and cut into thick slices

leeks – 300g (trimmed weight), approx. 4–6, cut into thick slices

maincrop potatoes – 300g, peeled and cut into 2cm dice

soft lemon thyme leaves – 1 teaspoon

sea salt, black pepper

salted butter – 50g, diced

dry white wine – 200ml *

chicken or vegetable stock – 1.2 litres (see page 24)

## Variations

**Low-carb Vegetable Soup:** Omit the potatoes and use 500g each of carrots and leeks instead.

**Farmhouse Vegetable Soup:** Use a medium cider in lieu of the wine.

### Prepare the vegetables
Combine the **carrots, leeks** and **potatoes** in a large saucepan. Scatter over the **thyme leaves** and season with a generous dose of **salt**. Dot with the **butter** and pour over the **wine**.

### Cook the vegetables **
Place the pan over a medium heat, bring to the boil, and then cover and simmer for 8 minutes. Take off the lid, give the vegetables a quick stir and cook, uncovered, over a high heat until all the wine has evaporated. Pour in the **stock**, bring to the boil and simmer for 10 minutes or until the vegetables are tender.

### Liquidise the soup
For a textured soup with a little bite, blitz the soup to a coarse purée in a food processor. For a thicker, smooth soup, liquidise the soup in a blender.

### Dish up
Return the puréed soup to the saucepan, season with **black pepper** and a little more salt if needed, and reheat over a low heat. Serve in warm bowls.

*Serving suggestion*
— Scatter over some chopped flat-leaf parsley or chervil.

### The knack

\* **The wine** adds a much-needed piquancy to the soup.

\*\* **Glazing the vegetables:** The vegetables are steamed first with the butter and wine, and then glazed to give the soup an intensely buttery flavour that you wouldn't acquire by simply frying them.

# Butternut Piri-piri Soup

Serves **6** / Start to Finish **1 h 15 m**

Butternuts keep for an age, months, so they serve as a good storecupboard vegetable. And quite likely you will have onions, tomatoes and chillies as a matter of course, so this is a great fallback soup. Pep it up by serving with a few of your favourite pickled chillies.

butternut squash – approx. 1.5–1.6kg, peeled, deseeded and cut into chunks a few cm in size

large onions – 2, peeled, halved and fairly thinly sliced

medium tomatoes (preferably on the vine) – 4, halved

medium-hot red chilli – 1, approx. 5–7cm in length *

extra virgin olive oil – 4 tablespoons

sea salt

chicken or vegetable stock – 900ml (see page 24)

**To serve**

soured cream

fresh coriander, coarsely chopped

pickled piri-piri or jalapeño peppers (optional)

### Roast the vegetables **

Preheat the oven to 200°C fan/220°C electric/gas 7. Arrange the **squash**, **onion** and **tomatoes** in a couple of large roasting pans so that they fit in a crowded single layer, adding the **chilli** to one of them. Drizzle a couple of tablespoons of **olive oil** over each roasting pan and season with **salt**. Roast for 55 minutes, stirring halfway through.

### Liquidise the vegetables in batches

Remove the roasted vegetables from the oven and discard any of the onion strands that are particularly dark. Cut the chilli in half lengthways and scrape out and discard the seeds. Tip one tray of vegetables into a blender, add the chilli and half the **stock** and liquidise until smooth. Pass through a sieve into a clean saucepan. Liquidise and strain the remaining tray of vegetables in the same way with the remaining stock.

### Dish up

Reheat the soup over a low heat and ladle into bowls. Serve with a spoonful of **soured cream**, some **chopped coriander** and a **pickled chilli** if you wish.

### The knack

* **Which chillies?** Bear in mind that smaller chillies tend to pack the biggest punch. For this you'll need a medium-sized one, about 5–7cm in length. It is the seeds in a chilli that provide the heat, which is why we discard them; there should be just the right amount of resonant warmth in the juices and flesh that remain. For a hotter soup, simply scatter over more pickled chillies at the end.

** **Roasting the vegetables:** The onion is likely to colour more quickly than the rest, so you need to keep an eye and stir the vegetables halfway through. Tuck any onions that look as though they are darkening too quickly under the other veg to protect them.

# Simple Watercress Soup

Serves **4–6** / Start to Finish **30 m**

I first ate this beautiful and austere soup at Le Gavroche and was on the phone for the recipe the minute I got home. I was delighted (and amazed) to discover there was no veal stock or anything else that might hamper a first go, and I have been cooking it ever since. The method itself is brilliant for any leafy green of this nature, so this is a great prototype soup.

chicken or vegetable stock – 1 litre *

unsalted butter – 50g

watercress – 250g (3 good-sized bunches), leaves and fine stalks

maincrop potatoes – 280g, peeled and finely sliced **

sea salt, black pepper

flat-leaf parsley – 25g, leaves and fine stalks ***

**Variations**

**Wild Garlic Soup, Rocket Soup or Spinach Soup:** Substitute the watercress for wild garlic, rocket or spinach.
You could play around with different mixtures, if you wish, flavouring with a little sorrel.

**Prepare the soup base**
Bring the **stock** to the boil in a small saucepan. Melt the **butter** in a large saucepan over a medium heat, add the **watercress** and stir until it wilts. Add the **sliced potatoes** and stir for a minute longer, then pour in the boiling stock and season with **salt and pepper**.

**Simmer the soup and liquidise**
Simmer the soup for 6 minutes or until the potatoes are just tender, and then liquidise in a blender with the **parsley**.

**Dish up**
Season to taste and ladle into bowls.

*Serving suggestion*
— Finish with a dollop of crème fraîche or a swirl of soured cream.

The knack

\* **Which stock?** Being such a simple soup, the ideal is a good homemade chicken broth (see page 24), but otherwise water would be preferable to a stock cube, which will likely overwhelm it.

\*\* **Why slice the potatoes?** Slicing the potatoes very finely means they cook in no time. This soup has everything to do with speed – the idea is to capture the vibrant green of the watercress, which would dull with lengthy simmering.

\*\*\* **Adding the parsley:** I like to liquidise the soup with some raw flat-leaf parsley, which gives it added vibrancy, but this isn't essential. Alternatively you could scatter the finished soup with some chopped parsley instead.

# Icy Gazpacho

Serves **4** / Start to Finish **15 m**

The call for gazpacho gets ever stronger as the temperature rises, and it remains the greatest of all chilled soups. Try to think of it as a salad in liquid form, the ultimate savoury smoothie, so the flavour of your tomatoes is all-important, even if their texture is lacking.

cherry tomatoes – 1kg *

cucumber – 1, peeled and cut into pieces (ends discarded)

garlic clove – 1, peeled and roughly chopped

medium-hot fresh red chilli – 1 heaped teaspoon, finely chopped

onion – 2 heaped teaspoons, finely chopped

extra virgin olive oil – 125ml **

red wine or sherry vinegar – ½ tablespoon

caster sugar – 2 heaped teaspoons

Maldon sea salt – 2 rounded teaspoons

black pepper

day-old white bread (e.g. sourdough or pain de campagne) – 3 thick slices, crusts removed and broken into pieces (trimmed weight approx. 90g) ***

**Liquidise the ingredients ***
Place **all the ingredients** for the soup – **except for the bread** – in a blender and reduce to a purée, then pass through a sieve into a clean bowl. You will have to do this in batches. Rinse out the blender and purée the soup again, this time with the **bread**. Pour the soup into a large serving bowl, cover with clingfilm and chill for at least an hour, but don't keep it longer than necessary.

*Serving suggestions*
— Serve with some olive oil splashed over each bowl.
— Scatter a few cooked shelled prawns, some slivers of smoked salmon and a spoonful of crabmeat over each bowl.
— Scatter over a chopped hard-boiled egg and some diced avocado.
— Spoon into small cups and accompany with a big plate of Parma ham and some cocktail gherkins or caper berries. This makes a great appetiser when you have friends round for a barbecue.

The knack

* **Which tomatoes?** As a rule of thumb, the smaller the tomato the sweeter the flavour – so during those months when tomatoes aren't in season I would choose cherry tomatoes. However during the summer, when they are plentiful, a ripe plum tomato is hard to beat. If you happen to have a farm shop or know a market stall that puts the slightly misshapen and mushy ones in a box to the side for sauces, these would be excellent too.

** **Which olive oil?** A good olive oil will come into its own here, my own preference being for a Sicilian or Umbrian one – something elegant but not too peppery.

*** **Liquidising tips:** You need to liquidise the soup twice, straining in between to attain a smooth vegetable purée. The bread, which is added when you purée the soup for the second time, will plump up while the soup is chilling, thickening it in the process.

# All-round Lentil Soup

Serves **6** / Start to Finish **1 h**

This was a staple in my fridge when I was weaning my children, as I could titrate the consistency from smooth and creamy to gradually more textured, all the while being assured that every spoonful came loaded with mother love and goodness. At any other time, lentil soup is the equivalent of a family supper wearing a onesie, glam doesn't really come into it.

Of the many lentils on offer, it is the humble tiny bead-like red ones that make for the most satisfying soup. Not only do they collapse to a wholesome mush as they simmer, but also they act as a sponge for other flavours, their own contribution to the party being their nourishing sweetness and mealy quality.

extra virgin olive oil – 4 tablespoons

leeks – 2, trimmed and thickly sliced

carrots – 4, trimmed, peeled and thickly sliced

celery heart – 1, trimmed and thickly sliced

fresh root ginger – 1 heaped tablespoon, finely chopped

medium-hot red chilli – 1 heaped teaspoon, finely chopped

garlic cloves – 4, peeled and finely chopped

red lentils – 500g, rinsed

cider vinegar – 3 tablespoons

chicken or vegetable stock – 2 litres (see page 24)

sea salt

**Prepare the soup base**
Heat the **olive oil** in a large saucepan over a medium heat, add the **leeks, carrots, celery, ginger** and **chilli** and fry for about 10 minutes until softened and starting to colour. Then add the **garlic** and cook for a few minutes. Stir in the **lentils**, add the **cider vinegar** and pour in the **stock**.

**Skim the soup and cook the lentils** *
Bring the soup to the boil, skim off any surface foam, and then simmer for 30 minutes or until the lentils are tender. Season with **salt**.

**Liquidise the soup and dish up**
Purée the soup in batches in a blender and taste for seasoning. Return the soup to the pan and reheat over a low heat. **

*Serving suggestions*
— For Oriental flair, scatter over some coarsely chopped coriander, finely sliced spring onion, finely sliced red chilli and coarsely chopped roasted peanuts.
— Garnish with a dollop of yogurt and some chopped flat-leaf parsley.
— Scatter over some crispy lardons or snippets of ham.
— Drizzle over some olive oil and finish with a grating of fresh Parmesan.

The knack

* **Skimming the soup:** The foam that rises to the surface when you simmer lentils contains the impurities. Unless you skim this off, it is liable to cook back into the soup.

** **Reheating the soup:** Occasionally lentil soup will thicken if allowed to cool. If this is the case, reheat gently and then thin it to the desired consistency with a drop of water.

# Moroccan Spicy Lamb & Split Pea Hotpot

Serves **6** / Start to Finish **2 h**

There are lots of flavours and textures jumbling around in this hotpot, which makes a comforting cold weather bowlful scented with turmeric, ginger and cinnamon, with tender shreds of lamb and mealy split peas.

lamb neck fillet (or boneless shoulder meat) – 1.2kg, cut into approx. 2cm medallions

medium onions – 2, peeled and quite finely chopped

head of garlic – 1, cloves peeled

thyme – a small bunch (approx. 10 sprigs), tied

sea salt

water – 2 litres

yellow split peas – 300g

celery sticks – 4, trimmed and finely sliced

crushed chilli flakes – ¼ teaspoon

ground turmeric – 1 teaspoon

ground ginger – 1 teaspoon

ground cinnamon – ½ teaspoon

saffron filaments – a pinch (approx. 30)

medium tomatoes – 4, skinned (see page 18) and coarsely chopped

plain flour – 1 heaped teaspoon

lemon – juice of ½

fresh coriander and flat-leaf parsley – 3 tablespoons of each, finely chopped

**Variation**

**Spicy Lamb and Split Pea Hotpot with Noodles:** Add a handful or two of fine vermicelli noodles a few minutes before the end.

### Simmer the lamb
Place the **lamb** in a large cast-iron or other heavy casserole with the **onion**, whole **garlic cloves**, **thyme**, some **salt** and the **water**. Bring to the boil and skim off the foam that rises to the surface. Cover with a lid and simmer over a low heat for 30 minutes.

### Add the split peas and flavourings
Add the **split peas**, **celery**, **chilli**, **spices** and **tomatoes**, cover with a lid and simmer for a further hour.

### Finish the soup and dish up
Whisk the **flour** with the **lemon juice** in a small bowl, and stir this into the soup. Bring back to the boil and simmer for 3–4 minutes to cook out the flour. Discard the thyme, stir in the chopped **herbs** and season to taste. Serve in warm bowls.

# Chicken Noodle Laksa

Serves **6** / Start to Finish **30 m**

Sweet, spicy and soothing. Like many Asian dishes, this recipe might initially appear complex with its different flavouring ingredients, but in fact it is one of the quickest soups on the block, taking some 10 minutes to cook once everything is prepared. Very much a main course soup.

groundnut oil – 2 tablespoons

garlic – 1 teaspoon, finely chopped

fresh root ginger – 1 teaspoon, finely chopped

medium-hot red chilli – 1 teaspoon, finely chopped, plus a little extra to serve

button mushrooms – 200g, stalks trimmed and thinly sliced

carrots – 2, trimmed, peeled, halved and thinly sliced

celery heart – 1, thinly sliced

ground turmeric – 1 teaspoon

thread fine noodles (straight-to-wok) – 300g

cooked chicken – 500g, shredded

chicken stock – 800ml (see page 24)

caster sugar – 1 teaspoon

dark soy sauce – 2 tablespoons

lime – juice of 1

coconut milk – 1 x 400ml tin

fresh coriander, coarsely chopped, to serve

**Stir-fry the vegetables, noodles and chicken**
Heat the **oil** in a large saucepan over a medium heat. Add the **garlic**, **ginger** and **chilli** and stir-fry briefly to release their flavour. Add the **mushrooms** and stir-fry for a couple of minutes until soft. Then put in the **carrots** and **celery** and stir-fry until these too are softened and glossy, while slightly crisp, approx. 5 minutes. Stir in the **turmeric**, **noodles** and **cooked chicken**.

**Add the stock and other flavouring ingredients**
Pour in the **stock** to cover the ingredients and bring to a simmer. Season with the **sugar**, **soy sauce** and **lime juice**. In a separate small saucepan, heat the **coconut milk** without allowing it to boil and stir into the soup.

**Dish up**
Ladle the soup into warm bowls and serve scattered with some coarsely chopped fresh **coriander** and a little **fresh chilli**.

# Birds

4

# About **Birds**

**Chicken**

The difference in quality between a free-range and an intensively reared bird is that between a flavour that is deeply savoury and satisfying and one that tastes of diddly squat, and on top of that there is the depressing scenario of the life an intensively reared bird has led.

As it is, most supermarkets do offer up a decent free-range bird, but if it doesn't advertise this, assume it isn't. One small, niggling caveat: always rummage to the back of the shelf to get the chicken with the longest shelf-life. I have never cooked a bird within 48 hours of its use-by date and found it to be fresh enough. So look for a minimum of 4 days.

Variety too plays its part, and I particularly favour French birds that are tasty with a firm toothsome flesh. Label Rouge is a good marque, should you get the choice. Equally, though, neither you nor the bird is likely to be gaining by paying silly sums of money.

**Duck**

Even the plumpest duck will cook down to half its original size in the throes of roasting, given the generous layering of fat that is the secret to its succulent flesh. This renders during cooking and can be saved and put to all manner of uses such as frying up or roasting potatoes. Do look for a bird that has its giblets, which can be used for making stock; the liver is delicious, sliced and briefly fried in a little butter.

**Pheasant**

Always go for a hen over a cock, especially if you are roasting the bird. The female of the species might come up a little bit smaller than the male, but it makes for more tender eating. And, equally, a young bird is likely to be more scrumptious than an older one, which will be good for little other than the stockpot. In this sense, a good butcher will serve you well, as most are picky about what they sell, and with a bit of luck might know the sex as well as the age of the bird.

The great *faux-pas* with pheasant is overcooking. A bird that weighs in at 700–800g – half the size of an average chicken – will be roasted to perfection in just 30 minutes.

**Guinea fowl**

Guinea fowl is everything you could hope for in a good chicken, and more. Succulent, dark meat with a deep flavour and the kind of texture we value in really well-reared chickens, French ones especially. Guinea fowl can be used interchangeably for any of the roasts and pot-roasts in this chapter. Simply take its size into account – on average they come up the size of a small chicken, approx. 1.2kg, so cook for 45 minutes.

**Whole bird or jointed meat?**

It is always more economical to buy a whole rather than a jointed bird; breast fillets are especially pricey. So you could do worse than buy from a butcher who can joint your bird for you. If it is the breasts you are after, you will be left with a handful of wings and legs that can be chucked in the freezer for another day.

**Storage**

There are some serious health hazards associated with raw poultry, as a significant amount is contaminated, hence we are advised not to wash chickens, which will only activate the bacteria. By extension, the incidence of contamination is radically lower in dry-plucked birds, which being labour-intensive are by default reared in small flocks. If you buy online, a producer is likely to flag this. But otherwise, the rather rough-looking birds with singed feather-stubs that you find at farmers' markets are the ones to seek out.

For supermarket birds, always cook them right through and be aware of possible cross-contamination. For instance, if you have marinated the chicken, avoid spooning the residue over the cooked meat, or putting it back on the plate that contained it raw. For information on defrosting, see page 110.

**Cooking**

To check if a whole bird is cooked, insert a sharp knife into the thickest section of the thigh; the juices should run clear. If they seem at all bloody, give the bird a little longer. The legs should also feel loose and as though you could pull them away from the body with ease.

**Resting**

Resting allows the juices to distribute evenly and the flesh time to relax, making the bird infinitely more tender. See individual recipes for recommended resting times.

**Carving**

Carving a chicken is almost self-explanatory. Most of us are after nice, thin slices of breast, and are familiar with that 'you first' offering at the table, which means you are unlikely to end up with the top sliver with crispy skin that is the prize piece. So cut across it, and ease the legs and wings away from the body before detaching them with a tug. And do remember to hang on to the carcass if you fancy making soup or have the need for stock (see page 24).

**What to do with leftovers**

Students could do worse than roast up a chicken once a week, for the myriad ways of stretching it out in the days that follow. Let your imagination wander towards Thai Green Chicken Curry (see page 96), Caesar Salad (page 259), Bang Bang Chicken Salad (page 278), toasted sarnies with lettuce, mayo, bacon and gherkins, stir-fries (pages 241–2) and Chicken Noodle Laksa (page 76).

# Homecoming Roast Chicken with Gravy

Serves **4–6** / Start to Finish **1 h 15 m**

It is this sort of basic that inspired me to write this book, far too simple for the average remit or a restaurant, it is unthinkable that a whole generation stands to grow up without knowing how to cook it. This is the simplest possible rendition of roast chicken and gravy, worth learning by heart. Even if you never learn to cook it any other way, you will still keep many a close one happy. Served with a pan of sautéed potatoes (see page 212) and a lovely green salad, this is home cooking at its best. (For roast chicken variations, see pages 84–5.)

free-range chicken – 1 x 1.6kg, untrussed *
extra virgin olive oil
sea salt, black pepper
dry white wine – 150ml
plain flour – 1 heaped teaspoon (optional)
chicken stock – 300ml (see page 24)

**Chicken Roasting Times**

| 190°C fan/210°C electric/gas 6½ | |
| --- | --- |
| 1.2kg bird | **45 m** |
| 1.4kg bird | **50 m** |
| 1.6kg bird | **50–55 m** |
| 1.8kg bird | **1 h** |
| 2kg bird | **1 h 10 m** |

**Prepare and roast the chicken**
Preheat the oven to 190°C fan/210°C electric/gas 6½. Select a roasting pan that leaves a little space around the outside of the bird, without swamping it – cast iron or another sturdy pan will allow for making gravy on the hob. Place the **chicken** in the pan, drizzle over a little **olive oil** and season the skin with **salt and pepper**. Transfer the bird to the oven and roast for 50–55 minutes (or according to the time in the chart). If you're after crispy skin, there is no need to cover with foil or baste during cooking. To see if your bird is cooked, pierce the thickest section of the thigh using a small sharp knife – the juices should run clear. If at all bloody, give the bird another 5–10 minutes and test again.

**Rest the chicken and make the gravy**
Transfer the chicken to a warm serving plate, tipping any juices from inside the cavity back into the pan, and leave it to rest for 20 minutes, uncovered. To make the gravy, spoon off the excess fat from the pan and set over a medium heat. Add the **wine** and simmer until reduced by at least half, stirring well to incorporate all the sticky residues on the base of the pan. Stir in the **flour** if you want a slightly viscous gravy (don't worry about small lumps as it will be strained), and then work in the **stock** with a wooden spoon. Simmer until the gravy tastes rich and balanced, seasoning it if necessary.

**Carve the chicken and dish up**
Carve the chicken, adding any juices given out on carving to the gravy. The breast or white meat is traditionally sliced across the grain, while the darker legs and wings are easiest removed whole. To serve, pass the gravy through a sieve into a warm jug or bowl and accompany with the carved meat.

The knack
* **Why untrussed?** If you cook your chicken trussed, so the legs are tightly secured to the breast, the air cannot circulate around it, which makes for a much longer cooking time, and that means an overcooked breast.

# Roast Chicken Variations

## Roast Chicken with Allspice & Thyme

Serves **4–6** / Start to Finish **1 h 20 m**

This is a great roast for serving with salads during the summer.

extra virgin olive oil – 2 tablespoons
lemon juice – 2 tablespoons
paprika – ½ teaspoon
allspice – ¼ teaspoon
thyme leaves – 1 tablespoon
free-range chicken – 1 x 1.6kg, untrussed
sea salt, black pepper

**Preheat the oven and prepare the marinade**
Preheat the oven to 190°C fan/210°C electric/ gas 6½. Combine the **olive oil, lemon juice, paprika, allspice** and **thyme leaves** in a small bowl. Spoon over the **chicken** in a roasting pan, coating the surface of the skin. (If you have time, you can marinate the chicken at this stage: simply cover with clingfilm and chill in the fridge overnight, basting well before roasting.)

**Roast the chicken**
Season the skin all over with **salt and pepper** and roast in the oven for 50–55 minutes, basting a couple of times during roasting.

**Rest the chicken and dish up**
Transfer the chicken to a warm serving plate, tipping any juices from inside the cavity back into the pan, and leave it to rest for 20 minutes. Serve the chicken with the roasting juices spooned over, skimming them of fat.

## Lemon & Butter Roast Chicken (Cold-oven Method)

Serves **4–6** / Start to Finish **1 h 20 m**

This method is particularly useful if you're running late and don't have time to preheat the oven. The skin benefits from that little extra bit of time, and dries out and colours even more than usual.

softened unsalted butter – 75g
free-range chicken – 1 x 1.6kg, untrussed
lemon – 1, halved
sea salt, black pepper

**Prepare the chicken**
Smear the softened **butter** over the **chicken** and place the bird in a roasting pan that will hold the chicken with a little room to spare. Squeeze over the juice of the **lemon** and pop the squeezed-out halves inside the cavity. Season the skin all over with **salt and pepper** and transfer the bird to a cold oven.

**Roast the chicken ***
Set the oven temperature to 200°C fan/220°C electric/gas 7 and roast for 1 hour, basting halfway through.

**Rest the chicken and dish up**
Transfer the chicken to a warm serving plate, tipping any juices from inside the cavity back into the pan, and leave to rest for 20 minutes. Serve the chicken with the roasting juices spooned over, skimming them of fat if you wish, but otherwise indulge in the butter.

**The knack**

* **Cooking time:** Note that the roasting time is 10 minutes longer for this method to allow for the oven heating up.

# Rustic Garlic Roast Chicken

Serves **4–6** / Start to Finish **1 h 20 m**

This is an easy version of this classic, where instead of peeling the cloves you simply roast the heads whole around the bird and squeeze the insides from the casings as you eat.

thyme sprigs – 20g
free-range chicken – 1 x 1.6kg, untrussed
sea salt, black pepper
lemon – 1, halved
softened unsalted butter – 30g
whole garlic heads – 4–6, tops sliced off through the cloves
dry white wine – 150ml
water – a few tablespoons
crème fraîche – 2 tablespoons

**Preheat the oven and prepare the chicken**
Preheat the oven to 190°C fan /210°C electric/ gas 6½. Scatter two-thirds of the **thyme sprigs** over the base of a roasting pan that will hold the chicken with a little room to spare. Place the **chicken** on top and **season**. Pull half the thyme leaves off the remaining sprigs and sprinkle over the chicken with the sprigs. Pop the **lemon** halves, cut-side up, at either end of the bird and dot the chicken and lemon with **butter**.

**Roast the chicken**
Roast in the oven for 20 minutes, then arrange the **garlic** heads around the bird and baste well. Return to the oven for a further 20 minutes, then pour the **wine** into the base of the pan and baste again. Roast for a further 10 minutes.

**Rest the chicken and make the gravy**
Transfer the bird to a warm serving plate, tipping any juices from inside the cavity back into the pan, and leave to rest for 20 minutes. Make the gravy as on page 82, discarding the lemon and adding a few tablespoons of **water** and the **crème fraîche**.

# Nordic Butter-basted Chicken

Serves **4–6** / Start to Finish **1 h 20 m**

There is something about the marriage of dill with seed mustard, one we know well from gravadlax, but just as lovely here.

lemon – 1, pierced all over with a skewer
free-range chicken – 1 x 1.6kg, untrussed
softened unsalted butter – 75g
dill leaves – a large handful, coarsely chopped
sea salt, black pepper
grainy mustard – 1 heaped tablespoon
dry white wine – 4 tablespoons
water or chicken stock – 4 tablespoons

**Preheat the oven and prepare the chicken**
Preheat the oven to 190°C fan/210°C electric/ gas 6½. Pop the **lemon** inside the **chicken**. Blend 50g of the **butter** with the **dill** and some **salt and pepper** in a bowl. Starting at the neck end of the chicken, slip your fingers beneath the skin to loosen it over each breast. Spread the herb butter over the flesh and pat the skin back into place, spreading it out evenly.

**Roast the chicken**
Place the chicken in a roasting pan. Smear over the remaining butter and season. Roast for 30 minutes, and then brush the **mustard** over the skin and baste well. Return the chicken to the oven for a further 25 minutes until the skin is deep golden.

**Rest the chicken and make the gravy**
Transfer the bird to a warm serving plate, tipping any juices from inside the cavity back into the pan, and leave to rest for 20 minutes. To make the gravy, skim off any excess fat from the juices, add the **wine** and simmer until reduced by about half. Add the **water** or **stock** and simmer for 2–3 minutes. Strain the gravy before serving.

# Roasting Tray Chicken & New Potatoes

Serves **4** / Start to Finish **1 h 40 m**

With this all-in-one there is a little bit of juggling at the start, but after that you can relax as it all comes out of the oven at the same time. This is one of the most useful bakes – roast chicken thighs with little golden potatoes in their skins, scented with garlic and bay. Lavish it with mayonnaise or aioli and dish up with a crisp green salad, and it whisks Sunday lunch into the present day.

small new potatoes such as Charlotte or Jersey Royal – 1kg, scrubbed

bay leaves – 4

extra virgin olive oil

sea salt, black pepper

free-range chicken thighs, or chicken pieces – 8

paprika

medium red onions – 3, peeled, halved and thinly sliced

garlic – 1 head, broken into cloves

lemon – juice of ½

mayonnaise (see page 260) or aioli (see page 168), to serve (optional)

**Parboil the potatoes and arrange in a roasting pan**
Preheat the oven to 190°C fan/210°C electric/gas 6½. Bring a large pan of salted water to the boil and parboil the **potatoes** for 10 minutes, then drain them. Arrange in a large roasting pan with the **bay leaves**, pour over 4 tablespoons **olive oil**, season with **salt and pepper** and roast for 10 minutes.

**Colour the chicken pieces**
Meanwhile heat 1 tablespoon oil in a large non-stick frying pan over a medium-high heat, season the **chicken thighs** with salt and **paprika**, and fry on both sides until really golden. You might have to do this in batches.

**Finish assembling the traybake and cook in the oven**
Stir the **onions** and **garlic cloves** into the potatoes, coating them with the oil, and then tuck in the chicken thighs, skin-side up. Drizzle over the **lemon juice** and roast in the oven for 50 minutes. Accompany with **mayonnaise** or **aioli** if you wish.

# Duck Leg & Parsnip Roast with Orange

Serves **6** / Start to Finish **3 h 15 m**

Duck legs make a sumptuous and comparatively inexpensive treat that spans the divide between pink and tender breasts and crispy Peking-style duck. This all-in-one roast makes a virtue of the duck fat given out in roasting the legs to cook the potatoes and parsnips, while the roasting juices form the basis of an aromatic and creamy sauce.

duck legs – 6 (total weight approx. 1.5kg)

sea salt

maincrop potatoes such as Maris Piper – 1.2kg, peeled and cut into pieces the size of a plum

parsnips – 600g, trimmed, peeled and cut into wedges

orange – 1, cut into slim wedges

bay leaves – 4

soured cream – 150ml

**Variation**

**Duck Leg & Parsnip Roast with Green Peppercorn Sauce:** Add 1 tablespoon chopped green peppercorns in brine to the sauce with the soured cream.

**Preheat the oven and slow-roast the duck legs**
Preheat the oven to 140°C fan/160°C electric/gas 3. Season the **duck legs** with **salt** and arrange in a large roasting pan, skin-side up. Cover with foil and roast in the oven for 2 hours.

**Parboil the potatoes and parsnips**
Towards the end of this time, bring a large pan of salted water to the boil and cook the **potatoes** and **parsnips** for 8 minutes; drain into a colander and set aside for a few minutes to steam-dry. Return the vegetables to the pan and give them a shake to roughen the surface slightly, ready for roasting.

**Roast the potatoes and parsnips**
Turn the oven up to 200°C fan/220°C electric/gas 7. Pour off the rendered fat and juices from the duck legs into a measuring jug, and then drain off the top layer of fat into a separate bowl, leaving the roasting juices behind in the bottom of the jug – these will be added to the sauce later. Spoon 5 tablespoons of the duck fat over the potatoes and parsnips, toss well and season with salt. Divide the potatoes between 2 large roasting pans, leaving room to add the duck legs later. Roast in the oven for 40 minutes.

**Crisp up the duck legs**
Remove the roasting pans from the oven, turn the vegetables and nestle the duck legs, **orange wedges** and **bay leaves** in among them. Return to the oven for a further 25–30 minutes, and then transfer everything to a large serving platter.

**Make the sauce and dish up**
To make the sauce, skim off any excess fat from one of the roasting pans and set over a medium heat on the hob. Pour in the reserved duck roasting juices and the **soured cream** and simmer gently for a minute or so to form a rich creamy gravy. If the sauce is very thick, you might need to thin it with a little water. Serve the duck and roasties with the sauce.

# Peking-style Duck with Hoisin Sauce & Rice Pancakes

Serves **4** / Start to Finish **3 h 20 m**

Those tantalisingly crisp golden ducks, which are all papery sheathes of skin and meltingly tender flesh, that hang in the windows of Chinese cafés in Soho, have pretty much done for any other way of cooking this bird. And while apocryphal stories abound about the best way to achieve the hallowed skin (days of drying the duck in a draught or setting up an air-dryer), this slow-cooking method is both simple and foolproof. Duck lends itself to Asian spices like no other bird, hence the five-spice – fab with smacked cucumber, hoisin sauce and Chinese pancakes. But equally you could leave this out and dish it up with the usual classic roast asides.

oven-ready duck (ideally with giblets) – 1 x 2.2–2.5kg *

sea salt, black pepper

Chinese five-spice powder

**To serve**

rice pancakes, warmed

hoisin sauce

spring onions, cut into fine strips

**Variation**

**Crispy Duck with Rich Sherry Gravy:**
Cook the duck as above and set aside to rest for 15 minutes. To make the gravy, drain off all of the fat from the pan and pour in 90ml medium sherry. Set the pan over a medium heat and simmer until reduced by half, scraping up all the sticky residue on the bottom. Stir in 2 teaspoons plain flour and allow to seethe momentarily, then gradually whisk in 300ml giblet or chicken stock (see page 24). Bring to the boil and simmer for several minutes until rich and amalgamated, and then season to taste. Serve the sauce with the duck.

### Prepare and roast the duck
Preheat the oven to 140°C fan/160°C electric/gas 3. The ideal here is a rack to roast the bird on, so that the rendered fat can run off and the skin can crisp on the bottom as well as the top. Generously season the **duck** all over with **salt, pepper** and **five-spice**, rubbing it into the skin. Place the duck, breast-side up, on the rack in a roasting pan and roast for 2½ hours. (If you are roasting without a rack, drain the rendered duck fat into a bowl at approximately hourly intervals.)

### Crisp up the skin
Increase the oven temperature to 200°C fan/220°C electric/gas 7 and roast the duck for a further 30 minutes to colour and crisp up the skin.

### Rest the duck and dish up
Remove the duck from the oven and set aside to rest for 15 minutes, transferring it to a plate if it isn't on a rack. To serve, loosely shred the duck meat with two forks, making sure you get all of the skin, which should be oily and crisp top and bottom. Pile onto a serving plate, discarding the bones, and serve with the **pancakes, hoisin sauce** and **spring onions,** placing everything centrally so everyone can help themselves.

*Serving suggestion*
— Accompany with the Korean Smacked Cucumber on page 264 or some simple cucumber batons.

The knack

\* **What to do with the giblets?** If the duck comes with giblets, don't let the liver go to waste: cut it into fine slices, fry briefly in butter and serve with the meat. You can use the heart, neck and gizzard to make stock (see page 24).

# Pot-roast Chicken with Wild Mushrooms

Serves **4** / Start to Finish **1 h 30 m**

I have to include this one, as Lou described it as 'the best chicken and mushroom dish' he had ever eaten, and he's a fussy boy. It is the generous jug of thick, creamy mushroom sauce that does it.

free-range chicken – 1 x 1.6kg, untrussed

groundnut or vegetable oil

sea salt, black pepper

Madeira or Marsala – 150ml

chicken stock – 150ml

garlic cloves – 8, peeled

bay leaf – 1

unsalted butter – 25g

mixed mushrooms – 400g, trimmed, quartered or sliced

crème fraîche – 50g

watercress, to serve

### Chicken Pot-Roasting Times

| | |
|---|---|
| 1.2kg bird | **50 m** |
| 1.6kg bird | **1 h** |
| 2kg bird | **1 h 10 m** |

### Colour the chicken
Preheat the oven to 160°C fan/180°C electric/gas 4. Heat a large non-stick frying pan over a high heat. Meanwhile, using your hands, lightly coat the **chicken** with a little **oil** and season all over with **salt and pepper**. Place the oiled bird in the hot pan and colour it on all sides.

### Prepare the pot for the oven *
Transfer the golden bird to a large casserole, breast-side up, and add the **Madeira** or **Marsala**, **stock**, **garlic cloves** and **bay leaf**. Bring the liquid to the boil, and then cover the pan with a lid. Transfer the pan to the oven and cook for 1 hour (for larger or smaller birds, see left).

### Fry the mushrooms in two batches
Ten minutes before the end, heat a knob of **butter** with 1 teaspoon oil in a large non-stick frying pan over a medium-high heat. Add half the **mushrooms**, season and fry for 3–5 minutes until golden, stirring frequently. If any liquid is given off, continue to cook until this evaporates. Transfer the cooked mushrooms to a bowl while you cook the rest in the same way.

### Rest the bird and finish the sauce
Transfer the chicken to a warm plate to rest for 15 minutes, lifting it cavity-downwards so that any juices inside trickle back into the pan. To finish the sauce, skim off any fat from the surface and discard the bay leaf. Set the pan over a medium heat, add the fried mushrooms and simmer for a few minutes. Using a slotted spoon, remove one-third of the mushrooms and all of the garlic cloves to a blender, along with 1 ladleful cooking liquor. Blitz to a smooth purée, and then stir the mixture back into the sauce. Stir in the **crème fraîche** and gently reheat the sauce.

### Carve the bird and dish up
Carve the chicken into hearty chunks and accompany with a jug of the mushroom sauce. Serve with a pile of **watercress** on the side.

### The knack
* Which pot? A decent cast-iron casserole is one of the best investments you can make. It should last you a lifetime, getting better with wear. The most useful will fit a chicken with a little room to spare around the edge. My vote goes to oval (approx. 30cm) rather than round, since if there is too much surrounding space the bird can dry out.

# Pot-roast Chicken with Watercress Sauce

Serves **4** / Start to Finish **1 h 20 m**

This particular pot-roast takes me back to our very first meal as a family in Normandy, when we had just started house-hunting there. The raw brutality of a five o'clock start off the ferry failed to dampen our enthusiasm as we chanced across a market just setting up on the fringes of Caen. Half an hour later – pepped up by a couple of industrial strength *cafés noirs* and the sugar-rush of *brioche aux pepites de chocolat*, those to-die-for pastries stuffed with custard and chocolate chips – we returned to the car laden with a fine-looking chicken, a tub of sticky yellow cream, a bunch of watercress and some rosy-hued garlic.

Our gîte was perhaps more idyllic from the outside than in the kitchen stakes, at any rate, with its wonky gas oven and one pan. But, it was large enough to pot-roast the chicken with a glass of wine and some garlic, with a mass of chopped watercress and cream thrown into the sauce at the end. I still look back on it as one of the finest chicken suppers I can recall.

vegetable oil

free-range chicken – 1 x 1.6kg, untrussed

sea salt, black pepper

bay leaves – 2

thyme – 3 sprigs

dry white wine – 150ml

softened unsalted butter – 1 teaspoon

plain flour – 1 teaspoon

watercress – 1 bunch (approx. 100g), trimmed and coarsely chopped

crème fraîche – 1 x 200ml tub

**Variation**

**Pot-roast Chicken with Tarragon Sauce:** Replace the bay with 4 x 5cm sprigs of tarragon, discarding them at the end. Omit the watercress and stir in 1½ tablespoons tarragon leaves along with the crème fraîche at the end.

**Colour the chicken and prepare the pot for the oven**
Heat a large non-stick frying pan over a medium-high heat. Pour a little **vegetable oil** into the palm of your hand, rub your hands together and coat the **chicken** all over. Season with **salt and pepper**. Colour the chicken thoroughly on all sides until it is an even golden brown. Transfer the chicken to a large cast-iron casserole, breast-side up, and add the **herbs** and **wine**. Bring the wine to a simmer, and then cover the pan with a lid.

**Pot-roast the bird and make the beurre manié**
Move the pan onto the smallest ring and cook over a very low heat for 1 hour (for larger or smaller birds, see chart on page 90). Meanwhile blend the **butter** and **flour** to a paste in a small bowl.

**Rest the bird and finish the sauce**
Uncover the chicken and leave it to rest in the pan for 15 minutes. Remove the chicken to a warm plate, pouring any juices from inside the cavity back into the pan, and carve it into hearty chunks. Skim any excess fat off the juices in the pan and remove the herbs. Place the pan over a medium heat and bring the cooking liquor back to the boil. Add the butter and flour paste in small pieces and keep stirring until it has melted. To finish, stir in the **watercress** and **crème fraîche** and taste for seasoning. Allow this to heat through and serve poured over the chicken.

# Provençal Chicken with Olives *&* Pistou

Serves **4** / Start to Finish **1 h 40 m**

All my summer pot-roasts are invariably variations on a theme of this one – tomatoes and garlic, the scent of rosemary and some olives. A salad in the background and I'm in a sunny clime. This dish has a light, clean profile, compared to the creamy indulgence of the richer ones described previously.

**For the chicken**

extra virgin olive oil

free-range chicken – 1 x 1.6kg, untrussed

sea salt, black pepper

onions – 3 medium or 2 large, peeled, halved and thinly sliced

garlic cloves – 3, peeled and finely sliced

beefsteak tomatoes – 2, skinned (see page 18) and coarsely chopped

rosemary – 2 sprigs

small dried red chilli –1, finely chopped

dry white wine – 150ml

mixed pitted green and black olives – 150g

**For the pistou (optional)**

basil leaves – 4 large handfuls

extra virgin olive oil – 9 tablespoons

salt

**Colour the chicken**
Heat a large cast-iron casserole over a medium-high heat. Pour a little **olive oil** into the palm of your hand, rub your hands together and coat the **chicken** all over. Season with **salt and pepper**. Put the chicken in the hot pan and colour it on all sides. Remove it to a plate and turn the heat down to medium-low.

**Fry the onions and add the aromatics and wine**
Add 2 tablespoons oil to the pan and the **onions** and fry until soft and translucent, approx. 5 minutes, stirring frequently. Once the heat calms down, you can turn it up a little. Add the **garlic** a minute or so before the end. Add the **tomatoes, rosemary, chilli, wine** and some salt, and settle the chicken into the sauce, breast-side up.

**Pot-roast the chicken**
Bring the liquid to a simmer, cover the pan with a lid and cook over a low heat for 1 hour (for larger or smaller birds, see chart on page 90).

**Make the pistou (optional)**
Combine **all the ingredients for the pistou** in a food processor and reduce to a smooth purée.

**Rest the chicken and finish the sauce**
Transfer the cooked chicken to a warm plate to rest for 15 minutes, tipping any juices from inside the cavity back into the pan. Leave the sauce to stand for 5–10 minutes to allow the oil to rise to the surface, and then skim it off with a large metal spoon. To finish the sauce, set the pan over a medium heat and simmer until the juices have reduced by half.

**Dish up**
Carve the chicken and serve with the sauce spooned over. Drizzle a little pistou over the chicken and sauce before scattering with the **olives**.

# Coq au Vin

Serves **4–6** / Start to Finish **1 h 50 m**

For everything that is good about a chicken stew, look no further than *coq au vin* with its copious red wine gravy, which is rich and lustrous without being gloopy. With button mushrooms and baby onions added just before the end, this is a hard act to beat.

vegetable oil – 1 tablespoon

sea salt, black pepper

free-range chicken – 1.6kg, jointed into 6–8 pieces *

rindless unsmoked streaky bacon (or lardons) – 75g, diced

plain flour – 1 heaped tablespoon

red wine – 600ml **

chicken stock – 150ml

bay leaf – 1

thyme – 2 sprigs

unsalted butter – 15g

baby onions – 100g, peeled but kept whole

button mushrooms – 100g, stalks trimmed if necessary but kept whole

flat-leaf parsley, coarsely chopped, to serve

**Colour the chicken and assemble the stew**

Preheat the oven to 130°C fan/150°C electric/gas 2. Heat the **oil** in a large casserole over a medium-high heat. **Season** the **chicken pieces** all over and colour them in batches until golden brown on both sides. Remove them to a bowl, add the diced **bacon** to the pan and stir until it is just beginning to colour. Pour off all but a tablespoon of the fat. Return the chicken to the casserole, sprinkle over the **flour** and cook, stirring, for about 1 minute. Pour in the **wine** and **stock**, and add the **bay leaf** and **thyme** and a little more seasoning. Bring briefly to the boil and cover with a lid.

**Cook the stew**

Transfer the casserole to the oven and cook for 1½ hours until the chicken is tender, turning the top pieces halfway through to stop them drying out. You can prepare the stew to this point in advance, in which case leave it to cool, and then cover and chill. ***

**Fry the onions and mushrooms and finish the stew**

Either on removing the casserole from the oven, or just before serving, melt the **butter** in a small frying pan over a low heat, add the **onions** and fry for 10 minutes until lightly coloured, stirring frequently. Add the **mushrooms** 3–4 minutes before the end and fry until lightly golden. Carefully skim off any fat floating on the surface of the stew and reheat if necessary. Add the onions and mushrooms, and serve straight away on warm plates, sprinkled with some coarsely chopped **parsley**.

*Serving suggestion*

— Mashed potato turns this into the ultimately comforting line-up.

The knack

\* **Which chicken?** The ideal here is a whole chicken that has been jointed into 6–8 pieces – a butcher should be able to do this for you. Failing that, a mixture of thighs and drumsticks will do nicely.

\*\* **Which wine?** The red wine needn't be anything special – cheap, cheerful and with plenty of character.

\*\*\* **Making it in advance?** Like many stews, this is almost better reheated, by which time the meat will have infused with the flavour of the sauce. The added advantage of making it in advance and chilling it until needed is you can easily scrape off any fat that has risen to the surface.

# Pheasant with Calvados & Apples

Serves **2–3** / Start to Finish **1 h**

If I had to name my favourite way of cooking pheasant then this would be it. The marriage of game with caramelised apples and earthy Calvados resonates with autumn.

unsalted butter – 30g

groundnut or vegetable oil – 1 tablespoon

sea salt, black pepper

pheasant – 1, trussed *

Calvados (or brandy) – 75ml

dry cider – 200ml

crème fraîche – 150g

eating apples – 2, peeled, quartered, cored and sliced lengthways

**Variation**

**Guinea Fowl with Calvados & Apples:** Use guinea fowl in place of the pheasant; adjust the cooking time according to the chart on page 90.

**Colour the pheasant**
Heat 15g **butter** and the **oil** in a large non-stick frying pan over a medium-high heat. **Season** the **pheasant** and colour it thoroughly on all sides in the hot fat. Transfer the golden pheasant, breast-side up, into a medium-sized cast-iron casserole.

**Flambé the Calvados ***
Gently warm the **Calvados** in a ladle over the gas or hob (you may need to do this half at a time), then light and pour it a little at a time over the pheasant, adding more as the flames die down. It's very important to do this in a controlled fashion and not to panic.

**Pot-roast the pheasant**
Add the **cider** – don't worry if the Calvados is still alight – and bring to the boil. Then cover the pan with a lid and cook on the smallest ring over a low heat for 30 minutes.

**Rest the pheasant and finish the sauce**
Remove the cooked pheasant to a warm plate and set aside to rest for 10 minutes. Meanwhile return the pan to a medium heat, add the **crème fraîche** and bubble away vigorously until the sauce appears to thicken slightly and seems richer.

**Fry the apples and dish up**
Heat the remaining 15g butter in a separate non-stick frying pan over a medium-high heat and fry the **apples** until well-coloured and just starting to burn around the edges, approx. 5 minutes. Meanwhile carve the pheasant breasts and remove any tender meat from the legs. Serve the pheasant with the sauce spooned over, scattered with the apple slices.

---

The knack

* **Why a trussed bird?** While I am forever telling you to untruss a chicken, pheasants do benefit from having their legs tied to the body during cooking otherwise they splay all over the place.

** **Flambéing** gets rid of the raw alcohol, while retaining the character of the liquid. I usually rope my husband in to help me because I am a bit timid when it comes to playing with fire. If you're totally fazed by the idea, simply add 2–3 tablespoons Calvados to the pan with the cider, foregoing the flames.

# Thai Green Chicken Curry

Serves **6** / Start to Finish **45 m**

Of all Thai curries this is the best known and loved, and there is usually a reason for popularity. It is as much about the gorgeous coconut gravy as it is about the chicken, and of course finding the treasure – those small pea aubergines (peas in this instance), basil leaves and the like. A big fluffy mound of plain, boiled rice is *de rigueur* (see page 220).

free-range chicken breasts – 6, skinned

groundnut or vegetable oil

sea salt

shallots – 8, peeled and thinly sliced

garlic cloves – 2, peeled and thinly sliced

Thai green curry paste – 2 level tablespoons *

chicken stock – 425ml

coconut milk – 2 x 400ml tins

lime leaves – 6

whole red chillies – 4, plus extra sliced to serve

mangetouts – 125g, stalk ends trimmed

shelled peas (fresh or frozen) – 200g

fish sauce – 3 tablespoons

caster sugar – 1 rounded tablespoon

fresh basil leaves – 20g

fresh coriander leaves – 20g

### Variation

**Quick Thai Green Chicken Curry:**
Replace the chicken breasts with 600g diced or shredded roast chicken or turkey, adding it at the same time as the peas. A great use for all that leftover turkey at Christmas.

**Colour the chicken**
Pull off the inner fillet on the underside of each **chicken breast** if present, and cut either side of the tendon to remove it, leaving two strips. Halve these if they seem long. Slice the remaining chicken breasts across into strips 1cm wide, again cutting out any white tendon, and halving any very thick slices into thin strips. Toss the chicken in a large bowl with just enough **oil** to coat it, and season with **salt**. Heat a large non-stick frying pan over a high heat and sear the chicken in batches until very lightly golden all over – don't worry if it isn't fully cooked. Transfer the chicken to a bowl and set aside while you make the sauce.

**Prepare the curry sauce ***
Heat 2 tablespoons oil in a large casserole or saucepan over a medium-low heat, and fry the **shallots** and **garlic** for several minutes until they soften, without colouring. Stir in the **green curry paste** and cook for a minute longer, then add the **stock**, 1 tin of **coconut milk**, the **lime leaves** and whole **chillies**. Bring to the boil over a high heat, and then simmer over a low heat for 10 minutes.

**Finish the curry**
The curry will take about 10 minutes from here. Bring the sauce back to the boil over a medium heat, add the chicken, **mangetouts** and **peas,** and simmer for 5 minutes. Pour in the remaining tin of coconut milk, stir in the **fish sauce**, **sugar** and **herbs,** and bring back to the boil. You can leave in the whole chillies and lime leaves and remove them as you are eating. Scatter with a few slices of fresh chilli to serve.

### The knack

* **Why bought curry paste?** Making a curry paste from scratch isn't the easiest of preparations, and more than likely to put you off making this mid-week, so buy in a good one. If you have access to a Thai deli then you should find an authentic range to choose from; my local makes their own curry pastes as well as importing them.

** **Making the sauce in advance:** You can prepare the curry sauce several hours in advance, in which case cover and set it aside. But leave cooking the chicken until shortly before you eat.

Thai Green Chicken Curry

# Bell Family's Favourite Chicken Curry

Serves **4** / Start to Finish **1 h 45 m**

There is something about the combination of tomatoes with fresh ginger, a fab marriage that lies at the heart of this simple curry. Unlike many chicken curries that skimp on the chicken, here you get a juicy piece or two each. Any of the usual asides will go down well in addition to rice – some poppadoms or naan bread, roasted cashews and a sticky mango chutney.

## For the curry

chilli powder or cayenne pepper –
1 level teaspoon

water – 300ml, plus 1 tablespoon

ginger purée or finely grated ginger
– 2 teaspoons

tomato purée – 2 heaped
tablespoons

caster sugar – 1 teaspoon

cloves – 6

green cardamom pods – 8

groundnut or vegetable oil –
4 tablespoons

garlic cloves – 6, peeled and finely
chopped

bay leaves – 2

cinnamon stick – 1 x 7cm, halved

turmeric – ½ teaspoon

medium-hot red chillies – 3

free-range chicken thighs and
drumsticks – 1.6kg

medium tomatoes – 3, roughly
chopped

sea salt

lemon or lime juice – 1 tablespoon

medium onions – 2, peeled and
coarsely chopped

fresh coriander – coarsely chopped,
to serve

## For the relish (optional)

green pepper – ¼, finely diced

medium red onion – ¼, peeled and
finely diced

medium tomato – 1, finely diced

lemon juice – squeeze

sea salt

**Prepare the chilli and tomato paste and make the spice bag**
Blend the **chilli powder** with 1 tablespoon **water** in a small bowl, then mix in the **ginger and tomato purées** and the **sugar**. Either wrap the **cloves** and **cardamom pods** in a small square of muslin, or cut the top off a teabag, empty out the contents and pop in the spices, pleating the top down to seal. Give the bag a couple of gentle bashes with a rolling pin to coarsely crush the spices, releasing their flavour.

**Cook the curry**
Heat 2 tablespoons **oil** in a large casserole over a medium heat. Add the **garlic**, **bay leaves** and **cinnamon** and cook briefly until they start to sizzle. Quickly stir in the **turmeric**, followed by the chilli and tomato paste and fry for about a minute. Then add the spice bag and **whole chillies**. Add the **chicken pieces** and **tomatoes**, stir to coat them in the sauce and spices and cook for 8–10 minutes, stirring frequently. Season with **salt**, add 300ml water and bring to a simmer. Then cover and cook over a low heat for 1 hour, stirring halfway through.

**Make the relish (optional)**
Combine **all the ingredients for the relish** in a small bowl, seasoning with salt at the last moment. Cover with clingfilm and chill until needed.

**Thicken the sauce**
Remove the cooked chicken pieces to a large bowl and set aside, covered with foil to keep warm. Skim off the fat from the surface of the sauce and remove the spice bag, cinnamon and bay leaves. Return the pan to a medium heat, stir in the **lemon or lime juice** and simmer until the sauce has reduced by about a quarter.

**Fry the onions and stir into the sauce**
Meanwhile heat the remaining oil in a large non-stick frying pan over a medium heat and fry the **onions** for 8–10 minutes until golden, stirring frequently. Stir the onions into the sauce and taste for seasoning. Return the chicken to the casserole, cover and reheat if necessary.

**Dish up**
Serve scattered with **coriander**, accompanied by the relish.

# Braised Chicken Legs with Dijon Mustard *&* White Wine

Serves **6** / Start to Finish **2 h**

For anyone who has grown up with English mustard or some other devil of the storecupboard, Dijon mustard is a completely different condiment, a shrinking violet by comparison that can be slathered with abandon inside a Croque Monsieur or down the length of a sausage. This opens a multitude of avenues, such as in this classic stew where in addition to contributing a deep golden crust it adds a delicious savour to the sauce and emulsifies it.

Dijon mustard – 2 tablespoons

whole free-range chicken legs – 6 (250–300g each)

sea salt, black pepper

unsalted butter – 50g, plus 1 teaspoon, softened

large onion – 1, peeled, halved and finely sliced

garlic cloves – 3, peeled

dry white wine – 300ml

tarragon – a couple of sprigs

bay leaf – 1

plain flour – 1 teaspoon

### Variations

**Rabbit with Dijon Mustard & White Wine:** Follow the recipe above, substituting the chicken legs for 1.5–1.8kg jointed rabbit meat.

**Guinea Fowl with Dijon Mustard & White Wine:** Follow the recipe above, substituting the chicken legs for 1.5–1.8kg guinea fowl, jointed into 6 pieces.

### Colour the chicken legs
Preheat the oven to 130°C fan/150°C electric/gas 2. Brush the **mustard** over the **chicken legs** and **season** them. Melt 50g **butter** in a large cast-iron casserole over a medium heat and colour the chicken pieces on all sides, working in batches so as not to overcrowd the pan. The mustard should ensure they turn a rich crusty gold. Transfer them to a bowl as they are done and set aside.

### Add the aromatics and wine
Add the **onion** and **garlic** to the pan and fry for a few minutes, stirring frequently, until a mid-golden brown. Return the chicken pieces to the pan and add the **wine, herbs** and a little more seasoning. Submerge the legs as far as possible, bring the liquid to the boil, and then cover with a lid.

### Cook the stew and make the beurre manié *
Transfer the casserole to the oven and cook for 1 ½ hours until the chicken is tender, turning the legs halfway through. Meanwhile blend the 1 teaspoon softened **butter** with the **flour** in a small bowl to form a paste.

### Thicken the sauce and dish up
Transfer the cooked chicken legs to a large bowl and discard the herbs. Skim off any fat on the surface and return the pan to a medium heat. Bring the juices back to the boil and whisk in the butter and flour paste in small pieces. Simmer until the sauce has thickened slightly. Serve the chicken legs with the sauce spooned over.

### *Serving suggestion*
— Keeping this in a French vein, if you happen to chance upon an escarole lettuce snap it up. This broad-leafed chicory is less bitter than most, and it is a natural choice whenever Dijon mustard or blue cheese abound. As ever with chicory, you want just the palest green or blanched sections of leaf.

### The knack
\* **Beurre manié:** Literally translated as 'kneaded butter', this is traditionally used to thicken sauces without creating lumps. To make, combine 1 teaspoon plain flour with 1 teaspoon butter in a small bowl and beat well until smooth.

# Braised Chicken Breasts with Garlic & Tarragon

Serves **4** / Start to Finish **50 m**

Chicken breasts are wasted in a stew as they generally cook too quickly, drying out before the sauce has a chance to enrich. A fricassée is a brilliant solution where the chicken remains beautifully succulent but you still end up with a sauce. The combination of chicken with tarragon and garlic will instantly transport you to a small French bistro, but there are plenty of other possibilities too – such as bay, thyme or rosemary.

unsalted butter – 50g, clarified *

sea salt, black pepper

free-range chicken breasts, skin on – 4 x approx. 200g, white tendon cut out

button mushrooms – 300g, base trimmed but kept whole

tarragon – 4 small sprigs (approx. 7cm long)

garlic cloves – 4, smashed

dry white wine – 100ml

crème fraîche – 100g

flat-leaf parsley – coarsely chopped, to serve (optional)

## Variations

**Chicken Thighs with Garlic & Tarragon:** Replace the breasts with 8 chicken thighs, frying them for 7 minutes on each side. Simmer the stew over a very low heat on the hob for 30 minutes, turning the meat halfway through.

**Chicken Breasts with Garlic, Tarragon & Peas:** Omit the mushrooms. Halfway into cooking the chicken, bring a medium-sized pan of salted water to the boil, add 200g shelled fresh peas and 150g topped and tailed mangetouts and cook for 2 minutes; drain well and stir into the finished sauce.

### Colour the chicken breasts
Preheat the oven to 130°C fan/150°C electric/gas 2. Pour the **clarified butter** into a large cast-iron casserole and set over a medium heat. Meanwhile **season** the **chicken breasts** on both sides. Once the butter is nice and hot, put in the chicken, skin-side down, and fry without turning until the skin turns golden brown, approx. 7 minutes. Turn briefly to colour the flesh on the other side, and then remove the chicken to a plate and set aside.

### Fry the mushrooms and cook the stew
Add the **mushrooms** to the pan and fry for 2–3 minutes, stirring frequently, until lightly coloured. Return the breasts to the pan, skin-side down, along with any juices, nestling them in amongst the mushrooms. Tuck in the **tarragon** and **garlic**, cover with a lid and cook in the oven for 25 minutes.

### Finish the sauce and dish up
Transfer the chicken and mushrooms to a bowl, discarding the tarragon and garlic, and cover with a saucepan lid or plate to keep warm. (If you prefer to skim off the excess butter in the pan, it's a good idea to leave the juices to settle for a few minutes before doing so.) To finish the sauce, set the pan over a medium heat, pour in the **wine** and simmer until reduced by half. Add the **crème fraîche** and simmer for a further minute or two until nicely enriched. Serve the chicken with the sauce spooned over, scattered with **parsley** if you wish.

*Serving suggestion*
— It's spuds in for this one: mash, boiled, sautéed, whichever way.

### The knack

* **Clarified butter:** For this recipe we want the flavour of butter with the higher frying temperature of oil. To make your own clarified butter, melt the butter in a small saucepan over a low heat, and then skim off and discard the surface foam using a metal spoon. Carefully pour off the clarified butter underneath into a jug or bowl, discarding the milky solids in the base of the pan. Ghee is an alternative here.

# Festival Jerk Chicken Wings

Serves **4** / Start to Finish **50 m**

For years I laboured under the illusion that I had conquered my Jerk Chicken, until I was informed by the Teenage Panel that it 'wasn't black enough'. 'Burnt, you mean?' I suggested, as they googled a picture of the perfect article, feeling that one too many festivals had corrupted their perception. But I got the point and went back to the drawing board, and this was the result, which takes more than spices. You can treat this marinade as a basic. Great for any small cut destined for the grill or barbie.

free-range chicken wings – 1kg

sea salt, black pepper

**For the marinade**

lemon or lime juice – 3 tablespoons

extra virgin olive oil – 5 tablespoons

spring onions – 4, trimmed and roughly chopped

fresh ginger root – 2cm, peeled

soft or lemon thyme leaves – 1 tablespoon

garlic cloves – 2, peeled

jerk seasoning – 4 teaspoons

### Marinate the chicken

Up to a couple of hours in advance of eating, prepare a paste by whizzing together **all the ingredients for the marinade** in a food processor. Transfer the mixture to a large bowl, add the **chicken wings** and turn to coat them. Cover the bowl with clingfilm and set aside in the fridge to marinate for a couple of hours if not cooking straight away.

### Roast the chicken

Preheat the oven to 200°C fan/220°C electric/gas 7. Arrange the wings in a single layer in a large roasting pan, and season them with **salt and pepper** on both sides. Roast for about 40 minutes until golden, turning them halfway through using tongs.

**Variation**

**Quick Jerk Chicken (Serves 6):** *Perfect for slipping into a wrap or taco shell along with some shredded crisp green lettuce and guacamole (see page 52).*

lemon juice – 2 tablespoons

extra virgin olive oil – 3 tablespoons

garlic clove – 1, peeled and crushed

jerk seasoning – 2 teaspoons

mini chicken fillets – 800g, white tendons removed

sea salt

Combine all of the ingredients in a bowl, cover with clingfilm and marinate for 2–3 hours in the fridge. Heat a large non-stick frying pan over a medium heat, season the chicken with salt and fry in batches for a couple of minutes on each side, until golden and firm when pressed.

# Sesame Teriyaki Chicken

Serves **4** / Start to Finish **30 m**

A big platter of Teriyaki Chicken smattered with sesame seeds is up there with Jerk Chicken. This teriyaki glaze tiptoes around the need for mirin and sake, two less bottles getting bored in the cupboard. It is the dynamism of sweet and salty we are after, chicken that is as savoury as it is caramelised and sticky.

Thigh fillets are a brilliant cut, everything that is good about the breast without the price tag. In addition they bring with them the succulence and flavour of the dark meat, and are more forgiving than a breast and less likely to dry out. This is a great choice for the barbie as part of a mixed grill, as well as making a speedy supper with some rice.

free-range chicken thigh fillets – 800g, skinned

toasted sesame seeds, for sprinkling

long fine strips of medium-hot red chilli and spring onion (6–7cm), to serve

### For the glaze
dark soy sauce – 4 tablespoons

runny honey – 4 tablespoons

sesame oil – 2 tablespoons

garlic cloves – 4, peeled and crushed to a paste

fresh root ginger – 1 tablespoon, finely chopped or grated

**Prepare the chicken thighs** *
Open out the **chicken thigh fillets**. Lay them between two sheets of clingfilm and gently bash with a rolling pin until they are about 1cm thick. This will ensure they cook quickly and evenly.

**Make the glaze**
Whisk **all the ingredients for the glaze** in a large bowl.

**Fry the chicken**
Add the chicken to the glaze and stir to coat the fillets. Heat a large non-stick frying pan over a medium heat for several minutes. Add half the fillets, or as many as will fit tightly together, and fry for 8 minutes, turning them after about 3 minutes once they have started to caramelise. Turn them back over again towards the end of cooking once the sugars have darkened and become stickier. If necessary, continue turning the chicken until it is evenly golden with a few singed bubbles; when fully cooked it should feel firm when pressed. Set aside on a warm plate and cover with foil. You can either fry the fillets in two goes, swooshing out the pan with water in between batches, or use two pans.

**Finish the glaze and dish up**
Towards the end of this time, pour the residual glaze into a small saucepan and simmer until reduced by half. Pass through a sieve into a small bowl and drizzle over the chicken. To serve, sprinkle some **sesame seeds** over the chicken and scatter with slivers of **chilli** and **spring onion**.

### The knack
* **Making this in advance?** The thigh fillets can be prepared several hours in advance and chilled in between sheets of clingfilm. You can also make the glaze in advance if you wish. I prefer not to marinate the chicken in the glaze as I find the honey draws out the juices from the chicken, which tends to toughen it.

# Sticky Duck Breasts with Asparagus & Beetroot Salad

Serves **4** / Start to Finish **35 m**

This is the recipe I turn to when I am after duck that is pink and tender. And the secret is to fry the breasts very, very slowly, so they remain slightly rare in the centre but without any hint of rawness. And then, to render them deliciously sticky and caramelised on the outside, they are glazed right at the end with honey and vinegar.

sea salt, black pepper

duck breasts – 2, (approx. 200g each) *

cider vinegar – 1 tablespoon

runny honey – 1 tablespoon

### For the salad

green or white asparagus – 500–600g, trimmed and halved into 6–8cm lengths (if the spears are finger thick, you may wish to peel them with a potato peeler to within 2cm of the base of the tip)

cooked and peeled beetroot (unvinegared) – 250g, ends trimmed, halved and thinly sliced

balsamic vinegar – 1 tablespoon

rapeseed oil – 3 tablespoons

baby leaves such as ruby chard and lamb's lettuce – a couple of handfuls

pistachios – 30g, coarsely chopped (optional)

**Prepare and cook the asparagus ***
Cook and cool the **asparagus** (see knack, below).

**Slowly fry the duck breasts**
Heat a large non-stick frying pan over a low heat. **Season** the **duck breasts** on either side, and fry skin-side down for 15–20 minutes until an even mid-golden brown. Drain off the rendered fat into a bowl (see below). Turn the duck breasts and cook the flesh side for 8–10 minutes, or until firm to the touch but still very slightly springy. Remove the duck breasts to a plate and drain off the rendered fat from the pan.

**Glaze the duck breasts**
Return the pan to the hob, turn up the heat to medium and add the **cider vinegar** and **honey**. Once this is simmering nicely, return the breasts to the pan, skin-side down, and cook for 1–2 minutes until a deep sticky gold, moving them around so they colour evenly. Turn and cook on the flesh side for 30–60 seconds, keeping a watchful eye so the sugars don't burn.

**Serve the salad**
Dress the **beetroot** with the **balsamic vinegar** and **rapeseed oil**, and season with salt and pepper. Divide the asparagus between four plates, arrange the beetroot slices over the top and scatter over a few salad **leaves**. Drizzle with the beetroot dressing. Thickly slice the duck breasts and divide between the plates. If you wish you can also scatter with chopped **pistachios**.

### The knack

* **Duck breasts:** On another occasion, four duck breasts will do as a main for 4–6 people, but you will need to have two frying pans on the go. Save the rendered fat for roast or sautéed potatoes; it will keep for weeks in the fridge.

** **Asparagus:** Cook fine asparagus or sprue for 2–3 minutes in boiling salted water, and finger-thick asparagus for 4–6 minutes, or until the thick end of the spear slices through with ease. If you are serving it cold, drain into a colander and pass under the cold tap (or plunge it into a sink of cold water) to preserve its colour and stop the cooking.

# Butterflied Chicken Breasts with Cherry Tomatoes

Serves **4** / Start to Finish **30 m**

I love the immediacy and freshness of this ensemble – the whole thing cooks in under 10 minutes, and both chicken and tomatoes are deliciously succulent.

**For the chicken**

skinless free-range chicken breasts – 4 x 150–200g

extra virgin olive oil – 2 tablespoons

lemon juice – 1 tablespoon

garlic cloves – 2, peeled and crushed to a paste

sea salt, black pepper

**For the tomatoes**

extra virgin olive oil – 4 tablespoons

banana shallots – 2, peeled, halved and thinly sliced

cherry tomatoes – 400g, halved or quartered

basil leaves – a handful, torn into pieces

**Prepare the chicken breasts ***
Cut out any visible white tendon from the underside of each **chicken breast**. Holding the knife parallel to the chopping board, slice each breast in half, leaving it attached at one side. Open up the breast like a book and gently pound it with a rolling pin between two sheets of clingfilm to an even thickness of about 1cm. Repeat with the rest of the breasts.

**Marinate the chicken**
Combine the **olive oil**, **lemon juice** and **garlic** in a large bowl, add the chicken escalopes and turn to coat. You can prepare them up to a couple of hours in advance, if you wish, in which case cover and chill.

**Grill the chicken**
Heat a ridged griddle over a high heat for several minutes until smoking hot. Season the chicken escalopes on either side with **salt and pepper**, and then grill in batches for 1–2 minutes on each side, turning them once you see the flesh is cooked through by about two-thirds. Once cooked, the meat should feel firm when pressed.

**Cook the tomatoes**
Halfway into cooking the chicken, heat 2 tablespoons **olive oil** in a medium-sized saucepan over a medium heat and fry the **shallots** for 4–5 minutes until soft but not coloured, stirring occasionally. Add the **tomatoes** and stir for 30–60 seconds – the idea is to warm them through rather than cook them. Remove the pan from the heat, stir in the **basil** with a little salt and drizzle over the remaining 2 tablespoons oil.

**Dish up**
Serve the chicken with the tomatoes and juices spooned over.

**The knack**

* **Pounding the chicken:** Unlike when you pound a steak, which serves to tenderise the meat, chicken is very delicate. The aim here is simply to level it to an even thickness, without damaging it. So gently does it.

# Meat

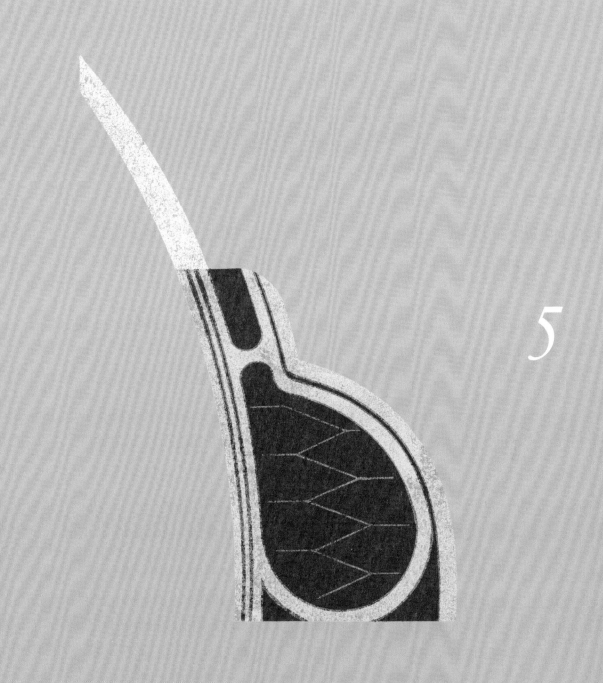

5

# About **Meat**

**Buying**

I buy 90 per cent of my meat from a good local butcher. They are always willing to oblige with those little extra requests, to remove and score the rind on my pork joint, or to go and see what's come in from market that morning that might fit the brief.

Essentially, I know the meat has been naturally reared and traditionally matured. Some supermarkets are better than others on this front, but even then there will likely be a massive differential between their welfare meat and the least expensive, when it is better to give it a miss altogether. Look out for high welfare marks such as the RSPCA's Freedom Food. While pork should be 'free range' or 'outdoor reared'.

In the case of red meats, such as beef and lamb, they should be streaked with fine threads of white or ivory fat. It is these that afford the meat its tenderness, succulence and flavour.

**Defrosting**

I usually defrost joints out of the fridge overnight, or remove them early on the morning for dinner that evening, while small cuts will defrost in about half a day. If you have a cast-iron casserole, this is perfect for keeping it cool and out of the sun, while protecting the meat from flies. If defrosting in the fridge, allow 24 hours for small cuts and about 24 hours per kilo for large joints.

**Room temperature**

Always allow meat to come back up to room temperature before cooking: give small cuts about 20 minutes out of the fridge, and larger ones 30–60 minutes.

**Vac-packed**

If the meat is vac-packed, it may appear slightly dark and also have a faint odour when unwrapped, which will disappear within about 20 minutes.

**Seasoning**

When to season your meat – whether well before, just before, or after cooking – is a hotly debated topic among chefs and cooks. I like to season meat immediately before it is cooked, which makes for a crispier and tastier exterior.

**Covering with foil**

I rarely baste the meat or cover with foil when roasting because this softens the outside, when what I am after is caramelised crispy skin.

**Meat thermometer**

I held off acquiring one of these for years, as I am not generally one for gadgets. But they are a foolproof way of assessing whether your meat is cooked as you want. A decent digital thermometer will allow you to accurately test the meat towards the end of cooking.

Insert the tip of the thermometer into the deepest section of the joint to register the very lowest temperature. The easiest way to assess this is to gently insert the probe right the way through the meat, watching carefully for the lowest temperature to register. (It is a good idea to let the joint stand for a few minutes on taking it out of the oven before testing, as the temperature will continue to rise.)

I recommend a Superfast Thermapen (www.thermapen.co.uk). However, more advanced thermometers allow you to set the desired temperature, insert a probe into the meat, and an alarm sounds when it is ready.

**Press test**

We've been cooking meat for thousands of years and meat thermometers have only been around for a few. Next best is the press test, something that gets easier with experience. Press the meat with your finger – squishy means rare, soft with some resistance means medium, and firm means well done.

**Resting**

All meat, burgers included, should be rested before being eaten, to allow the juices to distribute evenly. Give burgers and steaks about 5–10 minutes, and larger cuts 15–25 minutes.

You can also keep cooked meat on hold in a low oven (60°C fan/80°C electric/gas ¼) if you are not quite ready. Allow up to 30 minutes for small cuts and 60 minutes for larger joints. If your oven doesn't go down this low, you can turn it off and open the door to let out some of the hot air before placing the joint back inside.

**Carving**

In the recipes that follow, when it says carve across the grain, if you think how meat is made up of long strands, you are cutting through these to give a neat cross-section.

**Internal Temperature Guide**

| Beef | |
|---|---|
| Rare | 45–50°C |
| Medium-rare | 50–55°C |
| Medium | 55–60°C |
| Well done | 65–70°C |
| **Lamb** | |
| Medium | 55–60°C |
| Well done | 65–70°C |
| **Pork** | |
| Joint | 70–75°C |
| Fillet | 60–65°C |

# Essential Sauces for Meat

## Traditional Gravy

Serves **4–6** / Start to Finish **10 m**

Shamefully, my children's ideal gravy is something resembling Bisto. But that's fine, I can do Bisto, and save the discreet tasty *jus* made by stretching the caramelised juices at the bottom of the pan for when my husband and I are dining *à deux*.

Bisto basically translates as thick, dark brown and lots of it, and I can see the attraction. Albeit the two types of gravy are good for different reasons, something light with salads and summery veg, and Bisto-style for a hearty slap-up Sunday roast with all the trimmings.

**How to make traditional gravy**
Remove the roasted meat from the pan and set aside to rest. Skim off the excess fat from the roasting pan, otherwise the gravy will be greasy.

Place the roasting pan on a lowish heat, add a small glass of red or white wine (Madeira or medium sherry and port are also good with pork, beef, lamb and duck) and simmer for several minutes, scraping up the sticky residue on the bottom. Even when there appears to be very little in the way of roasting juices, it's surprising how far the flavour will stretch.

*For a thin jus:* Add about 100ml water, or 200ml stock (chicken for chicken, and beef for red meats). Simmer the gravy long and hard enough for the juices to amalgamate into a smooth sauce, then add any juices given out on carving.

*For Bisto-style gravy:* After simmering the wine, stir in 1 tablespoon plain flour, and cook for about a minute. Add 300–600ml good strong stock, working it in gradually as if you were making a white sauce, and simmer the gravy long and hard enough for the juices to amalgamate into a smooth sauce. Add any juices given out on carving, and then strain through a sieve into a jug at the last minute.

## Gravy from Scratch

Serves **6** / Start to Finish **50 m**

This is a useful little jug of knowhow that I gleaned from Jonny Haughton, the founding chef of West London's gastro pub, The Havelock Tavern. Perfect for whenever the meat fails on the sticky juices front (e.g. roast duck, chops, steak), in which case there will be no flavour on which to base the gravy. (This freezes beautifully, so you could always make double the quantity.)

groundnut or vegetable oil – 2 tablespoons

mixed vegetables (e.g. onion, celery, carrot and leek) – 500g (trimmed weight), diced

garlic cloves – 2, peeled and finely chopped

plain flour – 2 teaspoons

red wine – 150ml

beef stock – 400ml

sea salt, black pepper

**How to make gravy from scratch**
Heat the **oil** in a large saucepan over a medium heat, add the **vegetables** and fry for 30–35 minutes, stirring occasionally, until really well coloured, almost black (this is your gravy browning). Add the **garlic** a few minutes before the end, then stir in the **flour**.

Gradually add the **red wine**, which will thicken, and cook for a couple of minutes. Stir in the **stock** in two or three goes, add some **seasoning** and simmer for about 5 minutes.

Pass the gravy through a sieve, pressing out as much flavour as possible from the vegetables. If the gravy tastes at all thin, you can simmer it for a few minutes longer. Check the seasoning. If you let it stand for any length of time, there may be a little oil on the surface, which you can skim. Add any juices given out on resting the meat.

# Apple Sauce

Serves **6** / Start to Finish **1 h**

Any pork dish will lap this up. You could add some mint or fresh thyme, or a little chopped chilli, if you wish.

Bramley cooking apples – 400g, peeled, cored and sliced

golden caster sugar – 30g

water – 75ml

#### How to make apple sauce
Place the **apples** and **sugar** in a medium-sized saucepan with the **water**. Bring to the boil, and then cover and cook over a low heat for 15–17 minutes, mashing the apple to a coarse purée once or twice during cooking. Transfer the sauce to a bowl and set aside to cool.

# Mint Sauce

Serves **6** / Start to Finish **5 m**

This sauce is gentle and perfumed, and as such can be eaten with abandon, so you may like to double up on this amount with your roast lamb.

mint leaves – 25g

extra virgin olive oil – 5 tablespoons

red wine vinegar – 2 teaspoons

golden caster sugar – ½ teaspoon

sea salt, black pepper

#### How to make mint sauce
Whizz **all the ingredients** to a fine purée in a food processor. Taste and add a little more salt if necessary.

# Horseradish Sauce

Serves **4–6** / Start to Finish **5 m**

A jar of ready-made will pack the same kind of punch as English mustard, as well as being quite vinegary, so you will only ever want to spread it in a fine layer on your steak or beef. Whereas this rich and creamy horseradish, which is on the gentle side, has all the flavour, so you can smother your beef, roast potatoes and Yorkshires, and it melts into the gravy. Heaven.

crème fraîche – 100g

**Either** fresh horseradish root –
1–1 ½ tablespoons, finely grated *

**Or** shop-bought horseradish sauce –
1–2 teaspoons

sea salt

#### How to make horseradish sauce
Blend the **crème fraîche** and **horseradish** together in a small bowl and season with **salt**. Transfer the sauce to a clean bowl, cover and chill until required.

#### The knack
* **Grating the horseradish:** If anyone ever gives you the choice of either grating horseradish or chopping onions, go for the onions – the tears will be nothing compared to the howling flood that comes with finely grating this root by hand. Use a food processor.

# Sunday Lunch Rosemary Roast Shoulder of Lamb

Serves **4** / Start to Finish **1 h 35 m**

While some families sit around arguing whether Homer Simpson is saint or sinner, we spend our time debating shoulder of lamb or leg for dinner. I side with my mother here who always preferred a shoulder. It is the layers of fat that make for fabulously succulent meat and crispy outside slivers, which mysteriously disappear before the carver has a chance to sit down. Although the leg of lamb recipe that follows allows for lots of gravy, this one is lighter by comparison, and also quicker, perfect for a relaxed weekend.

lamb shoulder – approx. 1.7kg, knuckle removed but reserved

rosemary – a couple of sprigs, needles removed

medium red onions – 2, peeled, halved and thickly sliced

bay leaves – 2

extra virgin olive oil

sea salt, black pepper

dry white wine – 150ml

chicken stock – 300ml

### Variation

**French Rack of Lamb:** *A French rack of lamb with its tender noisettes and spindly shanks is a dainty treat that cooks in no time – just one rack makes a good supper for two.*

Preheat the oven to 210°C fan/230°C electric/gas 8. Drizzle a little olive oil over 1 x 500–600g rack of lamb, and season well. Heat a large non-stick frying pan over a medium-high heat and colour the fat. Remove the meat from the pan and place, bones uppermost, in a roasting pan. Roast for 25 minutes for rare and 30 minutes for medium. Rest for 15 minutes before serving.

### Shoulder of Lamb Roasting Times

190°C fan/210°C electric/gas 6½
**30 m per kg**
**PLUS 15 m**

### Prepare the lamb for the oven

Preheat the oven to 190°C fan/210°C electric/gas 6½. Calculate the total cooking time of your joint, allowing 30 minutes per kilo plus 15 minutes, so about 1 hour 10 minutes for a joint this size.

Make cuts all over the top of the **lamb** using a sharp knife and then, with the help of the tip of a teaspoon handle, stuff each hole with a few **rosemary needles**. Arrange the **onions** and **bay leaves** in the centre of a roasting pan that will hold the lamb snugly, and drizzle over a little **oil**.

Season the lamb all over with **salt and pepper** and place, fat-side up, on top of the onions, so they are tucked underneath and concealed from view. You can tuck the knuckle bone under the edge of the joint. Drizzle a little oil over the lamb.

### Roast the lamb *

Roast the lamb for 1 hour 10 minutes (or according to the time calculated). There is no need to baste.

### Rest the lamb and make the gravy

Transfer the lamb to a carving plate and set aside to rest, uncovered, in a warm place for 15–20 minutes. Discard the knuckle and the bay leaves from the roasting pan, and spoon off any excess fat. To make a light gravy, set the pan over a medium heat, add the **wine** and simmer with the onions, taking up all the sticky residue on the base of the pan, until reduced by half. Add the **stock** and continue to simmer for several minutes until the gravy tastes nicely rounded and rich.

### Dish up

Carve the lamb across the grain, adding any juices given out to the gravy. Pass the gravy through a sieve into a bowl or jug and serve with the lamb.

*Serving suggestion*
— The relatively high roasting temperature allows for classic roasties (see page 210). Accompany with some homemade mint sauce (see page 113).

## The knack

\* **Testing the meat:** Given its shape a shoulder is not a joint to test with a thermometer in the usual way, and is cooked medium rather than rare, though you may find the meat in the very centre surrounding the bone will be pink.

# Garlic Roast Leg of Lamb

Serves **6** / Start to Finish **1 h 50 m**

This is my favourite method for cooking leg of lamb for celebrations such as Easter, simple rustic fare at its best. Nestled in a thick blanket of rosemary and thyme, the scent of the lamb roasting is heavenly. It comes with a big jug of rich dark gravy.

leg of lamb – approx. 2.2kg

garlic cloves – 3–5, peeled and cut into long thin slivers

rosemary – a small handful of sprigs, plus 1 tablespoon needles

lemon thyme – a small handful of sprigs, plus 1 tablespoon leaves

extra virgin olive oil – 3 tablespoons

sea salt, black pepper

mixed vegetables (e.g. onion, carrot, celery and leek) – 500g (trimmed weight), diced

red wine – 150ml

chicken stock – 600ml

cornflour – 1 teaspoon (optional)

## Variations

**Roast Leg of Lamb with Anchovies:**
Replace the garlic with slivers of salted anchovy, or stuff the holes with a little of each.

**Garlic Roast Shoulder of Lamb:** This recipe can also be used for a shoulder. If smaller than 2.2kg, you will need to take the briefer cooking time into account when roasting the potatoes.

## Leg of Lamb Roasting Times

230°C fan/250°C electric/gas 9
**15 m PLUS**

160°C fan/180°C electric/gas 4
**17 m per 500g**

### Calculate the total roasting time
Preheat the oven to 230°C fan/250°C electric/gas 9. Calculate the total cooking time of your joint, allowing 17 minutes per 500g plus 15 minutes – so about 1 hour 30 minutes for a joint this size.

### Prepare the lamb for the oven
Make cuts about 1cm deep all over the **lamb** flesh at 3–4cm intervals using a fine sharp knife, and slip a sliver of **garlic** into each hole. Arrange the **rosemary and thyme sprigs** in a thick blanket over the base of a heavy-duty roasting pan (ideally cast iron) that will hold the lamb snugly.

Drizzle 1 tablespoon **olive oil** over the joint, season both sides with **salt and pepper** and place, fat-side up, on the bed of herbs. Scatter the **rosemary needles and thyme leaves** over the surface of the meat and drizzle over the remaining oil.

### Roast the lamb
Roast the lamb for 15 minutes, then turn the oven down to 160°C fan/180°C electric/gas 4 and continue to roast for a further 1 hour 15 minutes (or according to the time calculated).

### Rest the lamb
Transfer the joint to a warm plate and set aside to rest, uncovered, for 20 minutes. Discard as many of the herb sprigs in the pan as possible and skim off any excess fat to leave a couple of tablespoons.

### Make the gravy
Set the pan over a medium-high heat, add the **diced vegetables** and fry for 10–15 minutes until they are lightly golden and sticky with the roasting juices, stirring frequently. Add the **wine** and simmer briefly until well reduced, and then add the **stock**. (For thickened gravy, blend the **cornflour** with 1 tablespoon water in a small bowl and stir into the gravy with the stock.) Simmer the gravy for a further 5 minutes until it is nice and rich, and season to taste.

### Dish up
Carve the lamb across the grain, adding any juices given out to the gravy. Pass the gravy through a sieve into a bowl or jug and serve with the meat. (See Two Suppers for One, opposite, for what to do with any leftovers.)

# Two Suppers for One

Serves **4** / Start to Finish **3 h 30 m**

The chances are that you will be left with a fair amount of meat on the bone after roasting a leg or shoulder, which will be too stringy and tough to eat cold. Here you have the beginning of a completely different lamb supper. Slowly cook the leftovers for a few hours, and you should end up with a generous quantity of silky, succulent braised meat to serve approx. 4 people, the only waste being the bone itself. Any curry or tagine spice blend will turn it into a delicious stew for ladling over rice and couscous.

extra virgin olive oil – 2 tablespoons

medium onions – 2, peeled and finely chopped

garlic cloves – 3, peeled and finely chopped

medium-hot red chilli – 1 heaped teaspoon, finely chopped

fresh root ginger – 2cm piece, peeled and finely chopped

spice blend (e.g. ras-el-hanout or garam masala) – 1–2 teaspoons

chopped tomatoes – 1 x 400g tin

dry white wine – 150ml

chicken stock – 150ml

sea salt, black pepper

leftover roast lamb on the bone

**Prepare the stew base**
Preheat the oven to 140°C fan/160°C electric/gas 3. You need a lidded casserole long enough to hold the joint (if necessary, saw off the end bone to fit). Heat the **oil** over a medium heat and fry the **onion** for 8–10 minutes until golden, stirring frequently. Add the **garlic**, **chilli** and **ginger** a minute or two before the end. Stir in the **spices**, cook briefly, and then add the **tomatoes**. Continue to cook for several minutes until reduced by half. Stir in the **wine**, **stock** and some **salt** and settle the **lamb** into the sauce.

**Braise the lamb**
Cover the pan with a lid and braise the lamb for 3–4 hours, or until it is fork tender, turning it halfway through. (If the sauce seems to be drying out, add another glass of stock or water.)

**Shred the meat**
Pull the lamb off the bone using a couple of forks and coarsely shred the meat, discarding any fatty sections. Skim any fat off the surface of the sauce, stir the lamb back in and season to taste with **salt and pepper**.

# Crackling Roast Pork with Gravy

Serves **6** / Start to Finish **2 h 15 m**

Roast pork with crackling, apple sauce and a creamy gravy is an essential Sunday lunch classic. Cooked properly it is a feast, and more affordable than either lamb or beef. The crackling does away with the need for roast potatoes (and here you are roasting at a comparatively low temperature, in any case).

sea salt, black pepper

boned outdoor-reared pork shoulder – approx. 2kg, rind removed and scored, joint rolled and tied *

rosemary – a few sprigs

vegetable oil – 2 tablespoons

dry cider – 200ml

chicken stock – 300ml

double cream – 200ml

lemon juice – squeeze

apple sauce, to serve (see page 113)

**Shoulder of Pork Roasting Times**

230°C fan/250°C electric/gas 9
**15 m PLUS**

140°C fan/160°C electric/gas 3
**30 m per 500g**

### Calculate the roasting time

Preheat the oven to 230°C fan/250°C electric/gas 9. Meanwhile calculate the roasting time, allowing 30 minutes per 500g (joint weight, excluding the rind) plus 15 minutes. So a 2kg joint will weigh approx. 1.5kg without the rind, and take 1 ¾ hours in total.

### Prepare the pork and crackling for the oven

**Season** the **pork joint** all over and place, fat-side up, in a roasting pan that holds it with a little room to spare. Pull half the **rosemary** needles off the stalks and scatter these and the stalks over the pork, then drizzle over the **oil**. Place the **rind**, skin-side up, in another roasting pan and rub in a little salt.

### Roast the pork and crackling

Roast the pork and the rind for 15 minutes, then reduce the temperature to 140°C fan/160°C electric/gas 3 and continue to roast for a further 1 ½ hours (or according to the time calculated). There is no need to baste the meat or the crackling.

Once the time is up, you can check the internal temperature of the joint by inserting a meat thermometer in the centre, which should read 70°C.

### Rest the joint and crisp up the crackling

Transfer the joint to a warm plate and set aside to rest, uncovered, for 15–20 minutes. Meanwhile increase the oven temperature to 230°C fan/250°C electric/gas 9, and continue to roast the crackling while the meat is resting until the surface is crisp and pale and covered in small bubbles.

### Make the gravy

To make the gravy, skim the fat off the roasting pan and set over a medium heat on the hob. Add the **cider** and **stock,** and simmer vigorously for about 5 minutes until the sauce appears a little richer. Pour in the **cream** and simmer for a minute or two longer. Season to taste with salt and pepper, and sharpen with a little **lemon juice**. Strain into a warm jug or gravy boat at the last moment so the gravy is piping hot.

### Carve the joint and dish up

Drain any fat off the crackling into a small bowl (set aside to harden before throwing it away). Carve the roast across the grain, and serve with the crackling and gravy. Accompany with homemade **apple sauce**.

## The knack

\* **Separating the rind from the joint:** You can almost guarantee that a pre-packed joint will come rolled rind-on, in which case it isn't overly difficult to untie it, cut off the rind so the fat is evenly distributed between the two, and retie it. Or, rather easier, ask your butcher to do it for you, and score the rind as well if it hasn't been done already.

# Pork Belly Feast with Pumpkin Roasties

Serves **6** / Start to Finish **2 h 30 m**

This is a great basic method for cooking a belly joint, a feast of a cut that offers succulent strands of meat separated by equally thick strands of buttery fat, and a fab overcoat of crackling. Pork belly spans the East/West divide, and is equally good with Korean Smacked Cucumber (see page 264) or Sesame Spinach (see page 237) in place of the roasted pumpkin.

pork belly, ideally ribs in – 2kg, rind scored at 0.5–1cm intervals *
extra virgin olive oil, for coating
sea salt, black pepper
dry white wine – 100ml
water – 150ml

**Pumpkin Roasties:** *These make a change from potatoes, and pumpkin is particularly good with pork.*

pumpkin – 900g, trimmed weight (approx. 1.5kg whole), cut into chunky chips
extra virgin olive oil – 4 tablespoons
rosemary needles – 2 tablespoons
sea salt

Toss the pumpkin with the olive oil and rosemary in a large roasting pan. Place in the oven at the same time as turning the temperature back up again. Leave to roast while the pork is resting, carefully turning with a spatula halfway through. Scatter with sea salt before serving.

**Roast the pork** **
Preheat the oven to 230°C fan/250°C electric/gas 9 and place a large roasting pan inside. Meanwhile coat the **belly** with **oil** and season it generously with **salt and pepper**. Place the joint, rind-down, in the hot roasting pan and roast for 30 minutes.

Reduce the temperature to 150°C fan/170°C electric/gas 3½, turn the pork rind-up and roast for a further 1 hour 20 minutes.

Increase the oven temperature to 230°C fan/250°C electric/gas 9 and roast the pork for a further 10 minutes.

**Rest the pork and make the gravy**
Remove the pork from the oven and transfer it to a board to rest for 25–30 minutes. Skim any fat off the pork roasting pan and set over a medium heat. Add the **wine** and simmer until reduced by half, taking up all the sticky residue on the bottom of the pan with a wooden spoon. Add the **water** and simmer for a minute longer.

**Carve the meat and dish up**
Carve the pork into thick slices between the ribs, removing them if they come away easily. Serve the pork with the gravy, accompanied by some pumpkin roasties (see left) if you wish.

The knack

* **Which pork?** Try to buy your joint ribs-in, which will make for a sturdier cut that cooks more evenly; roasting on the bone always offers that little extra something in the way of flavour and succulence.

** **For extra crispy crackling:** The skin is given a head start by initially cooking it rind-down in a very hot roasting dish, and then the temperature is whacked back up at the end. Scoring the rind thinly at 5mm–1cm intervals makes a huge difference – a butcher should be able to do this for you.

# Traditional Roast Beef with Gravy

Serves **6** / Start to Finish **1 h 40 m**

This is the simplest possible rendition of roast beef with easy onion gravy, and lots of it. Silverside is a good family roasting joint with an excellent flavour, but you could trade up to sirloin for a special occasion. I like it cooked medium-rare, but if you prefer yours either side of this consult page 111.

banana shallots – 2, peeled, halved and sliced

groundnut or vegetable oil –
1 tablespoon

sea salt, black pepper

silverside joint – approx. 1.2–1.5kg

red wine – 150ml

beef stock – 400ml

horseradish sauce, to serve (see page 113)

## Variation

**Perfectly Rare Roast Beef:** *This is my default recipe whenever I am after rare beef, especially for serving cold.*

groundnut oil – 1 teaspoon

sirloin joint – 1.5kg

English mustard powder – 1 scant teaspoon

sea salt, black pepper

grainy mustard – 1 heaped tablespoon

Preheat the oven to 130°C fan/150°C electric/gas 2. Heat the oil in a large ovenproof frying pan over a high heat. Using a tea strainer, dust the fat and underside of the joint with mustard powder, and season. Sear the meat on all sides, making sure it is really well coloured as you'll be roasting at a low temperature. Brush the grainy mustard all over the joint, return to the frying pan and roast in the oven for 50 minutes or until the internal temperature reaches 45–50°C to leave it rare. Cover with foil and rest for 20 minutes before serving. Carve thinly.

### Prepare the joint
Preheat the oven to 230°C fan/250°C electric/gas 9. Calculate the total cooking time of your joint, allowing 16 minutes per 500g plus 15 minutes to leave it medium-rare – so a total of 55–65 minutes for a joint this size. Arrange the **shallots** in the centre of a roasting pan that will hold the beef snugly and drizzle over ½ tablespoon **oil**. **Season** the **beef** all over, place fat-side up on top of the shallots and drizzle over the remaining ½ tablespoon oil. Add a glass of water to the pan to a depth of a few millimetres.

### Roast the joint
Roast the beef for 15 minutes, and then turn down the oven to 180°C fan/ 200°C electric/gas 6 and continue to roast for a further 40–50 minutes (or according to the time calculated). If you wish, you can check the internal temperature with a meat thermometer (see page 111). If necessary, add a drop more water towards the end if the pan is drying out too quickly.

### Rest the joint and make the gravy
Transfer the joint to a warm plate and set aside to rest for 20 minutes, loosely covering with foil. To make the gravy, set the roasting pan over a medium heat on the hob, add the **wine** and simmer until reduced by half, stirring well to take up all the sticky golden residue on the bottom. Add the **stock** and continue to simmer for several minutes. Liquidise the contents of the pan in a blender, taste for seasoning and pour into a warm jug.

### Dish up
Thinly carve the beef and accompany with the gravy, Yorkshire puds (see page 124) if you wish, and **horseradish sauce** (see page 113).

# Yorkshire Puds

Serves **6** / Start to Finish **30 m**

The best Yorkshires are golden, risen and crusty, insignificant puffs that can be eaten in quantity. They enjoyed their finest hour when meat was roasted on a spit, and the pudding would bake beneath absorbing all the dripping and meaty juices. A far cry from the way we cook today, but we can still douse them in gravy. In fact, they cry out for it.

**For the batter**

plain flour – 110g, sifted

Maldon sea salt – ½ teaspoon

medium eggs – 2

whole milk – 75ml

water – 75ml

dripping, lard or vegetable oil, for greasing the tins *

you will need a fairy-cake or muffin tray

### Prepare the batter

*By machine:* The quickest means to a lump-free batter is to place **all the ingredients** in a blender and liquidise until smooth and creamy. Alternatively you could use a hand-held electric whisk.

*By hand:* Place the **flour** and **salt** in a bowl. Break in the **eggs** and roughly mix them in, then start to add the **milk** and **water** a little at a time, smoothing the mixture with a wooden spoon. If at the end the mixture is at all lumpy you can whisk it for good measure. Don't worry about resting the batter unless it fits in with your schedule, in which case set aside for 30–60 minutes.

### Bake the Yorkshires **

Preheat the oven to 200°C fan/220°C electric/gas 7. Liberally grease the inside of the fairy-cake or muffin tray with whatever **fat** you are using and place in the oven to heat up for at least 10 minutes. Rewhisk or blend the batter and pour into the moulds, filling them by two-thirds. Bake for 15–20 minutes until golden and risen.

### The knack

* **Fat:** Dripping is the ideal fat and gives the puddings a particular flavour. Next best is commercial lard and lastly vegetable oil.

** **Making the Yorkshire puds in advance?** Yorkshire puddings can be made in advance and reheated, especially handy should you be roasting your joint at a lower temperature. In this case, turn them on their sides to crisp up the base, and reheat for 5–10 minutes.

# Honey-glazed Ham

Serves **6–8** / Start to Finish **3 h**

Whole hams aren't just for Christmas, and if you get through anything like as much as we do in toasties and the like, then you may well find that it makes sense to cook one up every now and again.

smoked or unsmoked gammon – 2kg, boned and rolled *

celery – 3 outer sticks, trimmed and sliced

carrots (unpeeled) – 2, trimmed and sliced

leek – 1, trimmed and sliced

bay leaves – 2

runny honey – 2 tablespoons

English mustard – 2 teaspoons

### Variation

**Ham Glazed with Maple Syrup:**
Replace the honey with 2 tablespoons maple syrup blended with 1 teaspoon black treacle.

### Ham Poaching Times

in simmering water
**19 m per 500g**

### Simmer the gammon

Calculate the total cooking time of your joint, allowing 19 minutes per 500g. Place the **gammon** in a large saucepan (I use a preserving pan), cover with cold water and bring to the boil. Pour off the water and start again, covering the joint with fresh water. Add the chopped **vegetables** and **bay leaves** to the pan and bring to the boil. Simmer gently over a low heat for 1 hour 15 minutes (or according to the time calculated). Leave the pan uncovered and top up with boiling water halfway through, if necessary.

### Remove the rind and glaze the joint

Preheat the oven to 180°C fan/200°C electric/gas 6. Transfer the ham from the saucepan onto a board using two forks. Remove any string around the ham and pull or slice off the rind, keeping as much white fat on the joint as possible. Slice the fat at 2cm intervals with a crisscross pattern, avoiding cutting into the flesh. Blend the **honey** and **mustard** in a bowl, and spread in an even layer all over the ham. If you like you can tie another couple of pieces of string around the joint if it seems loose. Place the ham in a roasting pan, glazed-side up, and pour a few millimetres of the ham stock into the base to prevent any syrup that trickles down from catching.

### Finish in the oven

Roast for 35–45 minutes until the glaze is mahogany-coloured and dry. Set aside to rest for 20 minutes before carving, or serve cold. **

### The knack

\* **Do you need to soak the meat?** It is worth checking with your butcher to see if the joint needs soaking overnight to rid it of excess salt. I find a change of water during the cooking process usually does the trick.

\*\* **Cooked ham freezes well** and will be streets ahead of anything you buy ready-sliced.

# Hip Ham Hock

Serves **4** / Start to Finish **5 h**

A ham hock cooks down to gorgeously succulent flakes that are great in sarnies, omelettes or hash, as well as eaten hot with some lentils. It is also a good cut around Christmas, when the impecunious may find comfort in the economy of this dish as opposed to a prize gammon. The cooking liquor for an unsmoked hock can also be used as the basis for lentil or potato soup.

ham hock (smoked or unsmoked) –
1 x approx. 1.5kg

**Poaching ingredients**

carrots (unpeeled) – 2, thickly sliced

celery heart – 1, trimmed and thickly sliced

banana shallot (unpeeled) – 1, thickly sliced

cloves – 6

bay leaf – 1

dry white wine – 300ml

**Soak or pre-boil the ham hock**
Either soak the **hock** in cold water overnight, or bring it to the boil and change the water before adding the poaching ingredients.

**Cook the ham hock in the oven \***
Preheat the oven to 130°C fan/150°C electric/gas 2. Place the **hock** on its side in a casserole, add **all the remaining ingredients** and cover with **water** as far as possible. Bring to the boil, skim off any surface foam, and then cover with a lid. Transfer to the oven and cook for 4 hours, turning the hock halfway through and topping up with boiling water if necessary.

**Shred the ham hock**
Carefully lift the hock out of the casserole onto a plate, laying it on its side, and leave to rest for 15 minutes. Peel off and discard the rind and fat, and then pull the meat off the bone and shred it, discarding any more fat separating the pieces. You should end up with 450–500g shredded meat.

*Serving suggestion*
— Accompany with puy lentils (see page 240).

**The knack**

**\* Why cook the ham in the oven?** Anything that requires boiling for hours will turn the kitchen into a sauna in no time. But here the hock is cooked in a pot with a tight-fitting lid in the oven, giving a more even temperature and there is no risk of it boiling dry.

# Beef, Guinness & Cheddar Stew

Serves **4** / Start to Finish **2 h 30 m**

Of all the vegetables I want to find in a beef stew, carrots come top of the list – meltingly tender and sweet, mashed into a rich gravy with equally tender meat. And Guinness with its slight bitterness perfectly offsets their character. The little pockets of gooey Cheddar add flavour without being overly powerful. But equally it is a lovely basic stew without.

groundnut or vegetable oil

braising steak (ideally chuck) – 800g, cut into 3–4cm dice

plain flour – 1 tablespoon *

Chantenay carrots – 400g, trimmed, peeled and halved lengthways if large

bay leaf – 1

Guinness – 1 x 330ml bottle

beef stock – 450ml

tomato purée – 1 tablespoon

sea salt, black pepper

mature Cheddar – 150g, cut into 1cm dice

chives, finely snipped, to serve

### Colour the beef **

You will need to colour the meat in batches. Heat 1 tablespoon **oil** in a large casserole over a medium-high heat, add about one-third of the **steak** so the pieces are spaced well apart, and sear to colour them. Remove to a bowl and cook the remainder in the same way, adding more oil to the pan when necessary.

### Put the stew on to cook

Add all the meat back to the pan, sprinkle over the **flour** and stir, then add the **carrots** and **bay leaf**. Stir in the **Guinness**, **stock** and **tomato purée**, and some **seasoning**. Bring to the boil, cover and cook over a very gentle heat for 2 hours, stirring towards the end to make sure that it doesn't catch on the bottom of the pan. The stew can be made well in advance and reheated when necessary.

### Add the Cheddar and serve

Just before serving stir in the **Cheddar**, cover and leave for 2–3 minutes. Serve scattered with **chives**.

*Serving suggestion*
— Delicious served with mashed potatoes.

### The knack

* **Why flour?** Just a little flour in the sauce makes the difference between a water-thin gravy and a richer, slightly thickened one.

** **Colouring the meat:** The key to imbuing the braising juices with flavour lies with colouring the meat. It is really important to give the pieces sufficient space to caramelise; if you overcrowd the pan you risk drawing out the moisture and the meat will end up stewing. So, a few at a time.

# Beef Rogan Josh

Serves **8** / Start to Finish **3 h 30 m** *

Even today, after so many years of cooking, I find the curries that fit into my life are the ones that are redolent of my childhood. This was before we embraced the complexities of India's many regions and different styles. And I love all that, but the reality is half a day shopping, half a day cooking and a storecupboard full of ingredients that I probably won't use for another year. My ideal relies on easy to find ingredients, and an equally easy method.

tomato purée – 100g

saffron filaments – about 30

cayenne pepper – ½ teaspoon **

water – 600ml

groundnut or vegetable oil

sea salt, black pepper

lean braising steak (e.g. chuck) – 1.5kg, cut into 3cm cubes

medium onions – 4, peeled, halved and thinly sliced

garlic cloves – 4, peeled and finely chopped

garam masala – 1 level tablespoon

ground cumin – 1 rounded teaspoon

turmeric – 1 rounded teaspoon

bay leaves – 2

coarsely chopped coriander, to serve

**Herb Purée:** *For those curries that are complex and earthy in character this comes as a sprightly awakening.*

coriander leaves and fine stalks – 30g

mint leaves – 15g

medium-hot green chilli – ½ teaspoon, chopped

shallot – 1 teaspoon, chopped

fromage frais – 200g

caster sugar – ⅓ teaspoon

sea salt

Whizz the herbs, chilli and shallot in a food processor until very finely chopped and then scoop into a bowl. Stir in the fromage frais, sugar and a little salt, cover with clingfilm and chill for 30 minutes.

**Make the tomato sauce**
Preheat the oven to 140°C fan/160°C electric/gas 3. Place the **tomato purée**, **saffron** and **cayenne pepper** in a bowl and blend in the **water**.

**Brown the meat**
Heat 2 tablespoons **oil** in a large casserole over a medium-high heat. **Season** the **steak** and sear in the hot oil, a few pieces at a time. Add more oil to the pan as necessary and remove the browned meat to a large bowl as you go.

**Prepare the curry**
Turn the heat down to medium, add another 2 tablespoons oil to the pan and fry the **onions** for 5–8 minutes until golden and caramelised, stirring frequently. Add the **garlic** just before the end. Stir in the **garam masala**, **cumin** and **turmeric**, and then the tomato purée mixture and **bay leaves**. Return the beef to the pan, add some salt and bring to the boil. Cover and cook in the oven for 3 hours, stirring halfway through.

**Finish the curry**
Leave the juices to settle for about 5 minutes and then skim off the fat. The remaining juices should be rich and thick. Season the curry to taste and sprinkle over some chopped **coriander**.

*Serving suggestion*
— It is all the little bits that go with a curry that turn it into a celebration. So in addition to pilau rice (see page 221), lay on a pile of crispy poppadoms, some herb purée (see left) and a bowl of salted cashews.

The knack

* **Why the long cooking time?** This curry has a rich, rust-red sauce that relies on tomato purée for its body. The long slow cooking transforms both the sauce and the meat.

** **Tempering the heat:** The cayenne provides a definite bite for those who feel curry isn't curry without that tingling warmth. Omit it if your taste is milder.

Beef Rogan Josh

# Daube à la Provençale

Serves **6** / Start to Finish **1½ days** *

The leisurely pace of this dish perfectly fits our perception of lazy Provençal days, though its hearty character makes it just as apt on a chilly summer evening as a warm one.

chuck steak – 1.5kg, cut into 100–150g pieces, approx. 3–5cm thick **

extra virgin olive oil

sea salt, black pepper

smoked lardons – 150g

medium onions – 2, peeled, halved and thinly sliced

garlic cloves – 4, peeled and thinly sliced

ripe plum tomatoes – 400–500g, skinned (see page 18) and chopped

flat-leaf parsley – a handful, coarsely chopped (optional)

### For the marinade

thyme sprigs – 4–5

bay leaf – 1

juniper berries – 1 teaspoon, smashed

cloves – 6

strips of orange zest – 4, removed with a potato peeler

red wine (e.g. an inexpensive claret) – 1 x 75cl bottle

### Marinate the meat

Combine **all the ingredients for the marinade** in a large bowl, add the **steak** and press down to submerge it. Cover and chill for 24–48 hours, stirring now and again. (If you are pushed for time and you want to prepare it on the day, then a morning will do.)

### Strain the meat

Strain the marinade into a bowl and discard the aromatics, carefully removing any spices that have settled on the meat. Pat the meat dry using a double thickness of kitchen paper.

### Colour the meat and vegetables

Preheat the oven to 110°C fan/130°C electric/gas ½. Heat 1 tablespoon **olive oil** in a large casserole over a medium heat. Lightly **season** the meat all over and colour, a few pieces at a time, until crusty and golden. Transfer the meat to a bowl as you go, and add more oil to the pan as necessary. Add 1 tablespoon oil to the pan and fry the **lardons** for a couple of minutes until starting to colour, stirring frequently. Add the **onions** and fry for 5 minutes until nicely golden, adding the **garlic** just before the end. Finally add the **tomatoes** and cook for 1–2 minutes until softened.

### Slow-cook the daube

Add the meat back to the pan and pour in the marinade, submerging the meat as far as possible. Bring to a simmer very slowly on the hob, skimming off any foam that rises to the surface. Cover and cook in the oven for 5 hours or until the meat is meltingly tender, stirring halfway through.

### Finish the sauce

Leave the stew to stand for 15 minutes before skimming off the fat on the surface. Strain the juices through a sieve into a clean medium-sized saucepan and add the contents of the sieve back to the casserole. Cover the casserole with a lid to keep warm. Simmer the juices over a medium heat until reduced by about half – they should be rich in colour and taste deeply savoury. Pour them back over the meat and taste for seasoning. Serve scattered with **parsley** if you wish.

### *Serving suggestion*

— All those rich red wine gravy juices are fab with buttery mashed potato spiced with extra virgin olive oil (see page 208), mashed cauliflower (see page 234) or macaroni with grated Parmesan.

### The knack

\* **Timing:** You won't be overdoing it if you start preparing this a few days
in advance. Traditionally a daube would have been cooked a day or two in
advance to allow the favours to develop fully. In this case, leave it to cool and
then cover and chill. Make sure you scrape off any hard fat from the surface
before gently reheating on the hob.

\*\* **Which beef?** You can replace half the chuck with about 1.2kg short-ribs if
you wish. *Onglet* and featherblade are also excellent cuts, and they're leaner
than chuck and ribs. Choose a combination of any of these.

# Lamb Tagine with Dates & Tomatoes

Serves **6** / Start to Finish **2 h**

I recall watching a Moroccan man squatting on his haunches beside a mountain road in the Ourika Valley as he prepared a tagine early one morning in a conical clay dish designed for the purpose. There was no table, no utensils, no kitchen, no running water, and that is the marvel of these very basic stews – a careful blend of spices and time are the magic ingredients – as by lunchtime his tagine had been transformed. An upturned crate was produced as a table as he and a friend, continuing to squat, shared the tagine straight from the dish, scooping it up with swathes of flatbread.

medium onions – 2, peeled and coarsely grated *

ras-el-hanout, or other tagine spice blend – 1 rounded tablespoon

boneless leg of lamb – 600g, trimmed of fat and cut into 3–4cm dice

lemon – juice of ½

plum tomatoes – 250–300g, skinned (see page 18) and chopped

stoned Medjool dates – 75g, halved lengthways

fresh coriander – 4 tablespoons, coarsely chopped, plus extra to serve

unsalted butter – 25g

sea salt

water – 500ml

### To serve

chickpeas – 1 x 400g tin, drained and rinsed

young spinach leaves – 150g

toasted sesame seeds – a sprinkling (optional)

**Assemble and simmer the tagine ***
Combine the **onions** and **spice mixture** in a medium-sized casserole, mixing so they are evenly blended. Add **all the remaining ingredients** and stir. Bring to the boil, skim off the surface foam, and then cover and cook over a very low heat for 1 ½ hours.

**Finish the tagine**
Stir in the **chickpeas**, scatter over the **spinach**, and then cover and cook for a further 5 minutes, stirring halfway through. Taste for seasoning and serve scattered with more coriander and a sprinkling of **sesame seeds** if you wish.

---

**The knack**

* **Grating the onions:** If the thought of grating onions by hand brings tears to your eyes, consider using a food processor. Alternatively you could finely chop them instead.

** **Authenticity:** While the method here of 'bung it all in a pan and go' may seem on the simplistic side, this is exactly how many tagines are made.

# Gratin of Meatballs in Plum Tomato Sauce

Serves **4** / Start to Finish **1 h 40 m**

Hard not to love anything that poses as a mini-hamburger, especially when it comes smothered with a chunky tomato sauce.

### For the meatballs

extra virgin olive oil – 4 tablespoons

medium onion – 1, peeled and finely chopped

rindless unsmoked streaky bacon – 100g, finely diced

thyme leaves – 3 tablespoons

minced beef – 700g

sea salt, black pepper

### For the tomato sauce

plum tomatoes – 1kg, skinned (see page 18), halved and chopped

tomato purée – 3 tablespoons

extra virgin olive oil – 1 tablespoon

garlic cloves – 2, peeled and finely chopped

dried red chilli – 1, finely chopped

caster sugar – ½ teaspoon

### To serve

freshly grated Parmesan

### Variation

**Pasta with Meatballs:** Allow 100g penne per person. Bring a large pan of salted water to the boil, add the pasta and cook according to the packet instructions until just tender; drain into a colander. Serve the meatballs spooned over the pasta, accompanied by some extra Parmesan.

## Make the meatballs *

Heat 2 tablespoons **olive oil** in a large frying pan over a medium-low heat. Add the **onion** and **bacon** and fry gently for about 5 minutes, stirring occasionally until soft and cooked through. Sprinkle over 2 tablespoons **thyme leaves** a couple of minutes before the end. Transfer the contents of the pan to a large bowl and set aside to cool. Add the **minced beef** and some **seasoning** to the bowl and work everything together using a spoon. Shape the mixture into balls about the size of a large walnut and reserve them on a couple of plates.

## Make the tomato sauce

Place the chopped **tomatoes** in a bowl and combine with the **tomato purée**, 1 tablespoon **olive oil**, **garlic**, **chilli**, **sugar** and some seasoning. The sauce and meatballs can be made to this point in advance, in which case cover and chill them.

## Colour the meatballs and combine with the tomato sauce

Heat ½ tablespoon olive oil in a large non-stick frying pan over a medium heat. Add half the meatballs and colour them on all sides. Transfer them to a shallow ovenproof dish that will hold them all in a single layer with a little space in between each one. Scrape the pan clean, add another ½ tablespoon oil and cook the remainder in the same way. Spoon the tomato sauce over the meatballs.

## Bake the meatballs and dish up

Preheat the oven to 180°C fan/200°C electric/gas 6. Scatter the remaining thyme over the meatballs, drizzle over 1 tablespoon olive oil and bake in the oven for 40–45 minutes until the tomatoes on the top have started to singe at the tips. Accompany with a bowl of **Parmesan** to scatter over.

*Serving suggestion*

— These are as good for scooping up with warm flatbreads as ladled over pasta with a shower of Parmesan (see left), or dished up with rice.

### The knack

**\* Getting the texture right:** Providing you handle the meatballs carefully they should hold together well, but for added insurance – or should you feel butter-fingered – you could add an egg yolk to the meatball mixture.

# Best Ever Beef Ragu

Serves **4–6\*** / Start to Finish **1 h 30 m**

My preferred ragu is made with pure beef, rather than a mixture of meats, as it makes for a greater depth of flavour and a satisfyingly hearty texture. This version is richly flavoured with tomato and scented with rosemary, and just a hint of chilli.

This recipe features throughout the book, wherever a ragu is called for – in dishes such as moussaka, as well as the pasta greats spag bol and lasagne.

unsalted butter – 25g

extra virgin olive oil – 1 tablespoon

medium onion – 1, peeled and finely chopped

slim carrots – 2, trimmed, peeled, halved lengthways and thinly sliced

celery stick – 1, halved lengthways and thinly sliced

garlic cloves – 3, peeled and finely chopped

minced beef – 800g \*\*

red wine – 150ml

chopped tomatoes – 2 x 400g tins

tomato purée – 2 tablespoons

small dried red chilli – 1, crumbled

bay leaf – 1

rosemary – 1 sprig

sea salt

**Fry the vegetables**
Heat the **butter** and **olive oil** in a medium-large saucepan over a medium heat. Add the **onion**, **carrot** and **celery** and fry for 7–10 minutes until softened and glossy, stirring frequently. Add the **garlic** just before the end.

**Add the meat and the remaining ingredients**
Add the **minced beef,** turn up the heat and fry, stirring frequently, until it changes colour. Add the **wine, chopped tomatoes, tomato purée, chilli** and **herbs,** and season with **salt.**

**Simmer the ragu**
Bring to the boil, and then simmer over a low heat for 1 hour, stirring now and again. At this point there should still be plenty of juices. If you prefer a drier ragu for serving with tacos or tortillas for instance, turn the heat up to medium and continue to simmer until it thickens to the right consistency. To serve, skim off any excess fat and season to taste.

**Beef Ragu**

**Variations**

**Spaghetti Bolognese:** Simmer the ragu for 1 hour so there are plenty of juices left to moisten the pasta. Cook 300–450g spaghetti according to the packet instructions and drain. Return the pasta to the pan, toss with a slug of olive oil and serve with the ragu spooned on top, showered with Parmesan.

**Chilli-con-carne:** Add ⅓ teaspoon cayenne pepper and 1 teaspoon ground cumin with the garlic. Stir in 1 x 200g tin of butter beans at the end and simmer for a further 15–20 minutes until firm.

**The knack**

\* **Doubling-up:** If you make up a double quantity of the ragu and freeze it, you are halfway to a number of different suppers. In particular, I find it makes time-consuming delights such as lasagne (see page 201) more accessible. Remember that everything takes longer when you are dealing with larger quantities. So choose a large saucepan, fry the veggies for longer – approx. 10–15 minutes – and simmer the ragu for 2–2½ hours, skimming off the fat now and again.

\*\* **Which mince?** Lean mince is no bad thing, but I would go for a happy medium of 10 per cent fat rather than 5 per cent, which will be too dry. Fat provides succulence as well as flavour.

# Tex Mex Fajitas

Serves **6–8** / Start to Finish **4 h 15 m**

This one has intrinsic teenager appeal – I have yet to meet one who doesn't love the hands-on ritual of rolling up tortillas with a variety of offerings and sauces, and that little bit of chilli goes a long way in spelling danger. The meat can be made in advance and gently reheated on the hob, making this one great for entertaining despite its lengthy cooking.

featherblade steak – 1.5kg, sliced 2–3cm thick *

large onions – 2, peeled, halved and sliced

tomatoes – 200g, cores cut out and chopped

water – 100ml

### For the spice blend

ground cumin – 1 heaped teaspoon

paprika – 2 rounded teaspoons

dried oregano – 2 rounded teaspoons

cayenne pepper – ½–1 rounded teaspoon **

ground allspice – 1 rounded teaspoon

Maldon sea salt – 1 heaped teaspoon

black pepper

garlic cloves – 3, peeled and crushed to a paste

extra virgin olive oil – 2 tablespoons

red wine vinegar – 1 tablespoon

**Prepare the beef and put it on to cook**
Preheat the oven to 140°C fan/160°C electric/gas 3. Combine **all the ingredients for the spice blend** in a medium-sized bowl. Combine the **steak**, **onions** and **tomatoes** in a large casserole, drizzle over the spice blend and turn to coat the ingredients. Pour over the **water**, cover and cook in the oven for 4 hours, turning the meat once or twice during cooking.

**Thicken the sauce and shred the meat**
Transfer the meat and onions to a bowl and simmer the sauce until it is golden and thick. Add the meat back to the pan a couple of pieces at a time, pressing with the back of a large spoon until it flakes, then stir to coat it in the sauce.

*Serving suggestion*
— Serve with warm tortillas, griddled corn (see page 249), sliced pickled chillies, small crisp Little Gem leaves, chunky guacamole (see page 52), soured cream and halved cherry tomatoes mixed with coarsely chopped coriander.

The knack

* **Which beef?** Featherblade steak might require a trip to the butcher, but it is a well-kept secret among chefs and food lovers. Fabulously tasty, it has a thick streak of gristle that runs down the centre, which reduces to an imperceptibly silky gel with long, slow cooking, and long strands of succulent meat.

** **How much chilli?** Add cayenne to your taste here, ½ teaspoon for an imperceptible warmth, and double that for a noticeable hit of chilli.

# Pulled Pork Baps with Simple Slaw

Serves **6** / Start to Finish **5 h**

The essence of pulled pork is meat that is cooked long and slow until it is so tender you can pull it apart with a fork. Although it enjoys a rugged profile of outdoor cooking and firepits, pulled pork readily translates to the home kitchen and makes for a lovely relaxed Saturday lunch if you've got friends coming over. The seasoning can be mixed in advance, the night before for instance, so you can throw it together at breakfast time, and then go back to bed.

pork shoulder – 1 x 2.5kg unrolled boned joint, rind removed and scored *

warm soft white baps or wraps – 6

### For the rub

Maldon sea salt – 2 tablespoons, plus extra for the rind **

light muscovado sugar – 2 tablespoons

sweet paprika – 2 heaped teaspoons

cayenne pepper – ½ teaspoon

**Simple Slaw:** *This is* de rigueur *with pulled pork, and this is a suitably simplistic take on it.*

white cabbage – ½ (approx. 300g), core cut out

banana shallot – 1, peeled and finely chopped

flat-leaf parsley – 3 heaped tablespoons, finely chopped

mayonnaise – 100g

cider vinegar – 2 teaspoons

sea salt, black pepper

Finely shred the cabbage using a food processor attachment, pick out any tough strands and mix with the shallot and parsley in a large bowl. Whisk the mayonnaise with the vinegar and some seasoning in a bowl, spoon over the shredded vegetables and toss to combine.

**Prepare the pork**
Preheat the oven to 200°C fan/220°C electric/gas 7. Line the base and sides of a large roasting pan with two sheets of wide foil, one going either way, allowing enough overhang to bring up over the pork to make a tent. Combine **all the ingredients for the rub** in a medium-sized bowl and rub over the **pork**, including the crevices.

**Roast the pork and crackling**
Place the joint, fat-side up, in the roasting pan and roast for 20 minutes, uncovered. **Season** the **rind** and place in a separate roasting pan on the shelf underneath. Turn the oven down to 130°C fan/150°C electric/gas 2, bring the foil over the pork to form a tent and pleat to seal, leaving plenty of room for air to circulate. Roast for a further 4 hours, turning the pork halfway through. Increase the temperature to 200°C fan/220°C electric/gas 7. Open up the foil parcel, turn the joint so it is fat uppermost and spoon off the juices, reserving them in a little jug. Pour the fat off the crackling and discard. Return the meat and crackling to the oven and roast for a further 20 minutes until the joint is golden and the crackling is crisp.

**Pull the pork and dish up**
Slip the joint off the foil into the roasting pan and shred or 'pull' the meat using two forks, discarding any fat. Skim off and discard any fat from the reserved juices, and then pour half of the juices over the pork. (You can throw away the rest.) Set the pan over a medium-low heat on the hob and stir the shredded meat until it has absorbed the juice, approx. 10 minutes.

Serve the pulled pork in warm soft **white baps or wraps** piled with the Simple Slaw (see left) and accompanied by the crispy crackling.

### The knack

* **Choosing the perfect joint:** A boned shoulder gives you a long, evenly thick piece of meat, which I find gives better results than cooking it on the bone. I also prefer to cook the crackling separately. While a 2.5kg joint sounds large, it shrinks considerably on cooking, giving out lots of juices.

** **Salt:** You want Maldon here; if using a finer sea salt you might need to halve the quantity to allow for the lightness of Maldon flakes.

# Slow-cooked Auvergne Lamb

Serves **6–8** / Start to Finish **8 h 30 m**

Long before pulled meat of all types became fashionable, this traditional French treatment for a leg of lamb was doing the rounds of gourmands' tables. A *gigot de sept heures* is a classic in the Massif Central and many a passionate cook has transported the recipe back home after holidaying in the region. I love meat cooked this way. Sitting down to a soupy plateful of meltingly tender lamb, which falls into soft skeins at the sight of a spoon, is a trip down memory lane.

medium onion – 1, peeled

cloves – approx. 15

flat-leaf parsley – 1 small bunch, tied with string

thyme – 1 small bunch, tied with string

bay leaves – 2

sea salt, black pepper

leg of lamb (bone in) – approx. 2.5kg, knuckle removed and reserved

garlic – 5 heads, cloves peeled but left whole

sweet or medium-dry white wine (e.g. Monbazillac, Barsac, Sauternes or Jurançon) – 1 x 75cl bottle

### Prepare the aromatic broth

Stud the **onion** with the **cloves**. Place this in a cast-iron casserole that will hold the lamb (I use an oval 30cm casserole) and put in the **herbs** and some **salt**. Fill halfway with water and bring to the boil, then cover and simmer over a low heat for 20 minutes. Discard the onion and herbs.

### Pre-cook the lamb

Preheat the oven to 110°C fan/130°C electric/gas ½. Add the **leg of lamb** to the pan, bring the liquid back to the boil, and then cover and simmer for 20 minutes. Drain off and discard the stock and transfer the lamb to a plate. Pat the inside of the casserole dry with kitchen paper.

### Slow-roast the joint

Place the lamb back inside the dry casserole. Arrange the peeled **garlic cloves** around or underneath the lamb, add the knuckle, pour over the **wine** and add a little seasoning. Cover the top of the casserole with a double thickness of foil and then the lid. Cook in the oven for 7 hours, turning the joint after 2–2½ hours, when you will find the lamb has given out some of its juices and the liquid is swelling. Turn the lamb back up the right way after 4½–5 hours, by which time it should be about two-thirds covered in liquid. Remove the lid and foil at this point in order to colour and crisp up the skin.

### Rest the lamb and finish the sauce

Transfer the leg of lamb to a warm plate, loosely cover with foil and set aside to rest for 20 minutes. Skim off the excess fat from the surface of the pan and discard the knuckle. You should be left with a clear aromatic broth and lots of garlic cloves. Set the pan over a lively heat and simmer vigorously until reduced by about one-third. Tip the contents of the casserole into a blender and whizz until smooth – you may need to do this in two batches. Pour the sauce into a warm jug or gravy boat and season to taste. The lamb is not carved so much as pulled apart with a spoon and fork.

### *Serving suggestion*

— I would opt for hearty chunks of sourdough over potatoes. And perhaps some glazed carrots with diced sheep's cheese or feta (see page 234).

# Shepherd's Pie

Serves **6** / Start to Finish **1 h 10 m**

The infamy of Jeffrey Archer's Bollinger and Shepherd's Pie parties for Tory grandees are perhaps the best example of the heights to which this humble pie aspires. But it is rarely more at home than when slathered in ketchup with a pile of *petits pois* to the side. And there are few line-ups as comforting – like Roast Chicken, I have lost count of the number of times I have placed one of these on the table.

**For the meat**

groundnut oil – 2 tablespoons

shallots – 3, peeled and finely chopped

carrots – 1 large or 2 small – trimmed, peeled and thinly sliced

leek – 1, trimmed, halved lengthways and thinly sliced

celery sticks – 2, trimmed and thinly sliced

bay leaf – 1

thyme – 2 sprigs

minced lamb – 750g

red wine – 150ml

tomato ketchup – 2 tablespoons

Worcestershire sauce – 1 teaspoon

sea salt, black pepper

**For the mash**

maincrop potatoes such as Maris Piper – 1.3kg, peeled and halved (or quartered if large)

unsalted butter – 120g, diced, plus an extra knob for baking

whole milk – 3 tablespoons

you will need a 20 x 30cm ovenproof dish

**Variation**

**Cottage Pie:** Shepherd's Pie, as its name suggests, is made with minced lamb. It is sweet and gentle in character, and slightly richer than Cottage Pie, which is made using minced beef. The two are interchangeable here.

**Cook the meat**

Heat the **oil** in a large saucepan and fry the **vegetables** and **herbs** for 8–10 minutes over a low heat until glossy and tender, stirring frequently. Add the **minced lamb**, turn the heat up to high and cook, stirring until it colours and separates. Add **all the remaining ingredients**, including plenty of **seasoning**. Bring to a simmer and cook over a low heat for 20–25 minutes. If there appears to be a lot of fat on the surface, then skim the excess off.

**Make the mash**

Meanwhile bring a large pan of salted water to the boil. Add the **potatoes**, bring back to a simmer and cook until tender – you should be able to insert a table knife with ease. Drain into a sieve or colander and set aside for a minute or two to steam-dry. Pass through a mouli-legumes or press through a sieve back into the pan. In a separate pan, gently heat the **butter** with the **milk** and **seasoning**, and once melted stir into the mash.

**Assemble the pie**

Spoon the meat into the dish, discarding the herbs. Spread the mashed potato over the surface and fork into a crisscross of furrows. You can prepare the pie to this point in advance – in which case, cover and chill until required.

**Cook the pie**

Preheat the oven to 180°C fan/200°C electric/gas 6. Dot the surface with butter and cook for 35–45 minutes until piping hot in the centre and golden brown on top.

# Moussaka

Serves **6** / Start to Finish **1 h 40 m** (+ making the ragu)

If you have ever holidayed in the Greek islands, this dish is likely embedded in the inner recesses of your being. It is a personal favourite, the layers of silky aubergine with the ragu and its gooey blanket of white sauce on top are heartstoppingly good. There are various routes to the white sauce, but this easy version made with Greek yogurt is the one that gets my vote.

Best Ever Beef Ragu – 1 batch (see page 135)
ground cinnamon – ½ teaspoon

**For the aubergines**
aubergines – 4 (approx. 1kg), cut into 1cm slices (ends discarded)
extra virgin olive oil
sea salt, black pepper

**For the topping**
Greek yogurt – 500g
medium eggs – 2, beaten
halloumi – 200g, coarsely grated
oregano or marjoram leaves – 2 heaped tablespoons (or 1 heaped tablespoon lemon thyme leaves, if you prefer)

you will need a 30 x 20cm gratin dish, approx. 5–6cm deep

**Make the ragu**
Make the **ragu** according to the instructions on page 135, stirring in the **cinnamon** after colouring the beef. You want the mixture quite dry for this, so the pie can be neatly cut into squares, so if necessary simmer it for a further 15–20 minutes at the end.

**Roast the aubergine slices \***
Preheat the oven to 190°C fan/210°C electric/gas 6½. Lay the **aubergine** slices out on one or two baking sheets, brush with **oil** on both sides and season the tops with **salt and pepper**. Roast for 30–35 minutes until golden, turning halfway through.

**Make the white sauce**
Whisk the **yogurt** with the **eggs** in a medium-sized bowl, and then stir in half the **cheese**.

**Assemble the moussaka**
Spread half the ragu over the base of a 30 x 20cm gratin dish, and lay half the aubergine slices on top, then repeat. Spread the white sauce over the top and scatter with the remaining cheese. Toss the **herbs** with 1 tablespoon oil and sprinkle over the surface.

**Bake the moussaka**
Bake for 40–45 minutes until puffy and golden. Serve 10–20 minutes out of the oven, though on a fine day it is also delicious eaten warm rather than hot.

The knack

\* **Roasting the aubergines:** I like a moussaka to have plenty of aubergines in proportion to the meat, and to this end I layer them with the ragu. Aubergines will drink up as much oil as you throw their way, so by simply brushing them with oil we can reduce the tendency of a moussaka to be oily.

# Toad-in-the-Hole

Serves **4** / Start to Finish **50 m**

One of those nursery dishes that extends into old age, with student life in between. When Toad is good – crispy and risen around the edges and set with fat juicy bangers – it is very good indeed. A big jug of gravy (see page 112) or a bottle of a particularly good brown sauce or chilli ketchup will be welcome, as will some extra mustard.

**For the batter**
plain flour – 110g, sifted
Maldon sea salt – ½ teaspoon
medium eggs – 2
whole milk – 150ml
water – 150ml
Dijon mustard – 1 teaspoon *
wholegrain mustard – 1 teaspoon

**For the sausages**
dripping, lard or vegetable oil
sausages of your choice – 450g

you will need a 2 litre gratin dish

**Prepare the batter**
If making the batter in a blender, whizz **all the ingredients** together until smooth. If making by hand, proceed as for Yorkshire Puds on page 124 adding the mustards towards the end.

**Colour the sausages**
Preheat the oven to 200°C fan/220°C electric/gas 7. Heat a teaspoon of **dripping, lard or vegetable oil** in a frying pan over a medium heat and slowly colour the **sausages** on all sides. Try to do this as evenly as possible, turning them frequently, so they are a nice golden colour, but not too dark since they will colour further in the oven.

**Heat the dish \*\***
Place 2 tablespoons **dripping, lard** or **vegetable** oil in an ovenproof dish and heat in the oven for 10 minutes. Pour the batter into the hot dish and lay the sausages on top.

**Bake the Toad and dish up**
Place the Toad-in-the-Hole in the oven and cook for 30 minutes or until the batter is risen and golden. Serve straight away.

**The knack**

\* **Why the mustard?** Batter is bland by nature, so I like to jazz it up with the addition of mustard. I also favour spicy sausages or ones containing leeks or bacon for added interest.

\*\* **Why heat the dish?** Heating the dish with plenty of dripping before the batter goes in ensures that it almost fries at the edges and comes out beautifully crisp and rich, with that particular flavour that is the hallmark of being a good Toad.

# The Queen's Steak Pie

Serves **6** / Start to Finish **3 h**

My mum used to live close to Windsor Great Park and when we visited her for the weekend with our children, she frequently took the short cut on a Friday evening of buying in some steak pies from a farm shop that had a connection to Windsor Castle. They were seriously good, and soon became known as The Queen's Pie, and they've been on request ever since. I'm sure I don't cook as well as HM but this one has received family approval. A big steaming pie is something to roll out for a special occasion like a Christmas Eve supper or New Year's Day, or any celebratory winter dinner.

shortcrust pastry, preferably homemade (see page 22) – 600g

plain flour, for dusting

1 egg yolk blended with 1 tablespoon milk to form an eggwash

### For the filling

vegetable oil – 3–4 tablespoons

leeks – 2, trimmed and thinly sliced

celery – 1 heart, thinly sliced

chuck steak – 950g, trimmed of fat and cut into 3cm dice *

plain flour – 2 heaped tablespoons

medium sherry – 90ml

red wine – 200ml

beef stock or water – 200ml

bay leaf – 1

thyme – 3 sprigs

sea salt, black pepper

lambs' kidneys – 250g, fat removed and cut into 5mm slices (optional) **

shiitake or other flavourful mushrooms – 200g, thinly sliced

you will need a 2 litre pie dish

### Make the filling

Heat 2 tablespoons **oil** in a large saucepan and fry the **leeks** and **celery** over a low heat for about 8 minutes until soft and just starting to colour, stirring occasionally. Remove to a bowl and set aside. You will need to sear the meat in two goes, since if you overcrowd the pan it tends to stew rather than colour. So turn up the heat to medium-high, add half the **steak** to the pan and toss to seal and lightly colour it, then remove it and cook the remainder. Return the meat and vegetables to the pan, sprinkle over the **flour** and stir to coat everything thoroughly. Pour over the **sherry**, **wine** and **stock or water**, stirring well to make a smooth sauce. Add the **herbs** and some **seasoning**. Bring the liquid to a simmer, and then cover and cook over a low heat for 45 minutes, stirring occasionally.

### Fry the kidneys and mushrooms

Meanwhile heat 1 tablespoon oil in a non-stick frying pan over a medium heat. Add the **kidneys** (if using) and toss to seal. Remove from the pan and set aside. Heat the remaining 1 tablespoon oil, add the **mushrooms** and toss well until soft and coloured. Remove from the pan and set aside with the kidneys. Once the meat is cooked, remove the herbs and **season** to taste. Then stir in the mushrooms and kidneys and set aside to cool.

### Assemble the pie

Thinly roll out two-thirds of the **pastry** on a **floured** worksurface and use to line your pie dish. Don't worry if you have to mend the pastry in places, it won't show once the pie is cooked. Tip the cooled steak and kidney mixture into the pie and paint the rim with **eggwash** using a pastry brush. Thinly roll out the remaining pastry and lay over the meat. Carefully trim the edges, leaving 1cm for shrinkage. Press the edges together using a fork and paint the surface of the pie with eggwash. Roll out some of the pastry trimmings, cut into leaf shapes and mark with veins. Arrange on top of the pie and brush these with eggwash too.

### Bake the pie

Preheat the oven to 200°C fan/220°C electric/gas 7. Bake the pie for 45–50 minutes until nice and golden and serve straight away.

### The knack

* **Which steak?** Beware steak packed and sold simply as 'casserole' or 'braising' steak; you don't know what cuts it includes and they may cook at an uneven rate. Chuck steak is a lovely cut for stews, with just the right amount of fat to keep the flesh soft and succulent.

** **Kidneys have a strong flavour** – just a few give the pie its essential character.

# Spicy Pork Fillet

Serves **4** / Start to Finish **30 m**

Pork chops are a lottery, so often dry and tough and disappointing. Would that the French *côtes de porc* were more widely available – laced with fat and cut thin they are a great steak for the barbecue or grill. Otherwise, I grow increasingly fond of pork fillet, which is guaranteed to be tender.

pork fillets – 2 x 350–400g

**For the marinade**
fennel seeds – 1 teaspoon
cumin seeds – 1 teaspoon
coriander seeds – 1 teaspoon
small dried red chillies – 2
sweet paprika – 1 teaspoon
Maldon sea salt – 1 teaspoon
extra virgin olive oil – 2 tablespoons, plus extra for drizzling

**Marinate the pork**
Grind **all the spices for the marinade** in a coffee grinder, along with the **salt**. Tip into a small bowl and blend with the **olive oil**. Place the **pork fillets** in a large bowl, spoon over the spice blend and coat the pork using your hands. You can do this several hours in advance, in which case cover and chill. (If marinating the meat, omit the salt from the spice blend and season just before cooking.)

**Cook the pork**
Preheat the oven to 220°C fan/240°C electric/gas 9 and place a flameproof roasting pan large enough to hold the two fillets side by side over a high heat. Sear the fillets for 2 minutes on each side until lightly coloured, drizzle over a little oil and then roast in the oven for 12 minutes, turning after 5 minutes and drizzling with more oil. Transfer to a plate to rest for 10 minutes before serving.

**Dish up**
Slice the pork into medallions 1cm thick and serve drizzled with any juices given out on resting. It is also delicious cold.

*Serving suggestion*
— Accompany with Pilau Rice (see page 221), with the addition of toasted almonds, raisins and coriander, or a selection of salads.

# Classic Burgers

Makes **4** x 150g burgers / Start to Finish **30 m**

Minced beef, chopped shallot, sea salt and black pepper is as fancy as a burger needs to get, and purists wouldn't have it any other way. Breadcrumbs? Egg? No, no, no. If anything, concentrate on the relish tray, which has always been one of the best bits, and add in an array of cheeky sauces – English mustard and ketchup being a classic duo, or chilli sauce to bring it up to date. Extras of fried onions, grated cheese, sliced lettuce, crispy bacon, or salsa are also good. Some of the best burgers in my neck of the woods are to be had at Byron, and I spent a happy hour positioned opposite their grill watching their chef at work when I was writing this recipe. These take their cue from their 6oz classic – a stab at doing something very simple very well.

**For the burgers**

best minced beef – 700g *

shallots – 2 heaped tablespoons, finely chopped

sea salt, black pepper

**To serve**

medium red onion – ½, peeled, halved and thinly sliced

cocktail gherkins – 8, sliced

soft hamburger buns – 4, slit in half

mustard mayo (see below)

beefsteak tomato – ½, sliced

**Mustard Mayo**

mayonnaise – 40g

soured cream – 40g

Dijon mustard – 1 teaspoon

Blend all the ingredients in a small bowl, cover and chill until required. This will keep well for several days.

**Make the burgers**

Blend together the **minced beef, shallots** and **seasoning** in a large bowl. For an especially professional finish to your burgers, shape the mince a quarter at a time inside a 12cm ring cutter with smooth edges. Otherwise, form it into balls using your hands, flatten between your palms and use a rolling pin to smooth the surface. Bear in mind that the burgers will shrink and fatten when you grill them, however if you make a small indentation in the centre of each burger using your finger this should help counter this. If you want to make them in advance, then cover and chill them.

**Grill the burgers ***

Heat a ridged griddle over a high heat and cook the burgers for 2 ½ minutes on each side until firm but with a slight 'give' to leave them medium (see 'Press test', page 111). You will probably need to cook them in two batches. Transfer the cooked burgers to a plate and set aside to rest for 5 minutes.

**Assemble the burgers**

Combine the **sliced onion** and **gherkins** in a small bowl. Either toast the **buns** on the griddle or under an ordinary grill. Place a burger in each of the buns and smear over some of the **mustard mayo**. Next lay over a slice of **tomato** and season with salt and pepper. Finish with a scattering of sliced onion and gherkin.

**The knack**

* **Which mince?** The best burgers are made with meat containing about 20–25 per cent fat, so pass over the very leanest mince and go for one specked with white that'll be nicely succulent once cooked.

** **Flame-grilled burgers:** We all know just how good a 'flame-grilled' burger tastes, and the closest at home we can get is a barbecue. Failing that, a ridged griddle will sear and singe the meat nicely.

# Nada's Koftas with Pomegranate Hummus

Makes **12** skewers / Start to Finish **40 m**

These Lebanese koftas come courtesy of the wonderful cookery writer Nada Saleh, who is always my first port of call whenever I want to understand some aspect of the food of this region. Her recipes have a quiet, authentic restraint. These are also good on the barbecue (see page 311).

## For the koftas

minced lamb – 500g

coriander leaves and fine stalks – 25g, finely chopped

flat-leaf parsley leaves and fine stalks – 25g, finely chopped

small onion – 1, peeled and finely chopped

cayenne pepper – ¼ teaspoon

ground cumin – 1 teaspoon

Maldon sea salt – 1 teaspoon

## For the pomegranate hummus

chickpeas – 1 x 400g tin, drained and rinsed

small garlic clove – 1, peeled and sliced

sea salt, black pepper

water – 50ml

lemon juice – 2–3 tablespoons

tahini paste – 75g

extra virgin olive oil – 1 tablespoon, plus extra to serve

fresh clementine or orange juice – 2 teaspoons

large pomegranate – ½, seeds only *

you will need 12 wooden skewers, soaked in cold water for 10 minutes

### Make and shape the koftas
Combine **all the ingredients for the koftas** in a large bowl. Remove a small handful of the mixture, approx. the size of a walnut, and mould it around one end of a skewer, closing your hand around it and squeezing to form a little sausage shape. Repeat to form two koftas per skewer, leaving a 1cm gap between each. Arrange the prepared skewers on a plate, cover with clingfilm and set aside in the fridge while you make the hummus.

### Make the hummus
Place the **chickpeas** in a food processor with the **garlic** and some **salt** and whizz to a paste, gradually adding the **water** through the funnel until you have a thick creamy purée. Add 2 tablespoons **lemon juice** and the **tahini**, and whizz until really creamy, and then add the **olive oil** and the **clementine (or orange) juice**. Taste for lemon and seasoning. Spoon the mixture into a bowl, cover with clingfilm and set aside in the fridge until needed.

### Grill the koftas
Heat a ridged griddle over a medium-high heat and cook the koftas for 7–10 minutes in total, turning to colour them on all sides.

### Dish up
To serve, spoon the hummus into a little bowl, drizzle over a liberal dousing of olive oil and garnish with the **pomegranate seeds**. Serve the koftas separately.

*Serving suggestion*
— Accompany with warm pitta bread.

The knack

* **How to seed a pomegranate:** Cut the pomegranate in half and, working over a bowl to collect any juices, press down on each half to loosen the seeds. Pick out any white pith attached.

# Lamb Chop Supper with Pea & Potato Crush

Serves **4** / Start to Finish **40 m**

Lamb chops are the quick route to luxury for this meat, along with lamb steaks. The perfect lamb chop supper comes with new potatoes and peas – here a crushed mélange of the two – and lots of mint sauce.

lamb cutlets – 12 (total weight approx. 600g)

extra virgin olive oil, for brushing

mint sauce (see page 113) – double quantity, to serve

### For the crushed potatoes

medium-sized waxy potatoes such as Charlotte – 800g, peeled and halved

sea salt, black pepper

caster sugar – ½ teaspoon

shelled fresh peas – 150g

extra virgin olive oil – 6 tablespoons

### Variation

**Lamb Steaks:** *Replace the cutlets with 4 x 150–200g lamb steaks, approx. 2–3cm thick.*

Heat 1 teaspoon olive oil in a large non-stick frying pan over a high heat. Season the steaks on either side and fry for 5–6 minutes in total until golden – if they 'give' slightly when pressed, without being too squashy, this is an indication they are medium-rare. Turn the steaks on their sides to colour the fat, and then remove to a warm plate to rest for a few minutes.

**Cook the potatoes and peas**
Bring a medium-sized pan of salted water to the boil, add the **potatoes** and boil for 20–30 minutes until tender. Shortly before the end of this time, bring a few centimetres of water to the boil in a small saucepan with a little **salt** and the **sugar**, add the **peas** and simmer over a medium heat for 2–3 minutes until tender; drain well.

**Crush the potatoes ***
Drain the potatoes into a colander and leave for few minutes to steam-dry, then return them to the pan and lightly crush with a fork to break them up. Stir in the **olive oil**, add some **salt and pepper**, and then mix in the peas.

**Cook the lamb chops ****
Halfway into cooking the potatoes, heat a ridged griddle pan over a medium-high heat. Brush the **cutlets** on either side with olive oil and season with **salt and pepper**. You may need to cook them in two batches. Grill the cutlets for 3–4 minutes in total to leave them pink in the centre – they should have a slight give when pressed. To finish, stand them on their sides to colour the fat. Set aside to rest for a few minutes.

**Dish up**
Serve the cutlets on a pile of crushed potatoes, accompanied by some homemade **mint sauce**.

### The knack

* **What texture should the crushed potatoes be?** The potatoes should be a mass of chunky nibs, about 1–2cm in size, rather than mash – a fork is the ideal tool.

** **Chargrilling tips:** When grilling meat on a ridged griddle, you can enhance the charred stripes by pressing down on the meat using a flat metal spatula.

# Flank Steak with Salsa Verde

Serves **3–4** / Start to Finish **30 m**

Sirloin aside, my own preference is for the French cuts *bavette* (flank steak) and *onglet* (hanger steak), something we are more likely to find on the menu of a gastro pub than in the local supermarket. In fact, you don't even see *onglet* that frequently in France – given how little there is on the animal it is a prize morsel to be ordered in advance, and usually gets snapped up as soon as it reaches the shelves.

Both are recognisable by their long strands of meat. Unlike the classic cuts that we usually cook as individual steaks, they are ideal for grilling as a single piece and then thinly slicing. So it's a good option for three to four people, or if you happen to have a double griddle then cook two to serve six to eight.

flank steak – 1 x 600g piece, approx. 2cm thick *

extra virgin olive oil

sea salt, black pepper

### For the salsa verde

basil – 3 tablespoons, coarsely chopped

mint – 2 tablespoons, coarsely chopped

flat-leaf parsley – 6 tablespoons, coarsely chopped

garlic clove – ½, peeled

salted anchovies – 6

capers – 2 tablespoons, rinsed

medium-hot green chilli – ¼ teaspoon, finely chopped

lemon juice – 1 tablespoon

extra virgin olive oil – 6 tablespoons

Dijon mustard – 1 teaspoon

sea salt

### Variation

**Steak with Mushroom Sauce:** For a wintery take on the above, dish up with creamy mushrooms (see page 36).

**Grill the steak** **
Heat a ridged griddle over a high heat for several minutes. Brush the **steak** on either side with **olive oil**, season well with **salt and pepper** and grill for 6–8 minutes on each side, until soft but with a slight resistance. A meat thermometer inserted into the centre should read 45–50°C. Try not to move the steak around on the grill, except when turning. Transfer the steak to a warm plate to rest for 10 minutes.

**Make the salsa** ***
Whizz the **herbs, garlic, anchovies, capers** and **chilli** together in a food processor. Gradually add the **lemon juice** and **olive oil** through the feeder tube, and finally add the **mustard** and a pinch of **salt**.

**Carve the meat and dish up**
Carve the steak into thin strips through the grain and accompany with the salsa verde. (If the meat is too rare, when you come to carve it, simply reheat the griddle and cook the slices briefly on either side until they change colour.)

---

The knack

* **How thick should the steak be?** If the steak is any thicker than 2cm it will be difficult to cook through without resorting to the oven. If necessary, you can pound it to an even thickness using a rolling pin.

** **Cooking tips:** *Bavette* needs to be cooked rare, or edging towards medium-rare – certainly well short of medium or well-done. Properly cooked, and the promise is for heartstoppingly loose and tender strands of meat.

*** **Making the salsa verde in advance?** If you want to make the sauce more than a couple of hours in advance, add the lemon juice shortly before serving to save the herbs from discolouring.

# Essential Steaks

## Skinny Minute Steaks

Serves **2** / Start to Finish **15 m**

Minute steaks, true to their name, are cooked in just that amount of time. The pounding ensures the rump cooks to an even tenderness.

rump steak – 1 x 250g, 3cm thick
extra virgin olive oil
sea salt, black pepper

**Beat the steaks**
Slice the **steak** to form two thin steaks, and then beat each piece with a rolling pin to a thickness of a few millimetres. (If you wish you could do this between sheets of clingfilm.)

**Griddle the steaks**
Heat a ridged griddle over a high heat. Brush the **steaks** with **olive oil** on both sides and season with **salt and pepper**. Grill for 30 seconds on each side to leave them medium-rare, or 45–60 seconds if you prefer them medium, pressing down with a spatula to help brand the steaks with stripes. Transfer the steaks to a warm plate to rest for 5 minutes, covering them with foil to keep warm.

*Serving suggestion*
— If serving with garlic butter (see right), half-melt the butter in a small saucepan and drizzle over the steak, rather than flashing them under the grill. Being so thin, you don't want to cook them any further.

## High End Fillet

Serves **4** / Start to Finish **15 m**

I am more inclined to eat steak when I am out than at home, it's the charcoal grill that does it. But on those occasions when the craving does set in, the first thing to consider is the pecking order, which goes rump, sirloin, fillet – their relative tenderness (and cost) increasing accordingly, but with a trade-off in flavour.

Fillets will always be a treat – they win on texture alone – and here a little port or sherry melds with the cooking juices to form a sweet and delicate gravy.

groundnut oil – 1 tablespoon
fillet steaks – 4 x 175g, 2cm thick
sea salt, black pepper
unsalted butter – 50g, diced
port, Marsala or sweet sherry – 3 tablespoons

**Fry and rest the steaks**
Heat the **groundnut oil** in a large non-stick frying pan over a medium heat. (If your frying pan isn't large enough to hold all the steaks then heat two, adding 1 tablespoon oil to each.) Season the **steaks** with **salt and pepper** and cook for 3 minutes without turning. Add the **butter**, which will fizzle, and then turn the steaks and cook for a further 3 minutes on the other side. Remove the steaks to a warm plate to rest for 5 minutes.

**Make the sauce**
Add the **port (or Marsala or sherry)** to the hot pan and cook briefly, scraping up any caramelised bits on the bottom. Add any juices given out by the steak to the pan.

**Dish up**
To serve, place the steaks on warm plates and spoon over the sauce.

# Steaks with Garlic Butter

Serves **2** / Start to Finish **20 m**

I see this as a supper for two, given that you can't fit more than two steaks in one pan. So a cosy night in.

sirloin or rump steak – 2 x 200g, 2cm thick
vegetable oil

**For the garlic butter**
garlic clove – 1, peeled and crushed to a purée
softened unsalted butter – 50g
flat-leaf parsley – 1 tablespoon, finely chopped
shallot – 1, peeled and finely chopped
brandy – 1 teaspoon
sea salt, black pepper

**Make the garlic butter**
Blend **all the ingredients for the garlic butter** in a bowl and season with **salt and pepper**. This can be made in advance and chilled.

**Fry and rest the steaks**
Heat a large non-stick frying pan for several minutes over a medium-high heat. Brush the **steaks** on both sides with **vegetable oil**, season them with salt and pepper and cook for 2 minutes on each side to leave them medium-rare. Remove the steaks from the pan and set aside on a warm plate to rest for 5 minutes.

**Finish the steaks with the garlic butter**
Meanwhile preheat the grill to high. Dollop the garlic butter over the steaks and flash briefly under the grill until the butter melts, leaving mounds of parsley.

*Serving suggestion*
— A glossy bunch of watercress is the most desirable accompaniment, along with a pan of sautéed potatoes (see page 212).

# Steaks with Tarragon Sauce

Serves **2** / Start to Finish **15 m**

The sticky crust that clings to the base of the frying pan is one of the best bits, here eked out with Madeira, brandy and cream.

sirloin or rump steak – 2 x 200g, 2cm thick
vegetable oil
sea salt, black pepper

**For the tarragon sauce**
Madeira or medium sherry – 2 tablespoons
brandy – 2 tablespoons
double cream – 150ml
tarragon leaves – 1 heaped tablespoon

**Fry and rest the steaks \***
Heat a large non-stick frying pan for several minutes over a medium-high heat. Brush the **steaks** on both sides with **vegetable oil**, season them with **salt and pepper** and cook for 2 minutes on each side to leave them medium-rare. Remove the steaks to a warm plate to rest for 5 minutes.

**Make the sauce**
Add the **Madeira (or sherry)** and **brandy** to the pan, turn down the heat to medium and cook, scraping up all the bits on the bottom of the pan, until reduced to 1–2 tablespoons. Add the **cream, tarragon** and juices given out by the steak and heat through. Serve the steaks on warm plates with the sauce spooned over.

**The knack**

**\* How to cook steaks to your liking:** If the steak feels very squidgy when gently pressed, it will be rare; for medium it should have some degree of 'give'; if it feels firm that usually indicates well-done, however that tends to mean tough. (See page 111 for more information.)

# Fish & Seafood

6

# About **Fish & Seafood**

**Sustainability**

The majority of people today will be much more familiar with farmed salmon than wild. The sea bass and bream on the slab are also increasingly likely to have been reared. While such offerings may not be identical to wild, it does take the pressure off stocks. But as with any farming there is good and bad practice, and it is worth genning up on the Marine Conservation Society's website, where you will also find a guide to sustainable fish and where to find them. www.mcsuk.org

**Shopping tips**

If you are buying fish whole then look it in the eye, which should appear dark and glassy, rather than cloudy which suggests the fish is past its best. With fillets, the best route to determining how fresh they are is to be straight to the point with whoever's serving you and ask: 'did these come in today?' If the answer's 'no', move on to the next counter.

Beyond this, look for the quality of filleting: this should be nice and neat and look as though it's been in the care of a sushi chef before reaching the slab. If the flesh looks ragged with bones here and there, again I would give it a wide berth. Good filleting is a fairly clear indicator of the overall quality of what you are buying.

Always go shopping with an open mind. If, for instance, you are making fish pie or soup, it really doesn't matter about specific types – go for what seems fresh, plentiful or on offer. And don't worry if you've never heard of it – be adventurous, there is every chance it won't have been overfished.

Without doubt, the best occasions on which to enjoy fish are when you are in the vicinity of the coast or river from where it derives. There is nothing quite like that sweet smell of really fresh fish, when it can be linked to a seashore you walked along earlier.

**Storage advice**

If I am buying fresh fish, unless I am going to cook it on the day I pop it straight into the freezer. It takes no time to defrost, a few hours inside a covered casserole, which will provide a cool and protective environment.

## Frozen

While I would advocate buying fresh over frozen in most instances, fish and seafood is the exception to this rule. Fish that has been frozen out at sea using rapid-freezing techniques, which protect the flesh, is sometimes a better option than whatever you might find fresh on the slab. This is not to say that it is preferable necessarily, but not to be sniffed at either – and for fishcakes, pies and soups is a perfectly respectable choice. The one consideration is to allow approx. 30 per cent extra weight for the loss of water once it is defrosted.

## Preparation

One of the great advantages of buying fish from a fishmonger, rather than the supermarket counter, is the quality of preparation. If you are buying it whole, then ideally you want it gutted and cleaned, and any scales scraped off. And when this is slapdash, you simply end up having to redo it yourself.

## COOKING TIPS

### Frying

Fish fillets are best fried. Should they come with the skin, I like to give this the lion's share of the cooking time, which will crisp it up, turning and cooking the flesh-side just briefly. Fish is incredibly delicate and will stick and tear on pretty much any cooking surface bar non-stick. And it really does need to be non-stick, rather than that overused pan that has half given up.

### Grilling

An overhead grill is the best route here; a griddle will simply cling and tear the delicate flesh. If you particularly want to barbecue, then go for whole fish rather than fillets, and use one of those clamps. For more on barbecuing, see page 311.

### Stews and soups

Morsels of fish and shellfish will poach within minutes. The trick here is to make a soup base first, which can be done well in advance, and then add the fish at the last moment.

### Pan to oven

Whole fish are best either roasted, or coloured just briefly in a non-stick frying pan, and then popped into the oven.

### Which Fish for Which Dish?

**Meaty Fish Fillets**
Plain Mackerel Fillets (page 178)
Sea Bass Fillets with Herbes de Provence (page 179)
Vietnamese Sizzling Salmon (page 183)

**Flat Fish Fillets**
Harbour Kitchen Plaice with Cheat's Tartare Sauce (page 180)

**Whole Small Fish**
Whole Roast Sea Bream with Lemon & Thyme (page 176)
Mediterranean Mackerel with Cherry Tomatoes & Olives (page 178)
Whole Lemon Sole (page 180)

**Whole Large Fish**
Big Party Salmon (page 182)

**Mussels**
Moules Marinières (page 170)

**Scallops**
Scallops with Parsley & Pistachio Pesto (page 162)

**King Prawns**
Pad Thai with King Prawns (page 184)

# Scallops with Parsley & Pistachio Pesto

Serves **4 as a starter** or **3 as a main** / Start to Finish **20 m**

Of all the ways of enjoying this luxurious shellfish, there is none quite so good as stuffing them inside a generously buttered crusty white roll, their warmth melting the butter that soaks into the crumb with their juices. Slathering them with this gentle pesto is just one step beyond.

medium-sized scallops – 400g *

extra virgin olive oil, to coat

sea salt, black pepper

pea shoots or lamb's lettuce, to serve

lemon wedges, to serve

### For the pesto

flat-leaf parsley leaves – 50g

pistachios – 25g

extra virgin olive oil – 8 tablespoons

sea salt

lemon juice – squeeze

### Make the pesto
Place the **parsley, pistachios, olive oil**, a little **salt** and a squeeze of **lemon juice** in a food processor and blitz to a smooth purée, scraping down the sides of the bowl as necessary. The finished pesto should be a thick, drizzling consistency.

### Prepare the scallops
Remove the small white gristle attached to the **scallops** if present, and slice each one into two or three discs, approx. 1–1.5cm thick. Toss the scallops with **olive oil** to coat them, and season with **salt and pepper**.

### Cook the scallops
Heat a large non-stick frying pan over a high heat for several minutes. Sear the scallops in batches for 30 seconds on each side, turning them with a palette knife.

### Dish up
Divide the scallops between 4 plates, scatter each one with a handful of **peashoots or lamb's lettuce** and drizzle with the pesto sauce. Accompany with **lemon wedges**.

### Other serving suggestions
— Serve the scallops in crusty bread rolls, as a snack.
— Serve over a pile of rich and creamy mashed potato, as a main course.

### The knack

* **Preparing the scallops:** Many scallops are sold without the corals, but there is no reason why you cannot cook these up too should they come attached. In this case, prepare according to the guidelines on page 172.

# Gravadlax with Mustard Sauce

Makes **600g** / Start to Finish **2 days**

It is hard not to get a thrill out of making gravadlax for the very first time. Anything home cured comes shrouded in mystery, and the illusion that it must require either skill or specialist kit, but here neither. As well as being every bit as good as something you might buy (or rather better), homemade gravadlax is also kind on the pocket – so if smoked salmon seems out of reach, especially for any number, this is a great alternative. And you get that lovely mustard sauce to boot.

**For the gravadlax**

rock salt – 100g

caster sugar – 100g

yellow mustard seeds – 20g

dill – a small bunch (approx. 20g), finely chopped, plus 2 tablespoons to serve

salmon fillet (skin on) – 2 x 450g pieces, preferably from the thickest part of a whole fish

**For the mustard sauce**

soured cream – 150g

Dijon mustard – 1 rounded tablespoon

grainy mustard – 1 rounded tablespoon

caster sugar – 1 scant tablespoon

### Wrap up the fish with the curing mixture
Combine the **salt, sugar, mustard seeds** and **dill** in a bowl. Scatter one-quarter of the mixture over a piece of clingfilm, making sure it is large enough to wrap up the two pieces of fish when they are placed on top of each other. Place one **salmon fillet** skin-down on top, scatter over two-thirds of the remaining mixture, and then lay the second fillet, flesh-side down, on top so the thick part of the fillet rests on the thin part beneath. Scatter over the remaining salt mixture, wrap the salmon up, and then wrap in foil.

### Cure the fish for 48 hours
Two heavy cast-iron roasting pans that fit one inside the other provide the best route to curing and weighting the fish. Place the salmon inside the larger pan, and place the smaller pan on top (anything lighter will require weighting with a tin can or two). Chill for 48 hours, turning the parcel every 12 hours. During this time the sugar and salt will draw the juices out of the salmon to create a sticky brine.

### Make the mustard sauce
Blend **all the ingredients for the mustard sauce** together in a bowl, and set aside to stand for 10 minutes. If making in advance, cover and chill.

### Rinse the gravadlax and coat with the chopped dill
Unwrap the salmon and carefully rinse the marinade off the flesh-side – some of the mustard seeds and dill should remain, but you want to get rid of any excess salt and sugar. Place the fillets, skin-side down, on a worksurface, lay a double sheet of kitchen paper over the top and press down to absorb any excess liquid. Sprinkle the flesh side of each fillet with 1 tablespoon chopped dill and press down well until it sticks.

### Slice the gravadlax
Trim the edge of the fillets if very thin, and then slice the gravadlax diagonally off the skin, thicker than you would smoked salmon, discarding the ends. The mustard sauce will need a quick stir before serving. (The fillets can be frozen whole or sliced.)

*Serving suggestion*
— Serve with buttered soda bread, accompanied by breakfast radishes.

# Sardine Pâté

Serves **4** / Start to Finish **10 m**

Aside from mashing them onto hot buttered brown toast with a shake of Tabasco, this is one of the best uses for a tin of sardines (especially the covetable 'Connétable'). Hard to believe anything quite so humble can be quite so good.

This has real old-world charm and is just as at home in a Mayfair gentleman's club as it is for a chilled-out Sunday tea or as an appetiser with drinks. I always associate sardine pâté with my father-in-law Tony Bell, who used to adore it, so this one's for him.

sardine fillets – 3 x 100g tins, drained

softened unsalted butter – 50g

flat-leaf parsley – 2 tablespoons, finely chopped

small shallot – 1, peeled and finely chopped

extra virgin olive oil – 1 tablespoon

lemon juice – 1 tablespoon

Tabasco – several shakes

sea salt

spring onion – a few slivers

**Variation**

**Salmon Pâté:** Replace the sardines with 2 x 200g tins of wild red or pink salmon. Increase the parsley to 3 tablespoons and the lemon juice to 2 tablespoons.

**Blend all the ingredients together**
Mash the **sardines** in a bowl using a fork. In another bowl, work the **butter** until it's really soft and creamy. Add the softened butter to the sardines and blend in with the **parsley** and **shallot**. Work in the **olive oil** and **lemon juice**, and season with a few shakes of **Tabasco** and a little **salt**. Pile into a pot and smooth the surface, and then cover and chill until required. Shortly before serving, scatter some slivers of **spring onion** over the pâté.

*Serving suggestion*
— Spread the pâté on thin brown toast. Accompany with a few breakfast radishes and some sticks of celery heart.

# Smoked Haddock Chowder

Serves **4** / Start to Finish **30 m**

As fish soups go, a fish chowder is one of the easiest to make and also the most comforting with its milky base and potatoes – and no fish stock required, which makes for one less hassle. Traditionally it is thickened with crumbled crackers, and then there is Manhattan clam chowder, with a tomato base – lovely if you can get the clams, but they don't abound in the environs where I shop. The smoked haddock is a given, and makes for one of the loveliest of chowders, with its crispy nibs of bacon.

unsalted butter – 40g

rindless smoked back bacon –
6 rashers, cut into 1cm strips

leeks – 3, trimmed, washed and
thinly sliced

whole milk – 600ml

maincrop potatoes such as Maris
Piper – 450g, peeled and cut into
1cm dice

bay leaf – 1

undyed skinned smoked haddock
fillet – 450g, cut into 2cm pieces

sea salt, black pepper

flat-leaf parsley, coarsely chopped,
to serve

### Fry the bacon and leeks *
Melt the **butter** in a large saucepan over a medium heat, add the **bacon** and fry for 7–9 minutes, stirring occasionally and separating out the pieces until lightly coloured. Add the **leeks** and continue to fry for about 7 minutes until softened and just starting to colour.

### Cook the potatoes and haddock
Meanwhile place the **milk** in another large pan with the **potatoes** and **bay leaf**. Bring to the boil, and then simmer over a low heat for about 8 minutes. Add the **haddock** and poach very gently for 5 minutes until the potatoes are tender and the haddock flakes.

### Combine the two sets of ingredients and dish up
Stir the bacon and leeks into the haddock base, and season with **black pepper,** and a little **salt** if needed. Serve scattered with **parsley.**

### Variations

**For a richer and more indulgent soup:** Substitute 200ml of the milk for whipping cream.

**For authenticity**: Stir in 4 crumbled small water biscuits (or the equivalent of cream crackers) at the very end.

### The knack

\* **Cooking method:** The trick here is to fry up the bacon and leeks in one pan, and to cook the haddock and milk separately, and combine them at the very end. This ensures the bacon and leeks remain caramelised and golden, whereas with simmering they would soften and the colour would seep into the soup. This method also prevents the liquid splitting.

# Bell Family's Fish Stew

Serves **4** / Start to Finish **1 h 10 m**

This is the recipe I turn to for a family supper, designed to capture something of that fish stew you ate on holiday. The stew base is no more complicated than making a simple pasta sauce.

## For the stew

extra virgin olive oil – 3 tablespoons

shallots – 4, peeled, halved and thinly sliced

fennel bulb – 1, trimmed and diced

garlic cloves – 4, peeled and finely chopped

tomato passata rustica – 400ml

saffron filaments – pinch (about 20)

dried chilli flakes – pinch

sea salt and black pepper

fish stock – 500ml

mixed skinned fish fillets – 600g, cut into 3–4cm chunks *

## For the aioli

medium organic egg yolk – 1, at room temperature

Dijon mustard – 1 teaspoon

fine sea salt – pinch

garlic – 3 cloves, peeled and crushed to a paste

groundnut oil – 150ml

extra virgin olive oil – 75ml

lemon juice – 1 teaspoon

pastis (e.g. Pernod) – 1 scant teaspoon (optional)

## For the croûtons

slim baguette or ciabatta

extra virgin olive oil, for brushing

### Make the aioli

Combine the **egg yolk, mustard, salt** and **garlic** in a medium-sized bowl and whisk together to blend, ideally using a magic whisk. Gradually whisk in the **oils,** following the instructions for mayonnaise on page 260. (It is very important that you add the oil very slowly to prevent the mayonnaise from splitting.) Add the **lemon juice** and **pastis** at the end. Cover the bowl with clingfilm and store in the fridge until needed; make sure you bring the aioli back up to room temperature before eating.

### Make the croûtons

*For proper croûtons:* Preheat the oven to 180°C fan/200°C electric/gas 6. Slice the **baguette** into thin slices – 5mm thick for slim croûtons, or 1cm thick for more robust ones. Lay them out on a baking sheet and toast in the oven for 5 minutes until they have dried out. Paint each side with **olive oil** and return to the oven for a further 5–8 minutes until golden and crisp. *For toasted ciabatta:* Cut the bread into slices, as above, and toast both sides under the grill or in a toaster. Brush with olive oil before serving.

### Prepare the stew base **

Heat the **olive oil** in a large cast-iron or other heavy-duty casserole over a medium heat and fry the **shallot** and **fennel** for about 10 minutes until lightly golden, stirring frequently and adding the **garlic** just before the end. Add the **tomato passata,** the **saffron, chilli** and some **salt** and simmer over a low heat for 15–20 minutes, stirring occasionally until you have a thick purée. Now stir in the **stock.** (The fish stew can be prepared to this point in advance, in which case set aside to cool and then cover and chill.)

### Poach the fish in the stew base

To serve, bring the stew base back to the boil. **Season** the **fish** and add to the pan, and then cover and cook over a low heat for 5–10 minutes until the fish is firm. Serve with the croûtons and aioli.

### The knack

* **Which fish?** You want three quite different textures and flavours of fish (e.g. sea bass, scallops and prawns), total prepared weight 600g. All the fish morsels should be roughly the same size to ensure they cook evenly.

** **A versatile method:** This soup is a good basic to have up your sleeve. First you prepare a thin fish soup with ready-made fish stock, which removes a great deal of the pain, and then you poach the fish in the broth at the last minute.

# Moules Marinières

Serves **2** / Start to Finish **30 m**

Our farmhouse in Normandy is only a stone's throw from the beaches of the Cotentin, where the seascape turns into a city of tall black-crusted poles at low tide, a massive maritime park where *moules de bouchot* are farmed. These are arguably the best mussels of all, deep orange in colour, small and very sweet. Once acquainted it is hard to settle for others, as by comparison larger mussels tend to be lacking in flavour.

The ritual of eating *Moules Marinières* makes it a great rustic supper party treat – it is leisurely, deliciously messy and hands-on. Not a dish we turn to that frequently, but it always has a celebratory feel. This is the true Norman version.

groundnut or vegetable oil – 3 tablespoons

onion – 2 tablespoons, very finely chopped

shallot – 2 tablespoons, very finely chopped

garlic clove – 1, peeled and finely chopped

dry white wine – 100ml

live mussels – 1.7kg, scrubbed *

crème fraîche or unpasteurised cream – 70g

flat-leaf parsley – a handful, coarsely chopped

To serve
sourdough bread and unsalted butter

**Prepare the stew base**
Heat the **oil** in a large saucepan over a high heat, add the **onion, shallot** and **garlic** and fry for about 1 minute until softened. Pour in the **wine** and simmer until reduced by half.

**Cook the mussels and finish the dish**
Add the **mussels**, clamp on the lid and cook for 5–6 minutes until they have all opened. Stir in the **crème fraîche** and **parsley** and serve with **sourdough bread** and **butter**.

## Variation

**Garlicky Mussels:** Combine 70g unsalted butter, 3 peeled garlic cloves, the juice of ½ lemon and a shake of Tabasco in a food processor. Add 5 tablespoons finely chopped flat-leaf parsley and whizz briefly to combine. Cook the mussels as above (you may like to double the quantity for 4–6 people), and then dot them with the garlicky butter. Cover and leave to stand for a couple of minutes.

### The knack

* **Cleaning the mussels:** Many years ago, as a novice cook, I decided to try my hand at cooking *Moules Marinières*. Duly following the recipe, which failed to tell me to wash the mussels in cold water, I thought the most logical way to do this was to wash them in hot water to get off as much of the dirt as possible. This did of course kill them, and I watched with dismay as one by one they floated to the surface, gaping open.

So lesson number one is that live mussels must be washed in cold water. The best way to do this is to fill a sink with cold water and tip in the mussels. They may be very dirty at this point, so keep swooshing them as you pull off the tough beards attached to the shell. Throw away any that are broken or fail to close when you tap them sharply on the side of the sink, as they may well carry the risk of food poisoning. Place the whole closed mussels in a large saucepan as you go, and then, unless they are particularly clean, give them a second rinse in cold water.

# Portuguese Fish Stew

Serves **6** / Start to Finish **1 h**

This is a great soup for all those little-known white fish fillets that greet us on the slab, which we're not quite sure what to do with. It has a more wintery feel than the fish stew on page 168 (hardly surprising with cabbage and potatoes in there) and yet it has a slightly exotic demeanour courtesy of the chorizo and coriander. It readily accommodates lots of people, is rustic and easy. Serve some grilled bread, drizzled with olive oil, alongside.

Savoy cabbage – 200g, outer leaves discarded

extra virgin olive oil – 2 tablespoons

chorizo sausage (cooked or uncooked) – 200g, skinned, thickly sliced and diced *

maincrop potatoes such as Maris Piper – 900g, peeled and cut into 1cm dice

dry white wine – 150ml

plum tomatoes – 3, skinned (see page 18) and coarsely chopped

fish stock – 1.5 litres

sea salt, black pepper

mixed skinned white fish fillets – 900g, cut into 2cm chunks

**To serve**

extra virgin olive oil **

fresh coriander, coarsely chopped

**Prepare the cabbage**
Slice the **cabbage** into fine strands, discarding the tough central vein.

**Prepare the stew base**
Heat the **olive oil** in a large saucepan over a medium heat, add the **chorizo** and fry for a few minutes, stirring frequently, until lightly coloured. Pour off the fat (leave this to harden before throwing away), add the **potatoes** and give them a stir. Pour in the **wine** and boil until reduced by half. Add the **tomatoes** and **stock**, bring back to the boil and skim off any surface foam. Reduce the heat to low and simmer for 15 minutes or until the potatoes are tender. Coarsely mash the potato using a potato masher and season to taste with a little **salt** – the chorizo should have done most of the work here.

**Finish the stew**
Just before serving, bring the sauce back to the boil, add the cabbage and simmer for 5 minutes. Season the **fish** with **salt and pepper**, add it to the stew and poach for 5 minutes.

**Dish up**
Serve in warm bowls with some **extra virgin olive oil** poured over and a scattering of fresh **coriander**.

The knack

* **Why chorizo?** The chorizo is multi-tasking here – as well as contributing alluring little bacon-like nibs to the stew, which always work a treat with white fish, its full-on garlicky disposition and paprika further flavour the soup.

** **Why extra virgin olive oil?** The soup is finished with a drizzling of olive oil, a good case for a really fine one where its flavour will shine through.

# Fisherman's Pie

Serves **6** / Start to Finish **2 h 20 m**

Of all the recipes that the architect John Pawson and I included in *Living and Eating*, this is the one that friends most often tell us they cook. It took shape in our farmhouse in Normandy, and has remained our family staple ever since. Aside from its obvious gustatory charm, the real joy of a fish pie is that you can prepare it, lock, stock and barrel, well in advance and pop it into the oven half an hour before you want to eat.

## For the fish

unskinned haddock fillets – 800g *

whole milk – 250ml

bay leaf – 1

sea salt, black pepper

scallops – 250g

unsalted butter – 60g

plain flour – 50g

dry cider – 150ml

crème fraîche – 150g

Dijon mustard – 1 heaped teaspoon

cooked peeled prawns – 200g

small capers (e.g. Nonpareille) – 1 tablespoon, rinsed

## For the mash

maincrop potatoes such as Maris Piper – 1.5kg, peeled and halved if large

crème fraîche – 100g

unsalted butter – 50g

large egg yolks – 2

you will need a 2.5 litre ovenproof dish; I use a 35cm oval gratin dish

### Poach the fish **

Place the **haddock fillets** in a large saucepan. Pour over the **milk**, tuck in the **bay leaf**, season with **salt and pepper** and bring to the boil. Cover with a lid, leaving a gap for the steam to escape, and cook over a low heat for 4 minutes until the fish loses its translucency. Strain the cooking liquor into a bowl. Once the fish is cool enough to handle, flake it as coarsely as possible discarding the skin. If any liquid is given out at this point, throw it away.

### Prepare the scallops

Pull off the white gristle at the side of each **scallop**, removing the surrounding girdle. Cut off the orange corals and slice the white meat into 2 or 3 discs. Set aside while you prepare the sauce.

### Make the white sauce

Melt the **butter** in a medium-sized, non-stick saucepan, add the **flour** and allow the roux to seethe for a minute. Remove the pan from the heat and very gradually work in the **cider**, fish cooking liquor, **crème fraîche** and **mustard**, beating well with a wooden spoon to avoid lumps. Bring to the boil, stirring constantly, and simmer over a very low heat for 10 minutes. Season to taste.

### Finish the fish base

Add the cooked fish, scallops, **prawns** and **capers** to the white sauce and stir in carefully. Transfer the mixture to an ovenproof dish that affords a large surface area and set aside to cool. (This will help prevent the potato from sinking when you smooth it on top.)

### Make the mash

Bring a large pan of salted water to the boil and cook the **potatoes** until tender, approx. 20–30 minutes. Drain into a sieve or colander and pass through a mouli-legumes or sieve back into the pan. In a separate pan, heat the **crème fraîche** with the **butter** and some salt and pepper. Pour the hot cream over the mash, beat this in and then add the **egg yolks**. Smooth the potato mixture over the top of the fish, forking the surface into furrows. ***

### Bake the pie

Preheat the oven to 180°C fan/200°C electric/gas 6 and bake the fish pie for 35–40 minutes until crusty and golden on the surface.

## The knack

\* **Which fish?** A fish pie can run to seriously big sums of money if you allow
your inner shopaholic to get the upper hand, but there is no need. Look over
the quantity and variety of fish suggested – here haddock provides succulent
flakes that hold their shape, with the luxury of a few scallops and prawns –
and shop accordingly. There is also a lot to be said for frozen fish – just bear in
mind that it may lose some 30 per cent of its weight in water once defrosted.

\*\* **Poaching the fish:** You can use this method for poaching both smoked and
unsmoked haddock fillets, be it for an omelette, kedgeree (see page 221) or pilaf.

\*\*\* **Making the pie in advance?** If you wish, you can cover and chill the pie
at this stage until required, for up to 24 hours. In this case it may need a little
longer in the oven.

# Thai Fishcakes with Dipping Sauce

Serves **4** as a starter / Makes **16** / Start to Finish **40 m**

These are laced with all the piquant flavour thrills we expect from Thai food, which suggests they might be complicated to make when in fact they are a doddle.

**For the fishcakes**

lime leaves – 5

spring onions – 2, trimmed and roughly chopped

fresh root ginger – 1cm piece, peeled and coarsely chopped

fresh coriander leaves – 4 tablespoons, coarsely chopped, plus extra to serve

fish sauce – 1 tablespoon

skinned white fish fillets (e.g. cod, bream, haddock, etc.) – 500g, cut into chunks

groundnut oil, for shallow-frying

plain flour, for coating

**For the dipping sauce**

white wine vinegar – 180ml

golden caster sugar – 25g

garlic cloves – 2 large or 3 small, peeled and finely chopped

medium-hot red chilli – 1 teaspoon, finely chopped

**Make the dipping sauce**
Place the **vinegar** and **sugar** in a small saucepan and simmer over a medium heat until reduced by two-thirds. Place the **garlic** and **chilli** in a small bowl, pour over the hot liquid and set aside to cool.

**Make the fishcakes**
Place the **lime leaves, spring onions, ginger** and 4 tablespoons **chopped coriander** in the bowl of a food processor and finely chop. Transfer the mixture to a bowl and mix in the **fish sauce**. Put the **fish fillets** in the food processor and give them about 3 bursts of the motor to reduce them to a textured purée. Add to the bowl with the other chopped ingredients and blend together. Take heaped teaspoons of the mixture about the size of a walnut and flatten into small fishcakes; set aside on a plate.

**Fry the fishcakes and dish up**
Heat a few millimetres **groundnut oil** in a large frying pan over a medium heat. Dip the fishcakes in **flour** to coat them on both sides, and fry them in batches for 1–3 minutes on each side until golden and crisp. Arrange on a plate, scatter with chopped coriander and serve with the dipping sauce.

# A Big Fishcake with Parsley Sauce

Serves **6** / Start to Finish **1 h 20 m**

If you are after a decent humble fishcake come suppertime, this is the one, a comforting, no-nonsense basic. You can use any white fish here, including all those whose names you don't recognise, which is never a bad thing with fish, as it probably means they haven't been exploited. This version is dished up with parsley sauce, but you could serve with tartare sauce if you prefer (see page 180).

## For the fishcakes

maincrop potatoes such as Maris Piper – 600g, peeled and halved, or quartered if large

skinned white fish fillets (e.g. cod, haddock, hake, etc.) – 500g

dry white wine – 100ml

unsalted butter – 30g

sea salt, black pepper

anchovy essence – 2 teaspoons (optional)

capers – 2 tablespoons, rinsed and chopped

medium eggs – 2

fresh brown or white breadcrumbs – 75g (see page 37)

groundnut oil, for shallow-frying

## For the parsley sauce

crème fraîche – 300g

Dijon mustard – 1 heaped teaspoon

flat-leaf or curly parsley – 5 tablespoons, finely chopped

### Cook the potatoes and fish

Bring a medium-sized pan of salted water to the boil, add the **potatoes** and simmer for 20–25 minutes until tender. At the same time, arrange the **fish** fillets in a single layer in the base of another medium-sized saucepan. Pour over the **wine**, dot with the **butter** and season with **salt and pepper**. Bring the wine to the boil, and then cover the pan with a lid and cook over a low heat for 7 minutes until the fish loses its translucency. Using a spatula, transfer the cooked fish to a plate, reserving the cooking liquor, and set aside to rest for 10 minutes.

### Make the fishcake mixture

Drain the potatoes into a colander, set aside for a few minutes to steam-dry and then mash. Pour any juices given out by the fish back into the saucepan with the rest of the cooking liquor and set over a medium heat until reduced to a few tablespoons of buttery emulsion. Stir in the **anchovy essence** (if using). Meanwhile flake the fish and stir into the mashed potatoes with the **capers**. Add the reduced cooking liquor, mix again and season to taste.

### Shape and coat the fishcakes

Using your hands, shape the mixture into 6 large fishcakes and set aside on a plate or tray. Beat the **eggs** in a shallow bowl, and place the **breadcrumbs** in another. Dip the fishcakes first in the beaten egg, and then in the breadcrumbs. Set aside on a plate. (The fishcakes can be made a day or two in advance, in which case cover and chill them.)

### Make the parsley sauce

Place the **crème fraîche** and **mustard** in a small saucepan and bring to the boil, whisking to blend. Simmer for several minutes until you have a thin creamy sauce, and then stir in the **parsley** and a pinch of salt. (The sauce can also be made in advance, in which case transfer it to a bowl and set aside to cool before covering the surface with clingfilm and chilling.)

### Fry the fishcakes

Heat approx. 1cm **groundnut oil** in a large frying pan over a medium heat, and cook the fishcakes in two batches for 2 minutes on each side until golden and crisp. To serve, gently reheat the parsley sauce, without allowing it to boil, and serve spooned over the fishcakes.

**Fishcakes**

# Whole Roast Sea Bream with Lemon & Thyme

Serves **4** / Start to Finish **40 m**

This is a recipe I turn to again and again for whatever small and meaty whole fish the fishmonger has to offer – including sea bream, sea bass or red mullet. First the fish are seared to colour the skin, and then they are baked with aromatics, which form the basis of a light sauce.

lemon – 1, thinly sliced (ends discarded)

medium tomatoes – 4, sliced

large onion – 1, peeled, halved and sliced across

sea salt, black pepper

whole sea bream – 4 x approx. 300g, cleaned (head on) *

extra virgin olive oil – 8 tablespoons, plus extra for brushing

soft-leaved or lemon thyme – handful of sprigs, plus 1 heaped teaspoon leaves

dry or sweet white wine – 75ml

caster sugar – pinch (optional)

**Arrange the aromatics in a roasting pan**
Preheat the oven to 200°C fan/220°C electric/gas 7. Arrange half the **lemon, tomato** and **onion** slices over the base of a roasting pan that will hold the fish in a single layer, top to tail, and season with **salt and pepper**.

**Sear the fish skin**
Score the flesh of the **sea bream** diagonally on both sides at 2cm intervals, and then brush the skin with **olive oil** and season. Don't worry overly if there are fish scales on the skin as you will be lifting this off when you fillet it. Heat a large non-stick frying pan over a medium-high heat and sear the fish for about 1 minute on each side to lightly colour the skin – you will probably have to do this in batches. Arrange the fish, top to tail, in the pan on top of the aromatics.

**Finish assembling the dish**
Stuff **a few thyme sprigs** inside the gut cavity of each fish, and then arrange the remaining lemon, tomato and onion slices on top and season. Drizzle 4 tablespoons olive oil and the **wine** over the fish.

**Roast the fish**
Roast the sea bream in the oven for 15–20 minutes, or until the flesh comes away from the bone if you insert a knife into the top by the fin.

**Finish the sauce and dish up**
Transfer the fish to plates, and tip the vegetables and cooking liquid into a sieve set over a bowl, pressing down to extract all the juices. Stir the **thyme leaves** and the remaining 4 tablespoons olive oil into the sauce and taste for seasoning – you may like to add a pinch of **sugar,** especially if you used a dry white wine. If you wish, you can gently reheat the sauce in a small saucepan, without boiling, but it is also good at an ambient temperature. Accompany the fish with the sauce, pouring it over as you fillet it.

The knack

* **Why whole fish, not fillets?** Fish cooked on the bone has the best possible chance of being flavourful, the only caveat being the diner needs to take care to remove all the bones when eating, which isn't difficult. In a way, removing the bones yourself turns dinner into more of an event – like eating crab or mussels.

# Mediterranean Mackerel with Cherry Tomatoes & Olives

Serves **4** / Start to Finish **35 m**

Mackerel comes to life if you give it the Mediterranean treatment with tomatoes, olives, rocket, olive oil and balsamic vinegar. (It has a pronounced flavour and spars beautifully with equally dynamic ingredients.) I would do away with the potatoes here in favour of a hearty crust of bread.

whole mackerel – 4 x approx. 300g, cleaned (head on)

extra virgin olive oil

sea salt, black pepper

cherry tomatoes on the vine – 500g

balsamic vinegar – 1 tablespoon

pitted black olives – 100g

rocket – 4 large handfuls

sourdough bread, to serve

**Variation**

**Plain Mackerel Fillets (Serves 4):**
*For any supper where you are after simple fried mackerel fillets, here is the way. You can use this method for any fish fillet of a similar size.*

Heat 1 teaspoon olive oil in a large non-stick frying pan over a medium heat. Season 4 x 150–200g mackerel fillets on either side with salt and pepper, and fry, skin-side down, for about 3 minutes until golden and crisp – by which time the flesh should be cooked through by about two-thirds. Turn and cook on the flesh side for 1 minute.

**Sear the fish skin**
Preheat the oven to 220°C fan/240°C electric/gas 9. Score the **mackerel** flesh diagonally at 3–4 cm intervals on both sides, brush with **olive oil** and season with **salt and pepper.** Heat a large non-stick frying pan over a medium-high heat and sear the mackerel one at a time for 1 minute on each side, just to colour the skin.

**Roast the fish**
Arrange the fish head to tail in a roasting pan that will accommodate them in a single layer. Lay the **tomatoes** on top and drizzle over 2 tablespoons oil and the **balsamic vinegar.** Roast in the oven for 15 minutes until the flesh comes away from the backbone with ease. Scatter over the **olives** and set aside to stand for 5 minutes.

**Dish up**
Arrange the fish on serving plates, spooning over the cooking juices. Pile some **rocket** on top or to the side of each mackerel and drizzle over a little more oil. Accompany with **bread.**

# Sea Bass Fillets with Herbes de Provence

Serves **6** / Start to Finish **25 m**

Roasting sea bass with lots of resinous herbs top and bottom infuses it with flavour, while you briefly drift off in spirit to some pine-fringed rocky shore. If your sea bass fillets come up smaller than this, simply cook a few more, overlapping them in the roasting dish.

rosemary sprigs – approx. 6 (a hand's length)

thyme sprigs – approx. 8 (a hand's length)

small sage leaves – 2 tablespoons

sea bass fillets – 6 x 150–180g

extra virgin olive oil

sea salt, black pepper

lemons – 2, thinly sliced (ends discarded)

dry white wine – 100ml

### Variation

**Varying the fish:** This recipe is great for any meaty white fish fillet of the sea bass ilk, including sea bream or daurade.

**Arrange the aromatics in a roasting pan**

Preheat the oven to 200°C fan/220°C electric/gas 7. Pull about half the leaves off half of the **rosemary and thyme sprigs** and scatter these and the **sage** over the base of a large roasting pan that will hold all the sea bass fillets in a single layer.

**Sear the fish fillets**

Heat a large non-stick frying pan over a high heat. Score the skin of the **sea bass fillets** diagonally with two or three cuts. Brush both sides with **olive oil** and **season**. Sear the skin-side only for 1 minute until lightly coloured (you will probably have to fry the fish in batches). Arrange the fillets, skin-side up, in the roasting pan on top of the herbs. Brush the **lemon slices** with oil on both sides and sear for about 1 minute on each side until coloured. Scatter the rest of the herbs over the fillets, again pulling half the leaves off the stalks. Lay the lemon slices on top, pour over the **wine** and drizzle over another couple of tablespoons of oil.

**Roast the fish and dish up**

Roast the fish in the hot oven for 7–8 minutes or until the flesh is just cooked. Perfectionists among you may like to pour the cooking juices into a small saucepan and simmer them for a few minutes to concentrate their flavour. Serve the fish drizzled with the cooking juices.

# Harbour Kitchen Plaice with Cheat's Tartare Sauce

Serves **4** / Start to Finish **25 m**

It is hard to believe looking at the estuarine Devonshire town of Salcombe today that a few decades back it was a sleepy seaside village where fishermen set out in small boats to catch mackerel with a line, and sailing dinghies breezed from one side of the estuary to another. My father's great pride was a small house halfway up the valley side of South Sands, with a cinematic view, and we spent every summer there. That generally meant matching souwesters and those scratchy Guernsey jumpers, and lunch of plaice, chips and tartare sauce at the Harbour Kitchen on the High Street, its windows steamed up with a welcoming fug.

### For the plaice

plain flour, for dusting

plaice fillets – 4 x 150–200g *

Dijon mustard – 1 tablespoon

grainy mustard – 1 tablespoon

unsalted butter – 40g

extra virgin olive oil – 2 tablespoons

### For the cheat's tartare sauce

mayonnaise – 100g

soured cream or crème fraîche – 50g

small capers (e.g. Nonpareille) – 1 tablespoon, finely chopped, plus a few extra to serve

cocktail gherkins – 1 tablespoon, finely chopped

flat-leaf parsley – 1 heaped tablespoon finely chopped, plus extra to serve

sea salt, black pepper

### Make the cheat's tartare sauce

Combine **all the ingredients for the tartare sauce** in a bowl, cover with clingfilm and set aside in the fridge until needed.

### Coat the fish fillets with flour and mustard **

Place some **flour** on a dinner plate, season the **plaice fillets** with **salt and pepper** and dip either side in the flour to lightly coat them. Blend the **two mustards** in a small bowl.

### Fry the fish fillets

Heat half the **butter** and half the **olive oil** in a large non-stick frying pan over a medium heat. Put in two of the plaice fillets, skin-side down, and cook for 2 minutes. Turn and cook the flesh for 1 minute, and at the same time brush one-quarter of the mustard over the skin of each. Flip the plaice back over and cook on the skin side for a further minute until golden and crisp. Transfer the cooked fish to a warm plate and cover with foil to keep warm while you cook the remaining fillets in the same way.

### Dish up

Serve with the tartare sauce, scattered with extra capers and parsley.

### Variation

**Whole Lemon Sole:** *Substitute the plaice for small whole lemon sole (approx. 200g each), cleaned with heads removed.*

Heat 15g unsalted butter with 1 tablespoon olive oil in a large non-stick frying pan over a medium heat. Flour the fish as above and fry in batches in the hot fat for 2 minutes on each side until lightly golden and firm when pressed. Serve scattered with chopped parsley, accompanied by some lemon wedges.

### The knack

* **Which fish?** The ideal here are nice big fillets, but if they come up smaller simply buy 600–800g in total.

** **The mustard** renders the skin especially golden and crisp, turning it into a delicate crust.

# Big Party Salmon

Serves **10** / Start to Finish **55 m**

If yesterday's weddings and summer splashes were about poached salmon and mayonnaise, today I would opt for a whole roast salmon. There is very little difference in the texture of the two, but a roast fish has a yummy factor and relaxed allure that a poached fish can lack – or to put it another way, if you have ever tried to photograph a whole poached salmon with its white beady eye you will know what I mean.

Here the roast fish has the additional succulence afforded by the olive oil and wine that anoints it, plus a lovely mass of green leafy herbs. So let's keep getting married and having lovely get-togethers, but change the method.

dill – 2 tablespoons, finely chopped

chives – 2 tablespoons, finely chopped

flat-leaf parsley – 2 tablespoons, finely chopped

fennel seeds – 1 teaspoon, coarsely ground

Maldon sea salt, black pepper

whole salmon – approx. 3kg, cleaned and scaled (head and tail removed, if necessary, to fit in your oven)

extra virgin olive oil – 4 tablespoons

lemon – juice of 1

dry white wine – 3 tablespoons

### Prepare the fish
Preheat the oven to 200°C fan/220°C electric/gas 7 and preheat the grill to high. Combine the **herbs** and **fennel seeds** with a teaspoon of **salt** and about the same amount of **black pepper** in a medium-sized bowl. Score the **salmon** flesh diagonally at 5cm intervals on both sides, making deep slits. Season the fish with salt and pepper.

### Grill the fish and stuff with the herbs
Line your grill pan with a double thickness of foil so it is a little longer than the fish. Lay the salmon on top, cupping the edges of the foil. Grill one side for 3–4 minutes until the skin blisters and colours, and then stuff half of the herbs into the slits. Turn and repeat on the other side.

### Roast the fish
Pour the **olive oil**, **lemon juice** and **wine** over the fish and transfer it to the oven to roast for 40–45 minutes. To check if it is cooked, slip a sharp knife between the backbone and flesh – if cooked, the flesh should lift off the bones with ease; if the flesh clings or looks translucent then it will need a little longer.

### *Serving suggestion*
— Serve hot or cold with a double quantity of Aioli (see page 168) or Tartare Sauce (see page 180). Dish up with plenty of salads.

# Vietnamese Sizzling Salmon

Serves **2** / Start to Finish **12 m**

Here we go again with those Three Musketeers, garlic, ginger and chilli. You can fry salmon in this way whenever you want crispy fillets. This is just as good eaten cold as hot.

skinned salmon fillets – 2 x 150g

vegetable oil, 1 tablespoon (optional)

large garlic clove – 1, peeled and thinly sliced

fresh root ginger – 2cm piece, peeled and cut into fine strips 2–3cm long

medium-hot red chilli – ½, cut into fine strips 2–3cm long

spring onions – 2, trimmed and cut into fine strips 5–7cm long

light soy sauce – 1 tablespoon

lime wedges, to serve

### Fry the fish

Heat a large frying pan over a medium heat, and fry the **salmon fillets,** top-side down, for about 5 minutes, or until the outside is golden and crispy and the flesh is cooked through by about one-third. Carefully flip the fillets over and cook for about 3 minutes on the other side, or until the fish has just lost its translucency in the centre. Transfer the cooked fish to serving plates.

### Add the aromatics

Drain off any excess oil in the pan to leave approx. 1 tablespoon – but if the pan seems dry you might need to add a drop of **vegetable oil**. Add the **garlic, ginger** and **chilli** and sizzle briefly until fragrant and the garlic is just starting to colour. Remove the pan from the heat and stir in the **spring onion**. Spoon the fried aromatics over the fish, splash over the **soy sauce**, and accompany with the **lime wedges**.

### Variation

**Varying the fish:** *This is a good way of serving any fish fillet such as sea bass or sea bream.*

Follow the cooking method for mackerel fillets (see page 178, variation), and spoon over the stir-fried garlic, ginger, chilli and spring onion at the end.

# Pad Thai with King Prawns

Serves **2** / Start to Finish **20 m**

Gap years weren't quite as prevalent in my time as they are today, but Jonnie and I did manage five weeks trekking around Thailand. Bangkok's Khao San Road brings back fond memories, as that is where the two of us would spend hours hanging out in the various cafés. I remember one in particular, where an elderly woman used to spend all day stooped over a wok on a one-ring burner stationed at the entrance turning out order after order of Pad Thai. It was mesmerising to watch.

lime juice – 2 tablespoons

fish sauce – 1 ½ tablespoons

golden caster sugar – 1 tablespoon

groundnut oil – 1 tablespoon

shallots – 2, peeled, halved and thinly sliced

raw peeled tiger prawns – 100g

medium eggs – 2

'ready-to-wok' Thai-style ribbon noodles – 300g

beansprouts – 100g

spring onions – 3, trimmed and thinly sliced

fresh coriander – 6 tablespoons, coarsely chopped, plus extra to serve

roasted and salted peanuts – 25g, coarsely chopped

crushed chillies or chilli powder, to serve

**Prepare the ingredients**
Whisk the **lime juice, fish sauce** and **sugar** together in a small bowl. Prepare all the other ingredients to the point indicated.

**Stir-fry**
Heat the **groundnut oil** in a wok or a large non-stick frying pan over a high heat. Add the **shallots** and fry for about a minute, tossing them constantly until they are soft and starting to colour. Add the **prawns** and fry briefly, turning them until they are pink. Break in the **eggs** and rapidly scramble, and then add the **noodles**, separating them with your fingers as you drop them into the pan. Add the lime juice and fish sauce mixture and cook for 1 minute, moving the ingredients around in the pan until the liquid has been absorbed. Finally add the **beansprouts** and **spring onions** and stir-fry for 1 minute longer.

**Dish up**
Remove the pan from the heat, toss in the chopped **coriander** and serve in deep bowls, scattered with the chopped **peanuts** and more coriander. Accompany with a small bowl of **crushed chillies** (or chilli powder) to sprinkle over at the table.

*Pasta*

7

# About **Pasta**

General de Gaulle had it easy when he famously declared: 'how can you govern a country that has 246 varieties of cheese?' In Italy they have literally hundreds of different shapes of pasta, and four times that number of names depending on which region you are in.

For the rest of us pasta devotees without Italian genes, it is actually quite difficult to think in terms of different pastas suiting different sauces. Without lowering the bar, the reality in the Bell household is usually whatever we have in the cupboard, combined with whatever sauce we are planning. Thankfully, whatever the shape, the means of cooking dried pasta remains the same. But there are a few simple rules or guidelines worth considering:

**Dried v. fresh**
Dried and freshly made pasta are totally different in character, each with its own strengths, so it is best not to see one as being superior to the other. Having done my share of knocking out lobster ravioli in Hebridean huts, the passion tailed off with a career and kids. Making your own ravioli is hobby cooking, and the aim of this book is to make your life easy. So dried it is. What does matter in the small print is the use of the term 'bronze-die'. These preceded modern extruders and result in a pleasing rough texture that encourages the sauce to cling to the pasta rather than slipping off.

**Which flour?**
The vast majority of dried pastas will be made with durum wheat or semolina flour, but the range doesn't stop there. Barley, buckwheat, rye, rice, maize, chestnut and chickpea flours are all contenders, spelt too has a growing fan-base, and as gluten intolerance increases these niche types allow for all sorts of different possibilities.

**A good match**
Try to think of dried pasta as belonging to one of two camps: *long* pasta shapes such as spaghetti and tagliatelle, as well as long hollow types such as bucatini, are well suited to tomato-based sauces made with olive oil; *squat* shapes such as penne, rigatoni and conchiglie welcome chunky sauces, which will settle in the nooks and crannies. Fine egg pastas are better suited to cream and butter sauces, and also seafood.

### Get jazzy
Once you've got past the long, squat, tubular, sheet-like, soup or stuffed considerations, there is the allure of 'flavoured' pastas, a word to be taken lightly. In my experience, the spinach, beetroot, tomato or whatever other vegetable used to dye the pasta very rarely comes through with any sense of the vegetable, the one exception being wild mushroom pasta, which does have a lovely earthy scent. I also find it hard to resist pasta dyed a daring shade of black with squid ink, so very 80s. Truffle pasta? Still 80s, but what a treat.

### COOKING TIPS
### Before you begin
As soon as you add your pasta to the pan of boiling water, you have initiated a runaway train. There is no time to be lost between draining, tossing, serving and eating, so you need to have everything at the ready. Leave pasta to sit around for 10 minutes while you make the sauce, and the dish will languish at the stodgy end of the spectrum.

### Boiling the pasta
Allow 100g dried pasta per person. Bring a pan of water big enough to afford the pasta plenty of space to a rolling boil. I always use my biggest saucepan, which has a handle either side to make it easy to drain. Generously salt the water with a heaped teaspoon of coarse sea salt. Add the pasta and give it a stir with a wooden spoon, pushing it down into the water if it protrudes. Cook until it is just tender or *al dente*, leaving it firm to the bite, stirring every now and again. Be guided by the cooking time on the packet, and start to test it by removing a piece and carefully biting into it a couple of minutes before you think it will be ready.

### Draining and dressing
It is a good idea to clear the sink before putting the pasta on to boil, placing the colander at the ready. I say this from experience; I have been undone by a lazy pile of dirty dishes once too often. Drain the pasta into the colander, giving it a few shakes, and immediately return it to the pan, still on the wet side because it will continue to absorb any water that clings. I find it helpful to keep back a small cup of the starchy cooking liquor as a handy insurance should the sauce seem dry.

# Essential Pasta Sauces

## Midnight Sauce

Serves **2** / Start to Finish **10 m**

This idea originated with a friend who had just returned from doing some serious partying in Mallorca, where evenings consisted of lots of liquid and very little food. On arriving home to their rented house in the early hours they needed something they could knock up quickly to quell their hunger – hence Midnight Spaghetti, a big plate of pasta and all the aromatics of a sauce without the hassle of making one.

| | |
|---|---|
| extra virgin olive oil – 4 tablespoons | |
| garlic cloves – 3, peeled and finely chopped | |
| medium-hot red chilli – 2 teaspoons, finely chopped | |
| flat-leaf parsley – 3 tablespoons, finely chopped | |
| sea salt, black pepper | |
| freshly grated Parmesan, to serve | |

### Prepare the ingredients for the sauce
Place the **olive oil**, **garlic** and **chilli** at the ready in a small saucepan. Just as you are about to drain the pasta, place the pan over a medium heat and fry the ingredients very briefly until the garlic starts to sizzle – don't let it brown. Tip the hot garlic mixture over the cooked pasta, toss in the **parsley** and season with plenty of **salt and pepper**. Serve with lots of freshly grated **Parmesan**.

### Variations
**Pasta with Chilli & Garlic:** Leave out the parsley.
**Pasta with Garlic & Oil:** Leave out the parsley and chilli.

## Pesto Sauce

Serves **4–6** / Start to Finish **10 m**

The greatest ever use for basil? I reckon. Despite the quantity of herb involved, this version has a quiet restraint. Use to explore pasta shapes you might not have tried before, but in particular long ones.

| | |
|---|---|
| pine nuts – 30g | |
| basil leaves – 90g | |
| small garlic clove – 1, peeled | |
| extra virgin olive oil – 8 tablespoons, plus extra to store | |
| Parmesan – 50g, freshly grated, plus extra to serve | |
| sea salt, black pepper | |

### Toast the pine nuts
Gently toast the **pine nuts** in a large frying pan over a medium-low heat for a few minutes, shaking the pan now and again, until golden. Transfer to a bowl or plate and leave to cool.

### Whizz the ingredients to a purée
Place the **basil**, toasted pine nuts, **garlic** and **olive oil** in a food processor and whizz to a coarse purée. Add the **Parmesan** and a little **seasoning** and whizz briefly again. Serve with lots of freshly grated Parmesan.

(Any leftover pesto sauce can be stored in a small bowl, sealed with a thin layer of olive oil. Keep in the fridge and use within a couple of days.)

### Serving suggestions
— Splodge over roasted veg.
— Thin with an equal amount of oil and drizzle over grilled meat or pizza.
— Stir a teaspoon through vegetable soups.
— Spoon a tablespoon or two over mashed potato or vegetable purées, and stir through to streak them.

# Puttanesca Sauce

Serves **4** / Start to Finish **15 m**

Pushed to come up with a reason why my family eats this to the exclusion of almost every other pasta sauce, I would put it down to its balance. A perfect storm of the four corners of taste: salty anchovies and olives, the heat of chilli, and the sweet sourness of tomatoes. It also helps that it is effectively a storecupboard sauce. I make a point of always having the ingredients for this dish in the larder – it's not a case of *if,* but *when.*

extra virgin olive oil – 3 tablespoons

garlic cloves – 2, peeled and finely chopped

salted anchovy fillets – 6, sliced

chopped tomatoes – 1 x 400g tin

small dried red chilli – 1, finely chopped

small capers (e.g. Nonpareille) – 1 heaped tablespoon, rinsed

pitted green and black olives – 100g, finely sliced

flat-leaf parsley – 2 heaped tablespoons, finely chopped

## Make the sauce

Heat the **olive oil** in a medium-sized, non-stick frying pan over a medium heat. Add the **garlic** and **anchovies** and cook for a minute, mashing the anchovies into a paste using a wooden spoon. Add the **tomatoes** and **chilli** and simmer for about 7 minutes until the sauce is glossy and thickened, stirring occasionally. Stir in the **capers, olives** and **parsley** and cook for one minute longer.

# Amatriciana Sauce

Serves **6** / Start to Finish **30 m**

In the same spirit as Puttanesca (left), if not as feisty, this dish relies on a tin of chopped tomatoes, lots of bacon and onions, and a chilli or two to spice it up. In other words, it is the kind of staple you can hope to have the wherewithal to cook on many an average day. Deriving from the Italian for lover, in its country of origin Amatriciana has aphrodisiacal status. Is there something we don't know about bacon?

extra virgin olive oil – 3 tablespoons

medium onions – 3, peeled, halved and thinly sliced

small dried chillies – 2, finely chopped

unsmoked streaky bacon – 250g, diced

chopped tomatoes – 1 x 400g tin

dried oregano – ½ teaspoon

freshly grated Parmesan, to serve

## Fry the onions

Heat 2 tablespoons **olive oil** in a large non-stick frying pan over a lowish heat and cook the **onions** with the **chilli** for about 15 minutes, stirring constantly, until they are golden and silky. You will need to do this slowly to ensure the onions soften fully and caramelise evenly.

## Fry the bacon and finish the sauce

Meanwhile heat the remaining tablespoon olive oil in another frying pan over a medium-low heat and cook the **bacon** until it is golden and beginning to crisp, stirring occasionally. Using a slotted spoon, transfer the crispy bacon to the pan with the onions. Add the **chopped tomatoes** and **oregano** and simmer for a few minutes until the sauce thickens. Serve with lots of freshly grated **Parmesan**.

**For Bolognese Sauce,** see page 135.

# Spaghetti Carbonara

Serves **4** / Start to Finish **30 m**

As Sophia Loren put it 'everything you see I owe to spaghetti,' including second helpings of Spaghetti Carbonara, so eat up. This famous Roman dish with its creamy egg sauce melded with Parmesan, and crispy bacon nibs, is thought to originate with the *carbonai* or charcoalmakers of the Apennine Mountains, and is testament to how good a humble dish can be.

extra virgin olive oil – 1 tablespoon

unsalted butter – 10g

unsmoked back bacon – 225g, sliced into thin strips (rind and fat discarded) *

dry white wine – 4 tablespoons

spaghetti – 450g

large organic eggs – 3

Parmesan – 75g, freshly grated, plus extra to serve

flat-leaf parsley – 3 tablespoons, finely chopped

sea salt, black pepper

### Fry the bacon
Heat the **oil** and **butter** in a large non-stick frying pan over a medium heat, add the **bacon** and fry until it turns crisp at the edges, stirring occasionally. Add the **wine** and cook for about 1 minute until well-reduced, and then remove the pan from the heat.

### Cook the pasta
Meanwhile bring a large pan of salted water to the boil, add the **spaghetti** and stir to separate. Cook according to the instructions on the packet until just tender.

### Whisk together the ingredients for the sauce
Lightly beat the **eggs** in a large bowl, blend in the **Parmesan** and the **parsley** and **season** well.

### Toss the pasta with the sauce **
Drain the spaghetti, though not too thoroughly, and rapidly toss into the bowl with the egg and cheese mixture. Quickly reheat the bacon and tip the entire contents of the pan over the pasta, tossing to combine. Taste for seasoning and serve straight away with more Parmesan scattered on top.

The knack

* **Which bacon?** This is one occasion where you want nice lean strips of back bacon rather than streaky, as the latter will make the dish greasy. Try to seek out dry-cured bacon for maximum flavour.

** **Tossing the pasta:** If there is any skill involved here, then it lies with the tossing. You need to be speedy in doing this, so the strands of pasta are evenly coated and the egg sets to a uniform creaminess. Be sure to have everything at the ready.

# Crab Linguine with Lemon & Chilli

Serves **4** / Start to Finish **20 m**

The River Café's seminal cookbooks look as fresh and relevant today as they did when they were first published, and I am sure this will still be the case 50 years from now. Their style and approach redefined Italian cooking in Britain, and gave birth to a new love and understanding of it. And they did everything with such panache.

Every cook of my generation is likely to have a desert island recipe taken from one of these books that evokes memories of long lazy lunches where too much Prosecco flowed. When my son Louis returned from a teenage holiday to Lucca raving about crab linguine I was so happy because it took me right back to those days.

400g linguine

For the sauce

mixed brown and white crabmeat – 200g

medium-hot red chilli – 1, finely chopped (core and seeds discarded)

garlic clove – 1, peeled and crushed to a paste

extra virgin olive oil – 6 tablespoons

lemon juice – 4 tablespoons

flat-leaf parsley – 2 heaped tablespoons, coarsely chopped, plus extra to serve

sea salt, black pepper

**Make the sauce** *
Combine **all the ingredients for the sauce** in a large serving bowl.

**Cook the pasta**
Meanwhile bring a large pan of salted water to the boil, add the **linguine**, pushing down to submerge it, and cook according to the instructions on the packet.

**Toss the pasta with the sauce and dish up**
Drain the pasta into a colander, shaking off the excess water without worrying about every last drop, and tip into the bowl with the crab sauce. Toss to coat and serve scattered with a little more parsley.

**The knack**
* **Simplicity itself:** The magic of this assembly lies with the speed and lack of pretension of the sauce, which is uncooked and can be prepared in the time it takes to whisk up a salad dressing.

# Orecchiette with Purple Sprouting Broccoli & Ricotta

Serves **4** / Start to Finish **40 m**

These chubby little 'ears' of pasta from Puglia are unique among the pasta family. They have a soft and pudgy texture unlike any other that goes halfway to being a dumpling. This way of serving them with flowering broccoli is particularly good.

purple sprouting broccoli – 700g

orecchiette – 250g

extra virgin olive oil –
3 tablespoons, plus extra to serve

garlic cloves – 4, peeled and finely chopped

small dried chilli – 1, finely chopped

sea salt, black pepper

Parmesan – 100g, freshly grated

ricotta – 125g, loosely broken up

**Variations**

**Orecchiette with Purple Sprouting Broccoli, Ricotta & Bacon:** Scatter over some crispy lardons at the end.

**Orecchiette with Asparagus & Ricotta:** Replace the purple sprouting broccoli with thin asparagus.

**Prepare the broccoli**
Cut off the flowering heads of the **broccoli** and set aside. Trim the tough bases from the stalks and cut the tender stems lengthways into long slices, approx. 1cm thick.

**Cook the broccoli and the pasta**
Bring two large pans of salted water to the boil. Add the **orecchiette** to one, give it a stir and cook according to the instructions on the packet. At the same time, add the broccoli to the other pan, bring to the boil and cook for about 2 minutes until just tender; drain into a colander.

**Fry the vegetables**
Towards the end of cooking the pasta, heat 3 tablespoons **olive oil** in a large non-stick frying pan over a medium heat. Add the **garlic** and **chilli** and cook momentarily until they are fragrant. Stir in the broccoli, season with **salt and pepper** and stir-fry for 1–2 minutes.

**Toss the pasta \***
Remove a small cup of boiling water from the pan of pasta and set aside. Then drain the pasta into a colander, leaving it on the wet side, and return it to the pan. Tip the broccoli mixture over the pasta and toss to combine. Scatter over the **Parmesan**, add a splash of the reserved cooking liquid, return the pan to a low heat and stir gently until the pasta is coated in a creamy emulsion.

**Dish up**
Dot the **ricotta** over the pasta and turn just once to combine. Drizzle over a little more olive oil.

The knack

\* **Tossing the pasta:** Here the Parmesan melds with the cooking liquid to form a creamy sauce that very lightly coats the pasta. Orecchiette encourages this, being a soft pasta that releases its starch.

# Gratin of Ravioli with Spinach & Crème Fraîche

Serves **4** / Start to Finish **30 m**

Making your own ravioli is a serious amount of work and no mean skill, the sort of cooking that is best left to keen breadmakers. Ready-made ravioli takes you halfway to the finishing line. This gratin is as simple as it is luxurious.

extra virgin olive oil
garlic cloves – 2, peeled and finely chopped
spinach – 500–550g
sea salt, black pepper
fresh ravioli – 500g
crème fraîche – 200g
Parmesan – 100g, freshly grated
freshly grated nutmeg

you will need a 30 x 20cm roasting pan

**Variations**

Whether they are called fiorelli, girasoli, tortelloni or ravioli, they are all a variation on a theme, so simply choose a filling that appeals. Most flavours work well here – sausage and fennel, pumpkin and pine nut, tomato and basil, Bolognese… Just bear in mind the quality does vary hugely, so aim for top-end.

**Fry the spinach**
Heat 1 tablespoon **olive oil** in a large non-stick frying pan over a medium heat, add one-quarter of the **garlic** and one-quarter of the **spinach** and fry, tossing constantly until it wilts. Transfer the cooked spinach to a bowl and cook the rest in the same way. Season with **salt and pepper** after frying to prevent the spinach from throwing out all of its juices.

**Cook the ravioli and make the sauce**
Meanwhile bring a large pan of salted water to the boil and cook the **ravioli** according to the instructions on the packet. To make the sauce, combine the **crème fraîche**, half the **Parmesan**, a little **nutmeg** and some seasoning in a small saucepan and bring to the boil. Drain the pasta into a colander, return it to the pan, pour in the sauce and toss well to combine. Towards the end of this time, preheat the grill to high.

**Assemble and grill the gratin**
Reheat the spinach in the frying pan and arrange it over the base of a 30 x 20cm roasting pan. Spoon the ravioli and sauce on top, scatter over the remaining Parmesan and drizzle with a little more oil. Set under the grill until golden and sizzling. Serve straight away.

# Gorgeously Gooey Macaroni Cheese

Serves **4–5** / Start to Finish **45 m** *

Such is the family appeal of this one (and its potential to be dull and stodgy) that I have played with this recipe endlessly over the years. Just how do you achieve pasta that is tender without being overcooked, and cheese that stays deliciously molten and gooey rather than disappearing into the sauce? Oven-baked macaroni cheese tends towards stodge, whereas this method marries the pasta and the sauce at the last moment just before it is served.

In France this pasta regularly turns up dressed to the nines – the most indulgent macaroni cheese I have ever eaten came studded with lobster, on the quayside in St. Tropez. Normally in our house we ring the changes by folding in a few prawns, however you could marry it with scallops or even chicken livers.

macaroni – 200g **
unsalted butter – 50g
plain flour – 45g
whole milk – 700ml
bay leaf – 1
Dijon mustard – 1 tablespoon
sea salt, black pepper
freshly grated nutmeg
Gruyère – 200g, cut into thin strips a few centimetres long ***
Parmesan – 50g, freshly grated
baby plum or cherry tomatoes – 200g, halved
extra virgin olive oil – 1 tablespoon

you will need a 20 x 30cm gratin dish

**Cook the macaroni**
Bring a large pan of salted water to the boil. Add the **macaroni**, give it a stir to separate out the pieces and cook according to the instructions on the packet until just tender. Drain into a colander and set aside.

**Make the cheese sauce**
Meanwhile melt the **butter** in a medium-sized, non-stick saucepan over a medium heat. Add the **flour** and cook for about 1 minute, stirring constantly, until it is seething nicely. Remove the pan from the heat and gradually work in the **milk** a little at a time using a wooden spoon. Return the white sauce to the heat and bring to the boil, stirring frequently until it thickens. Add the bay leaf and simmer over a low heat for 10 minutes, stirring occasionally. Remove the **bay leaf**, add the **Dijon mustard** and give the sauce a whisk to ensure that it is completely smooth and silky. (If lumpy, pass through a sieve into a large bowl.) Season to taste with **salt**, **pepper** and **nutmeg**.

**Finish the gratin**
Towards the end of this time, preheat the grill to high and place the gratin dish underneath to warm through. Stir the cooked macaroni into the sauce and reheat gently, then mix in the pieces of **Gruyère** and tip into the hot dish. Scatter the **Parmesan** over the surface.

In a small bowl, toss the **tomatoes** with the **oil** and season with salt and pepper. Scatter the tomatoes over the macaroni cheese and set under the grill until the tomatoes have softened and the cheese is golden and bubbling.

*Serving suggestion*
— Macaroni cheese has expanded its role at home from a suppertime classic to an elegant aside to the Sunday roast, doused in gravy. But for a simple supper all that is called for is a green salad.

### The knack

\* **Making the dish in advance?** Both the pasta and the sauce can be cooked a couple of hours in advance. Transfer the cooled drained pasta to a bowl and cover it with clingfilm; cover the surface of the sauce with clingfilm too, whisking it until smooth before finishing the recipe.

\*\* **Which macaroni?** Macaroni comes in any number of sizes. The small egg macaroni beloved in France makes for the most delicate dish, while larger types are more rustic looking. Be guided by your preference and what is on offer.

\*\*\* **Which cheese?** You want one of the fondue cheeses here rather than Cheddar, which will give out a lot of butter. Gruyère promises an especially gooey macaroni, while grated Parmesan provides a punchy topping.

# Lasagne

Serves **6–8** / Start to Finish **65–70 m** (+ making the ragu)

*Lasagne al forno* is the ultimate lavish pasta creation, a big-hearted bonanza that emerges from the oven golden and bubbling, oozing a rich ragu and silky white sauce. The real plus to this dish is its potential for being made in advance, which gives it the same relaxed entertaining appeal as a fish pie.

Best Ever Beef Ragu – 1 batch, simmered for 1 hour to leave it nice and juicy (see page 135)

Parmesan – 100g, freshly grated

yellow or green no-cook egg lasagne – approx. 275g *

**For the white sauce**

unsalted butter – 50g

plain flour – 40g

whole milk – 1 litre

bay leaf – 1

sea salt

freshly grated nutmeg

you will need a 38 x 25cm roasting pan or baking dish, approx. 5–6cm deep

### Make the white sauce **

Melt the **butter** in a medium-sized, non-stick saucepan over a medium heat. Add the **flour** and cook for about 1 minute, stirring constantly, until it is seething nicely. Remove the pan from the heat and gradually work in the **milk** a little at a time using a wooden spoon. Return the white sauce to the heat and bring to the boil, stirring frequently until it thickens. Add the **bay leaf** and simmer over a low heat for 10 minutes, stirring occasionally. Remove the bay leaf and give the sauce a whisk to ensure that it is completely smooth and silky. Season to taste with **salt** and **nutmeg**. (If lumpy, pass through a sieve into a large bowl.)

### Assemble the lasagne

Layer up the ingredients in a baking dish as follows: cover the base of the dish with one-quarter of the **ragu**, then drizzle over one-quarter of the white sauce. Scatter over one-quarter of the **Parmesan** and cover with a layer of **lasagne**, breaking the sheets to fit – you should get about 4 in a row lengthways, with one broken in half into long strips to fill the gaps. Repeat the layering process until all the ingredients are used up, finishing with a layer of white sauce and whatever Parmesan is left over on top. In total you should have 3 layers of pasta and 4 of ragu and white sauce. (At this point you can cover and chill the lasagne for up to 12 hours until needed.)

### Cook the lasagne

Preheat the oven to 170°C fan/190°C electric/gas 5. Bake the lasagne for 45–50 minutes until golden and bubbling on the surface.

---

#### The knack

* **Which lasagne sheets?** I find it somewhat disappointing that coloured pastas don't live up to their looks. Green lasagne has purely to do with aesthetics. Still, it cuts a dash, especially in *lasagne al forno*, but white or green will do.

** **How thick should the white sauce be?** Modern sheet lasagne does away with pre-cooking, the one requisite being you coat the pasta with enough sauce to moisten it as it bakes. This means starting out with a sauce that is sloppier than you would normally make to allow for the pasta drinking up the juices. Aim for the consistency of runny custard.

# Gnocchi Peperonata

Serves **4** / Start to Finish **40 m**

These plump little dumplings are as convenient as pasta. Here I have mixed them into a tray of roasted peppers with lots of molten mozzarella.

banana shallots – 3, peeled, halved and thinly sliced

mixed Romano peppers (e.g. red, yellow and orange) – 6, cut into thin strips 5–7cm in length (core and seeds removed) *

extra virgin olive oil – 6 tablespoons

sea salt

red wine vinegar – 2 tablespoons

gnocchi – 500g

buffalo mozzarellas – 2 x 125g balls, torn into 3–4cm pieces

freshly grated or shaved pecorino, to serve

a few tiny basil or mint leaves, to serve (optional)

**Roast the peppers**
Preheat the oven to 230°C fan/250°C electric/gas 9 and bring a large pan of salted water to the boil. Place the **shallots** and **peppers** in a large roasting pan and drizzle with 4 tablespoons **olive oil**, tossing well to combine. Season with **salt** and roast for 25 minutes or until lightly coloured. Remove the peppers from the oven and set over a low heat on the hob. Drizzle over the **vinegar** and cook for a further 1–2 minutes until the vinegar has completely evaporated, stirring frequently.

**Cook the gnocchi**
Just before the end of cooking the peppers, add the **gnocchi** to the boiling water and give it a stir. Cook for about 3 minutes until the dumplings rise to the surface.

**Drain and toss the gnocchi**
Drain the gnocchi into a colander, shaking it dry, and then tip it into the roasting pan with the peppers. Drizzle over 2 tablespoons olive oil and toss well to combine. Mix in pieces of **mozzarella** and finish off in the oven for 5 minutes until the cheese has melted. To serve, spoon into bowls, scatter with **pecorino** and garnish with a few tiny **basil or mint leaves** if you wish.

The knack

* **If using bell peppers:** Reduce the quantity to about 5. You may need to roast them for a bit longer.

# Potatoes, Rice & Grains

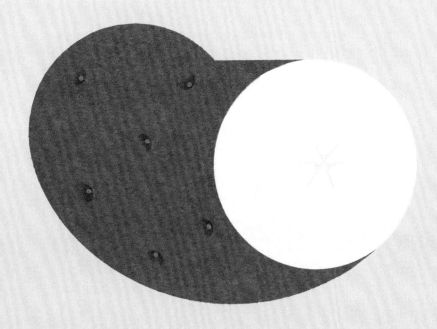

# 8

# About **Potatoes, Rice & Grains**

POTATOES
### Maincrop potatoes
These are our heritage, as much a part of our kitchens as a pot of tea and toast. They're big and mealy when cooked and, unless baked or sautéed, best peeled.
*Good for:* Classic roasties: nothing turns out a roast potato with a crisp exterior and meltingly tender insides in the same way. They make a light, fluffy mash, and a rustic gratin where the starch in the potatoes fuses the slices together. Baked potatoes are basically just large maincrops.

### New or salad potatoes
Once upon a time, 'new' potatoes heralded spring, and a bowl of Jersey Royals licked with butter and infused with a sprig of mint was as much of a treat at Easter as the chocolate eggs that followed. Today we have waxy-fleshed potatoes all year round, something to take advantage of given their unique character, even if Jersey Royals do remain the pinnacle.
*Good for:* Roasting in their skin. They make a dense, rich mash, and an excellent gratin where you want the slices to remain separate. They are also good for salads where you want some definition.

RICE
### Basmati
Basmati is king among long-grain rices and the best all-rounder – and out of some 8,000 varieties that is no mean accolade. It has a particular scent that comes with its provenance in the foothills of the Himalayas. That said, the variety itself can differ hugely in quality depending on the brand. Tilda basmati rice is recommended.

### 'Easy cook' rice
This is a bit of a misnomer. Par-boiled to harden and make the grains more resistant to overcooking, it actually takes longer to cook. And long-grain is simply a generic term, with no particular guarantees.

### Short-grain rice
Short-grain rices are high in starch, which they shed as they are cooking, making them ideal for recipes using liquid, which will thicken to an alluring limpid texture. Arborio is the best known of the risotto rices: Carnaroli is a premium type that remains firm and holds its shape; Vialone Nano is smaller and especially adept at absorbing flavours. It's worth knowing that the classic risotto rices can also be used for rice pudding, although the reverse of using 'pudding rice' for risottos isn't to be recommended.

### Wholegrain types
Wild rice is lovely stuff, although technically an aquatic grass rather than a true rice. Try to buy it on its own, rather than buying mixes that will have been treated so that the different types cook at the same rate. Other personal

favourites are Nanjing black rice and Carmargue red. The former, originally grown in the area as a delicacy for the Tang dynasty some 1,500 years ago, is tantalisingly delicate and creamy, and jet black. Red rice, grown in the wetlands of the Carmargue in the company of flamingoes and black bulls, has a gorgeous texture and delicate flavour, that much more subtle than brown basmati.

### Rice safety
Something worth knowing, in case you ever decide to feed the masses on rice, is the potentially dire effects of leaving cooked rice standing at room temperature for any length of time. This, and undercooked chicken livers, take care of the vast majority of food poisoning cases that occur. Fine to re-fry or use it for egg-fried rice, but chill it as soon as it is cool.

### Freezing leftover rice
A small bag of cooked pilau rice is one of the more useful things to have in the freezer, and can be stir-fried from frozen. The rice needs to be nice and dry before freezing, if it's wet it'll emerge a solid block.

GRAINS
### Bulgar
For information on different types, see page 228.

### Quinoa
This has a deep, satisfyingly bitter and nutty savour and a texture quite unlike any other, courtesy of the fine C-shaped tail or germ that separates out from the seed when it cooks. Cultivated in the Andes for over 6,000 years, the Incas referred to it as 'the mother of all grains'. As well they might, for it contains more protein than any other grain, up to 18 per cent, and unlike wheat and rice can boast all the essential amino acids, and is gluten-free.
*Good for:* Makes a great basis for salads with roasted veg, broad beans, asparagus, slivers of roast chicken or whatever else takes your fancy.

### Spelt
Spelt is often equated with 'farro', but it cooks up very differently. While farro requires soaking and always remains firm and chewy, spelt can be cooked like rice and turns creamy and yielding by comparison. And for the time-challenged among us, spelt is by far the most useful of the two products.
*Good for:* Makes a hearty foundation to any salad, and laps up the juices of roasted veg when the two are newly cooled.

### Couscous
Traditionally couscous was made by hand, using semolina or durum wheat, and then steamed twice, but modern mass-produced couscous has been pre-steamed and dried, making the preparation that much easier.
*Good for:* Salads and serving with soupy stews such as tagines.

# Essential Potatoes

## Mash

Serves **6** / Start to Finish **45 m**

The best comes liberally laced with butter or cream and plenty of milk, it should slop off the spoon rather than sitting as a dry lump.

waxy or maincrop potatoes such as Maris Piper – 1.5kg, peeled and cut into even-sized pieces if large

salted butter – 50g, diced

extra thick double cream – 4 generous tablespoons

sea salt

whole milk – splash

### Cook and mill the potatoes
Bring a large pan of salted water to the boil and cook the **potatoes** until tender. Drain into a sieve, leave for a few minutes to steam-dry, and then pass them through a mouli-legumes or potato ricer, or sieve back into the pan.

### Enrich the mash and dish up
Beat in the **butter** and **cream** and season plentifully with **sea salt**. Gently reheat the mash, adding a drop of **milk** to achieve the right consistency – it should be a thick purée as opposed to a spoonable lump. (Avoid freezing.)

### Variations
**Olive Oil Mash:** Replace the butter with 3 tablespoons extra virgin olive oil. This is good with chargrilled meat and fish, and roasted vegetables.

**Mustard Mash:** Beat Dijon mustard into the mash to taste.

**Saffron Mash:** Grind about 25 saffron filaments and infuse with a drop of boiling milk for 15 minutes. Stir into the finished mash.

**Lower-fat Mash:** Halve the quantity of butter and replace the cream with fromage frais.

## Champ

Serves **6** / Start to Finish **50 m**

This Irish classic is mash in its party frock, a great one when entertaining – not least because it is best to reserve this sort of OTT richesse for an occasional treat.

maincrop potatoes such as Maris Piper – 900g, peeled and cut into even-sized pieces if large

unsalted butter – 100g, plus a knob to serve

spring onions – 3 bunches (approx. 400g), trimmed and cut into 1cm slices

double cream – 200ml

sea salt and black pepper

### Cook and mill the potatoes
Bring a large pan of salted water to the boil and cook the **potatoes** until tender. Drain and leave to steam-dry for a few minutes, and then press through a mouli-legumes or potato ricer, or sieve back into the pan.

### Simmer the spring onions with the cream
Meanwhile melt the **butter** in a medium-sized saucepan and fry the **spring onions** for about 5 minutes until soft and silky, stirring occasionally. Add the **cream** and **seasoning**, bring to a simmer and cook for another few minutes until the mixture thickens.

### Combine the mash with the spring onions
Stir the cream and onion mixture into the mashed potato and adjust the seasoning – it should be nice and sloppy.

To serve, make a well in the centre and drop in the remaining knob of butter. (If you wish, you can cook this in advance and gently reheat it when required.)

# Jacket-on Roast Potatoes

Serves **4** / Start to Finish **1 h 5 m**

These are a hybrid between roast potatoes
and baked, a great way of cooking little new
or waxy-fleshed potatoes, with no peeling
or parboiling necessary. Ideal when you are
pressed for time. These are delicious with pretty
much everything, but keep in mind relaxed and
summery Mediterranean fare.

small or baby waxy or new potatoes such as
Charlotte or Jersey Royal – 900g, scrubbed if
necessary

extra virgin olive oil

thyme sprigs – 6 (optional)

sea salt

### Prepare the potatoes
Preheat the oven to 190°C fan/210°C electric/
gas 6½. Place the **potatoes** in a roasting dish,
drizzle over some **olive oil** and stir to coat.
Tuck the **thyme** in here and there (if using), and
scatter over some **sea salt**.

### Roast the potatoes
Roast the potatoes for 1 hour, stirring them
halfway through.

# Baked Potatoes

Serves **4** / Start to Finish **1 h 35 m**

Naff? Almost, but given the proper care too
good to pass up as a healthy convenient supper.
Lightly coated in oil with a smattering of sea
salt these emerge with a crisp golden skin and
creamy within.

baking potatoes such as Maris Piper, Desiree or
King Edward – 4 x 225–275g

extra virgin olive oil

Maldon sea salt

### Prepare the potatoes
Preheat the oven to 160°C fan/180°C electric/
gas 4. Scrub the **potatoes** and dry them. Make
an incision the shape of a lid on the top of each
one with a small sharp knife. Place a little **olive
oil** in the palm of your hand, rub your hands
together and then over the potatoes, to lightly
coat them.

### Bake the potatoes
Place them on a baking dish, sprinkle over some
crystals of **sea salt**, and bake for 1½ hours.

### *Serving suggestions*
— Scoop out the fluffy mashed potato from
the inside and mix with 5 tablespoons extra
virgin olive oil, 2 heaped tablespoons chopped
parsley, ½ crushed garlic clove and some salt
and pepper. Spoon the mixture back inside the
potato and serve.
— Scoop out the fluffy mashed potato from
the inside, pass through a sieve into a bowl and
mix with a knob of butter and some seasoning.
Pile half of the mixture back into the potato
skin and fill to the brim with grated Gruyère
or Emmental. Replace the lid and reheat in the
oven for 20 minutes.

# Bell Family's Favourite Roasties

Serves **4** / Start to Finish **1 h 30 m**

A week rarely goes by in our house without a roast of some sort, and the potatoes are just as important (if not more) than the joint they accompany. In fact, it is the potatoes that define the Sunday lunch element more than the roast, which frequently gets dished up with salads and a hearty loaf of bread mid-week. Here they are slathered in olive oil and have a fairly healthy profile, and they are divinely crisp.

It is hard to know whether to be gladdened or worried by the number of roasties that get consumed should you cook up more than is required. Double? Not unknown to disappear.

maincrop potatoes such as Maris Piper – 900g, peeled, and cut up *

extra virgin olive oil

sea salt

## Variations

**Goosefat Roasties:** For fabulously crisp and rich potatoes, trickle 80g melted goosefat over the potatoes in lieu of the olive oil.

**All Butter Roasties:** For roasties with a delicate, crisp shell infused with the flavour of butter, clarify 100g unsalted butter (see page 101) and trickle over the potatoes in place of the olive oil. Unlike olive oil, the butter should liberally swamp the potatoes. Turn and baste several times during cooking.

**Everyday Roast Potatoes:** If you want a milder flavour than olive oil or butter, go for cold-pressed rapeseed oil rather than vegetable oil, as the latter will have been refined.

### Parboil the potatoes
Bring a large pan of salted water to the boil and preheat the oven to 190°C fan/210°C electric/gas 6½. Add the **potatoes** to the pan and cook for 8 minutes. Drain into a sieve or colander and leave for a minute or two to steam-dry.

### Roughen the surface **
Return the potatoes to the pan and roughly shake from side to side, tossing them in the air until they appear textured and floury on the surface. You can be as rough as you like without the risk of them breaking up.

Tip the potatoes into a large roasting pan and trickle over some **olive oil**, without drowning them – they certainly shouldn't be sitting in a pool of it. Scatter over some **sea salt**.

### Roast the potatoes
Roast in the oven for 1 hour, turning them halfway through. For the best results, settle your tray of potatoes on the top shelf of the oven; if they go below the roast it will likely steal their thunder. Cook until evenly gold all over, the colour of a crisp. If you are roasting them at the same time as a joint, they may need a little longer than this. Equally if you are roasting at a slightly lower temperature, you can turn it up while the joint is resting.

### The knack
* **What size chunks?** Small roasties tend to be crispier than large ones. For the best results, cut them somewhere in between the size of a clementine and a large walnut.

** **Shaking the parboiled potatoes in the pan** to roughen the surface is the secret to a crisp shell. Hence the need for maincrop, which are guaranteed to be nice and floury.

# Sautéed Potatoes

Serves **3–4** / Start to Finish **1 h 15 m**

Given the right loving attention in the pan you should end up with lots of tantalisingly golden crispy bits as well as big silky slices. A combination of butter and olive oil gives an especially good flavour, but you could use olive oil alone, lard or goose fat if you prefer. This method is an endlessly useful way of using up any leftover boiled potatoes.

salad or waxy potatoes such as Charlotte – 600g, scrubbed

unsalted butter – 25g

extra virgin olive oil – 1 tablespoon

sea salt, black pepper

garlic clove – 1, peeled and finely chopped

flat-leaf parsley – 2 tablespoons, finely chopped

**Boil the potatoes**
Bring a large pan of salted water to the boil, add the **potatoes**, bring back to the boil and cook for about 15 minutes until tender when pierced with a knife. Drain into a colander, leave to cool and then slice 0.5–1cm thick.

**Sauté the potatoes**
Heat the **butter** and **oil** in a large non-stick frying pan over a low heat and sauté the potatoes for about 20 minutes, turning them every few minutes, until they are evenly golden and crisp, **seasoning** them a few minutes into cooking. Five minutes towards the end, add the chopped **garlic**. Sprinkle over the chopped **parsley**, toss to distribute and serve straight away.

# Oven-roasted Chips with Rosemary & Thyme

Serves **4–6** / Start to Finish **1 h 20 m**

Great for feeding the masses where sautéed potatoes would take up too many pans and too much attention. For a steak lunch or supper with friends, these answer the call for something in the shape of chips.

large waxy potatoes such as Charlotte – 1.2kg, peeled

thyme – 10 sprigs

rosemary – 5 small sprigs

lemon – finely grated zest of 1, plus 1 tablespoon juice

extra virgin olive oil – 2 tablespoons

unsalted butter – 40g

sea salt, black pepper

**Chip the potatoes and assemble**
Preheat the oven to 180°C fan/200°C electric/gas 6. Slice the **potatoes** lengthways 1cm thick, and then cut into thick chips. Arrange in a large roasting pan with the **thyme, rosemary** and **lemon zest**. Drizzle over the **olive oil** and **lemon juice**, dot with the **butter** and **season**.

**Roast the chips**
Cover the pan with foil and roast in the oven for 25 minutes. Loosen the chips with a spatula and give them a stir, and then return them to the oven to roast, uncovered, for a further 45–55 minutes until deliciously golden and caramelised. Give them another stir 10–15 minutes before the end.

# Roasted Sweet Potatoes with Middle Eastern Elixir

Serves **4** / Start to Finish **45 m**

They might look like potatoes, but sweet potatoes have more in common in terms of flavour and texture with a pumpkin or squash, only sweeter. So much so that any aside needs to be carefully gauged – I would go for something salty, such as ham or bacon, or a relatively austere meat like lamb or chicken. Alternatively just wallow in them as a vegetarian offering, as suggested below.

The Middle Eastern elixir is an all-purpose blend. Fab drizzled over simple green salads with avocado, or roasted veg (see page 244), or served alongside grilled and roasted meats – beef, lamb and chicken – or fish.

small orange-fleshed sweet potatoes – 1.2kg, peeled and quartered lengthways (halved if long)

extra virgin olive oil – 5 tablespoons

onion seeds – 1 level tablespoon

sea salt, black pepper

large red onions – 2, peeled, halved and thinly sliced

watercress – 2 handfuls, washed (optional)

For the Middle Eastern elixir

lemon juice – 3 tablespoons

runny honey – 2 teaspoons

large garlic clove – 1, peeled and crushed to a paste

medium-hot red chilli – 1 heaped teaspoon, finely chopped

ground cumin or coriander – ⅓ teaspoon

sea salt

extra virgin olive oil – 6 tablespoons

flat-leaf parsley – 3 tablespoons, finely chopped

**Roast the sweet potatoes**
Preheat the oven to 220°C fan/240°C electric/gas 9. Toss the **sweet potatoes** in a large bowl with 3 tablespoons **olive oil**, the **onion seeds** and some **seasoning**. Tip into a large roasting pan that will hold the potatoes in a crowded single layer and roast for 30–40 minutes, stirring halfway through.

**Roast the red onions**
Meanwhile toss the **onion slices** in a large bowl with 2 tablespoons oil, spread out on a baking sheet and roast for 15–17 minutes until golden and caramelised, stirring halfway through.

**Make the dressing**
Whisk the **lemon juice**, **honey**, **garlic**, **chilli** and **spice** with some **salt** in a small bowl, and then add the **olive oil**. Shortly before serving, stir in the **parsley**. (Avoid adding the parsley too far in advance or it will dull in flavour and colour.)

**Combine the ingredients and dish up**
To serve, mix the onions into the sweet potatoes and drizzle over the dressing. Transfer to a large serving bowl or platter and top with a pile of fresh **watercress** (if using).

# Hasselback Roasties

Serves **6** / Start to Finish **1 h 10 m**

I frequently cook these out in Normandy – partly because we have the biggest bay tree you have ever set eyes on in the garden, and partly because it is one of the best ways of roasting a waxy-fleshed potato; the French don't go in for maincrops, so classic roasties are off the agenda.

extra virgin olive oil – 5 tablespoons

medium waxy potatoes such as Charlotte – 1.2kg

fresh bay leaves – handful

sea salt, black pepper

unsalted butter – 20g

**Prepare and roast the potatoes**
Preheat the oven to 190°C fan/210°C electric/gas 6½. Drizzle 3 tablespoons **oil** over the base of a large roasting pan that will hold the potatoes in a single layer. Cut a thin slice off the bottom of each **potato** so that it sits flat. Finely slice each potato downwards to within about 1cm of the base – if you aim to cut halfway down there's a little leeway if you cut too far. If the **bay leaves** are small, you can slip them into the middle of each potato, otherwise scatter them in amongst them halfway through cooking. Drizzle over 2 tablespoons oil, season with **salt and pepper** and dot with the **butter**. Roast in the oven for 1 hour until golden top and bottom, basting them halfway through.

# Boulangère Potatoes

Serves **6** / Start to Finish **1 h 30 m**

Traditionally French villagers took advantage of the cooling communal bread oven to bake this dish of potatoes, hence the name. Its *raison d'être* is the gorgeously golden crusty top layer. Without the cheese and cream of a Gratin Dauphinois (see page 218), many is the time its lighter profile is welcome.

extra virgin olive oil

medium onions – 4, peeled, halved and thinly sliced

maincrop potatoes such as Maris Piper – 1.2kg, peeled and thinly sliced

sea salt, black pepper

chicken or lamb stock – 300ml *

you will need a 2 litre gratin dish, approx. 32cm in length

**Fry the onions**
Preheat the oven to 180°C fan/200°C electric/gas 6. Heat 2 tablespoons **olive oil** in a large non-stick frying pan over a medium heat, add half the **onions** and fry for 6–8 minutes, stirring occasionally, until silky and lightly golden. Remove from the pan and set aside on a plate while you cook the remainder in the same way.

**Assemble the gratin**
Arrange one-third of the **potatoes** over the base of the ovenproof dish, season with **salt and pepper** and smooth half the onions on top, then repeat. Arrange a final layer of potatoes on the surface, press everything down with your hands, and pour the **stock** evenly over the top to half cover them. Season and cover the gratin with foil.

**Bake the gratin ***
Bake for 45 minutes. Then turn up the oven to 200°C fan/220°C electric/gas 7 and remove the foil. Drizzle the surface generously with oil and cook for a further 25 minutes until golden on top.

The knack

* **For a particularly delicious version:** Make with leftover gravy, thinned with boiling water, in place of the stock. (Always worth storing leftover gravy in the freezer for this purpose.)

** **Crisping the surface:** If serving with roast lamb or chicken, you can always turn up the oven while the meat is resting in order to colour the top.

# Gratin Dauphinois

Serves **6–8** / Start to Finish **1 h 20 m**

If a bacon sarnie is the undoing of many a veggie, then this has to be the apple to lure a Low Carb Eve – golden and gooey on top and crisp in the corners below. Nothing like as rich as the majority of variations of this classic that involve buckets of cream or milk, this one still ticks all the boxes – tender layered potatoes infused with butter, garlic and thyme.

maincrop potatoes such as Maris Piper – 1.2kg *

unsalted butter – 50g, melted

garlic clove – 1, peeled and finely chopped

thyme leaves – 2 teaspoons (optional)

sea salt, black pepper

double cream – 4 tablespoons

Gruyère – 150g, grated

you will need a 20 x 30cm gratin dish or shallow ovenproof dish of an equivalent size

## Variations

**To accompany lamb:** Replace the thyme with finely chopped rosemary.

**For a lighter gratin:** Replace the butter with olive oil.

**Step up the garlic:** Layer the potatoes with fine slivers.

**Vary the cheese:** Replace the Gruyère with Emmental, Abondance or Comté. These all melt well and will return to being just as gooey if reheated.

**Slice the potatoes and mix with the butter and herbs**
Preheat the oven to 180°C fan/200°C electric/gas 6. Peel and slice the **potatoes** as thinly as possible – you can use the slicing attachment on a food processor. Toss these in a bowl with the melted **butter**, **garlic**, **thyme** (if using) and **seasoning**.

**Assemble and bake the gratin**
Tip the potatoes into the dish and press them level using your hands – don't worry about neat overlapping slices, a rustic take on this gratin is just as alluring. Cover tightly with foil and bake for 50 minutes or until the potatoes are tender when pierced with a knife.

**Crisp up the top**
Turn the oven up to 220°C fan/240°C electric/gas 9. Drizzle the **cream** over the potatoes and scatter over the **cheese**. Return the gratin to the oven for a further 15–20 minutes until the cheese is golden and bubbling. (If you wish, you can tip the corner of the dish and pour off any excess melted butter.)

The gratin can be reheated in an oven at 200°C fan/220°C electric/gas 7 for 20 minutes.

The knack

* **Which potatoes?** If you use maincrop potatoes such as Maris Piper or Desiree, the starch helps the slices to adhere into a thick cake. Waxy types such as Charlotte will give an equally tender gratin, but the slices will remain separate and more defined.

# Essential Rice

## Perfect Plain Rice

Serves **6 \*** / Start to Finish **35 m**

Given the prevalence of stodgy rice, it's good to know that perfection is so readily achieved with this 'two-to-one' method. No need for scales to be involved, simply use double the amount of water to rice. Supper for two? Fill a standard mug with rice by about two-thirds and add twice the volume of water. User-friendly, this rice will stand around for longer than the allocated 20 minutes if you're not quite ready to eat.

basmati rice – 400g

water – approx. 750ml \*\*

Maldon sea salt – 1 teaspoon

**Rinse and boil the rice**
Place the **rice** in a large bowl, cover plentifully with cold water and set aside to soak for 30 minutes. Drain into a sieve and rinse well under the cold tap. (If you are short of time you can skip the soaking step and simply rinse the rice instead.) Place in a medium-sized saucepan with a little under double the volume of **water** and the **salt**. Bring to the boil, skimming off any foam that rises to the surface, and simmer for 8–9 minutes until the liquid has been absorbed.

**Cover and leave to stand**
Clamp on a lid, turn off the heat and set aside for 20 minutes to dry out, then fluff up the rice with a fork.

**The knack**

\* **Doubling up:** Always worth cooking up extra plain rice to turn into egg-fried rice (see right).
\*\* **Adding flavour:** Chicken or vegetable stock will give a tastier rice than water, and you could always perfume it with herbs – such as bay, thyme or rosemary – or whole spices such as saffron, cardamom, cinnamon or cloves.

## Egg-fried Rice

Serves **2** / Start to Finish **10 m**

A big easy and favourite in our house. All the more reason for cooking up plenty of the Perfect Plain Rice (see left).

basmati rice – 125g, cooked as for Perfect Plain

medium eggs – 2

sesame oil – 1 tablespoon

sea salt, black pepper

vegetable oil – 1 teaspoon

slim spring onions – 4, finely sliced

**Stir-fry the rice with the eggs \***
Fluff the cooked **rice** using a fork. In a small bowl, whisk the **eggs** with the **sesame oil** and some **seasoning**. Heat the **vegetable oil** in a wok or large non-stick frying pan over a medium heat. Add the eggs and then straight away add the rice, stirring brusquely to coat. Fry for 2–3 minutes, turning occasionally, and then remove from the heat and stir in the **spring onions**.

*Serving suggestion*
— Fry a couple of handfuls of diced roast ham in a drop of oil until crispy and stir into the finished egg-fried rice.

**The knack**

\* **Speed:** This stir-fry is typical of the whizz-bang nature of Asian cooking, where you need to have everything at the ready because it is all done and dusted within a couple of minutes.

# Pilau Rice

Serves **4** / Start to Finish **50 m**

This is Perfect Plain Rice with added bling, by way of aromatics, whole spices, herbs and the like. It's a great fallback to have in the fridge, especially if you have children and are in need of frequent healthy offerings. From its most basic incarnation, when it makes a lovely aside to a curry that is a tad more glam than plain rice, there are a myriad of ways of dressing it up.

basmati rice – 250g

groundnut or vegetable oil – 3 tablespoons

shallots – 4, peeled and thinly sliced

raw cashew nuts – 50g

cinnamon stick – 1

green cardamom pods – 8, smashed

cloves – 4

black peppercorns – 10

bay leaves – 2

lemon zest – 2 strips, removed with a potato peeler

chicken stock or water – 450ml

Maldon sea salt – 1 teaspoon

black pepper

**Rinse the rice and prepare the pilau base**
Soak the **rice** as opposite. Heat the **oil** in a medium-sized saucepan over a medium heat, add the **shallots, cashews, spices, bay leaves** and **lemon zest** and stir-fry for 3–5 minutes until lightly coloured. Stir in the rice, pour in the **stock** and season with **salt and pepper**.

**Cook the rice and then set aside to stand**
Bring to the boil, skimming off any foam that rises to the surface, and simmer for 8–9 minutes. Clamp on a lid, turn off the heat and set aside for 20 minutes to dry out. To serve, fluff up the rice with a fork. Remove the aromatics as you are eating.

## Variations

**Rice Salad:** Set aside to cool and then stir in some chopped leafy herbs, spring onions, olives, capers or gherkins. Dress with olive oil and lemon juice.

**Retro Risotto:** A stir-fry or old-fashioned risotto is a good way of making odds and ends in the fridge spread. Fry up some lardons or diced chorizo, a few cooked green beans, a punnet of wild mushrooms and some slivers of leftover roast chicken. Add the leftover pilau rice and stir-fry until heated through. Serve with toasted almonds and chopped flat-leaf parsley or coriander, and accompany with a dollop of chutney or chilli sauce.

**Kedgeree:** Stir-fry some cooked leftover pilau rice with some cooked smoked haddock (see page 172) and stir in some chopped coriander. Serve scattered with salted nuts and chopped boiled egg.

# Stove-top Saffron Risotto

Serves **4** / Start to Finish **35 m**

On the louche side of decadent with way more butter and Parmesan than the food police would ever sanction, the star here is the pinch of saffron filaments that both scent and dye the rice.

Lovely with any beef stew (and for that matter roast chicken), but never better than when it is eaten on its own, with a crisp green salad to follow.

saffron filaments – approx. 30 *
boiling water – 1 tablespoon
chicken or vegetable stock –
1.2 litres (see page 24)
sea salt and black pepper
unsalted butter – 100g
medium onion – 1, peeled and
finely chopped
risotto rice (e.g. Carnaroli or
Vialone Nano) – 300g
dry white wine – 150ml
Parmesan – 100g, freshly grated,
plus extra to serve

### Variation

**Lemon Risotto:** Omit the saffron. Stir the finely grated zest of 2 lemons, 2 tablespoons lemon juice, 50g freshly grated Parmesan and 2 tablespoons double cream into the finished risotto. Finally add 100g grated Emmental, 3 tablespoons finely chopped flat-leaf parsley and a generous grinding of black pepper.

### Prepare the saffron
Grind half the **saffron filaments** in a pestle and mortar and blend with the **boiling water**, then stir in the remaining whole filaments.

### Put the stock on to simmer **
Bring the **stock** to the boil in a small saucepan, season to taste with **salt and pepper** and keep it at a simmer at the back of the stove, half-covered with a lid to stop it evaporating.

### Prepare the risotto base
Heat half the **butter** in a medium-large saucepan over a medium heat and fry the **onion** for several minutes until it is glossy and relaxed, without colouring. Add the **rice** and stir for a minute or two until it is translucent and coated in the butter.

### Gradually add the simmering stock
Add the **wine** and saffron liquor. Once this has been absorbed, turn down the heat to low and start to add the chicken stock a ladleful at a time, stirring and making sure it has been absorbed before you add the next one. At no stage should the rice be flooded, but at the same time care must be taken that the rice doesn't dry out to the point where it sticks. The risotto should take 20–25 minutes to cook once you start to add the liquid.

### Finish the risotto and dish up
Remove the pan from the heat while the grains still have some resistance, leaving it on the sloppy side as it will continue to absorb the liquid. Stir in the **Parmesan** and the remaining butter, taste for seasoning and serve on warm plates with a little extra Parmesan sprinkled over.

### *Serving suggestions*
— Scatter over some roasted veggies at the end – peppers and onions are especially good (see pages 245–6).
— Stir through a dollop of pesto at the end (see page 190).
— Add 125g diced mozzarella, or other fonduesque cheese such as Emmental, at the end and leave for a few minutes to melt.

**Stove-top Risotto**

### The knack

* **Which saffron?** For a full-on hit that combines saffron's golden hue and its honeyed scent, use both filaments and ground. If you're in a hurry, opt for ground saffron.

** **Adding the stock:** The stock needs to be boiling when it is added to the rice, otherwise it stops the cooking process every time you add more. Care must be taken with each addition that the rice doesn't dry out to the point where it sticks, hence the need to stir it frequently when you're cooking risotto on the hob. (If you haven't got the patience to keep stirring, you can always opt for the oven risotto on page 224 instead.)

# Oven-baked Tomato & Herb Risotto

Serves **4** / Start to Finish **50 m**

Cooked traditionally, a risotto demands you hover attentively by the stove for some 20 minutes, adding a little more boiling stock to the rice each time it is absorbed. It is worth learning how to cook it properly (see page 222), even if you are forgiven for opting for this oven-baked cheat's version thereafter. This one, made with tomatoes and masses of herbs, is perfect summer fare.

## For the risotto

chicken or vegetable stock – 1 litre (see page 24)

unsalted butter – 25g

medium onion – 1, peeled and finely chopped

beefsteak tomatoes – 800g, skinned (see page 18) and coarsely chopped

risotto rice (e.g. Carnaroli or Vialone Nano) – 300g

dry white wine – 150ml

saffron filaments – approx. 25, ground and blended with 1 tablespoon boiling water

sea salt, black pepper

Parmesan – 100g, freshly grated, plus extra to serve

## For the herb purée

mixed fresh herbs (e.g. flat-leaf parsley, basil and mint) – 50g, roughly chopped

extra virgin olive oil – 6 tablespoons

### Prepare the risotto
Preheat the oven to 170°C fan/190°C electric/gas 5. Bring the **stock** to the boil in a small saucepan. Melt the **butter** in a large cast-iron casserole over a medium heat and fry the **onion** for a few minutes until translucent. Add the chopped **tomatoes** and cook for a few minutes longer, stirring frequently until they start to become mushy. Add the **rice** and cook for 1–2 minutes, stirring to coat it in the butter and flavourings. Add the **wine** and continue to cook until it has all been absorbed. *

### Cook the risotto
Add the **saffron** liquid, pour in the hot stock and season with plenty of **salt and pepper**. Bring to the boil, cover the pan with a lid and cook in the oven for 25 minutes.

### Make the herb purée
Meanwhile place the **herbs** and **olive oil** in a food processor and blitz to a smooth purée.

### Dish up
Just before serving, stir the grated **Parmesan** into the risotto, dollop the herb purée on top and fold over a few times to streak it. Serve with extra Parmesan to hand around.

The knack

* **Making the risotto in advance?** If you wish you can prepare the risotto to this point in advance.

# Butternut Squash Quinotto with Pomegranate

Serves **4** / Start to Finish **50 m**

This is a lovely light risotto made with quinoa, an exquisitely delicate and highly nutritious grain. Lighter than other risottos, with no cheese, it's halfway to a pilau but slips down that much more easily being on the soupy side.

extra virgin olive oil – 1 tablespoon

1 x 700g butternut squash, peeled, halved lengthways and cut into 1cm slices (seeds discarded)

sea salt, black pepper

unsalted butter – 50g

medium onion – 1, peeled and finely chopped

garlic cloves – 2, peeled and finely chopped

fennel seeds – 1 teaspoon, coarsely ground

quinoa – 300g

dry white wine – 150ml

chicken or vegetable stock – 1.2 litres (see page 24)

cinnamon stick – 1

bay leaf – 1

lemon juice – generous squeeze

pomegranate – 1, seeds only (see page 150)

flat-leaf parsley – 5 tablespoons, coarsely chopped

**Fry the squash**
Preheat the oven to 180°C fan/200°C electric/gas 6. Heat the **olive oil** in a large non-stick frying pan over a medium heat. Add enough **squash** to cover the base of the pan (you will probably need to do this in two goes), **season** and colour well on both sides. Transfer to a bowl and set aside.

**Prepare the risotto base**
Heat half the **butter** in a large cast-iron casserole over a medium heat and fry the **onion, garlic** and **ground fennel seeds** until glossy and relaxed, stirring occasionally. Add the **quinoa** and stir for a minute until you hear it popping. Pour in the **wine** and, once it has been absorbed, add the squash and give everything a good stir. Pour in the **stock**, add the **cinnamon stick** and **bay leaf**, and season with salt and pepper. Bring to the boil, and then cover and cook in the oven for 25 minutes until the quinoa is just tender – the risotto should still be on the wet side.

**Dish up**
Stir in the remaining butter with the **lemon juice** and taste for seasoning. Combine the **pomegranate seeds** with the **parsley** and scatter over the quinotto at the last moment.

# Nada's Bulgar & Tomato Kibbeh

Serves **4–5** / Start to Finish **25 m**

If the potential downside of grains and pulses is their tendency towards stodge, this Syrian recipe for *Kibbeh al-hammam* from the Lebanese cookery writer Nada Saleh overwhelmingly refutes that reputation. With a creamy base of bulgar and tomatoes, smothered with chopped parsley and pomegranate seeds, it can be made well in advance, which makes for easy entertaining, and it will stand in for any of the usual carb offerings. I first tasted this as part of a pre-Christmas buffet that Nada had prepared, and it had us all going back for seconds and thirds.

onion or banana shallot – 100g, peeled and finely chopped

extra virgin olive oil – 4 tablespoons

tomato purée – 1 heaped teaspoon

fine bulgar – 170g *

water – 3 tablespoons

ripe tomatoes – 650–700g, skinned (see page 18) and finely chopped

sea salt

pomegranate syrup – 2 tablespoons

flat-leaf parsley – handful, coarsely chopped

spring onions – 2, trimmed and finely sliced

pomegranate – 1, seeds only (see page 150)

**Prepare the onion base**
Place the **onion, olive oil** and **tomato purée** in a medium-sized bowl and stir to blend.

**Prepare the bulgar**
Place the **bulgar** in a mixing bowl, sprinkle with the **water** and stir. Cover with the **tomatoes** and generously season with **salt**. Spoon the onion mixture over the tomatoes, drizzle over the **pomegranate syrup** and stir to combine. Using your fingers and palms knead the mixture, crushing the nibs of tomato until well-blended.

**Dish up**
Give the mixture a stir, transfer it to a shallow serving dish and smooth the surface. Scatter over the **parsley, spring onion** and **pomegranate seeds**. Leave to stand for at least 30 minutes. The kibbeh can also be prepared several hours in advance, in which case loosely cover and set aside in a cool place. Any leftovers will be delicious the following day.

*Serving suggestion*
— Spoon the kibbeh into Little Gem lettuce leaves and serve as an appetiser or as finger food.

The knack

\* **Fine bulgar:** Middle Eastern delis will stock coarse bulgar (Nada spells it burghol) for pilau and serving like rice, and fine bulgar for making kibbeh. The coarse variety is the norm in most supermarkets, however you can give this a whizz in an electric coffee grinder or mill. You're after the consistency of coarse granulated sugar.

# Vegetables

9

# About **Veg**

### Shopping tips

It will always be more satisfying to buy and cook vegetables that are locally produced, with which we have an innate connection. Seasons for individual vegetables seem to stretch with every year, but we are all aware of the sense of bounty in the shops when a vegetable is 'in season'; it may well be on offer too. Unlike with meat and fish, where you should be very wary if it is discounted, a glut of any one vegetable that has forced the price down generally means it is at its best.

Always go for loose over bagged: you can choose what you want, checking it in the process; it won't have suffered the indignity of plastic wrapping; and frequently it will be less expensive. Always avoid 'prepped' veg; you will end up having to trim the ends of those beans all over again. The majority of stir-fry mixes are only fit for the compost heap: try to buy the freshest of beansprouts instead, and combine them with freshly sliced vegetables of your choice.

If the organic looks better, fine, but I have never found there to be a radical difference in quality. And if it's misshapen, give it a home; the conformity enforced by major supermarkets makes for the most appalling waste.

### Storage advice

Vegetables like to breathe, so if they come plastic wrapped, at the very least open this up. The ideal environment is cool and airy. I store my veg in a couple of wire mesh apple baskets, kept well away from sunlight. And I transfer anything ripening too quickly to the bottom drawer of the fridge.

### Preparation

You can prepare a stir-fry mix or sliced vegetables such as carrots and courgettes up to about a day in advance, but as a rule of thumb do this as close to the time of cooking as possible to avoid them browning and drying out (see page 241).

### COOKING TIPS

The five methods to keep close to heart when considering how to cook any one veg are boiling, braising, stir-frying, grilling and roasting.

### Boiling

Sometimes very lightly boiled veg are exactly what we are after to serve alongside a slow-cooked dish or a roast with lots of gravy. But boiled vegetables are also the gateway for including in other composite dishes.

*Method:* Bring a pan of water to the boil over a highish heat, big enough to give the vegetables plenty of space, and season with sea salt. I use a coarse sea salt for this, and by adding a good dose this has a real effect in bringing out the flavour of the vegetable. Add the prepared vegetables and bring back to the boil, then turn the temperature down to a simmer and cook until they are just tender. For roots, this is when a knife can be inserted with ease; green veg such as beans should be only just tender or very slightly under-cooked – it is best to remove one and bite or cut into it. Drain the veg either into a sieve or a colander, and leave to steam-dry for a few minutes if serving them hot. If you are serving the veggies cold, plunge them into a sink or large bowl of cold water in order to stop the cooking.

*To serve:* If serving hot, dot the veg with good salted butter, ideally a Norman or Breton one that is laced with sea salt crystals, and sprinkle over some grated Parmesan or chopped flat-leaf parsley if you wish. Alternatively, you can drizzle over a good extra virgin olive oil and season with a sprinkling of sea salt. You can also squeeze over a little lemon juice, or drizzle over a few drops of balsamic vinegar.

## Braising
This goes one step beyond boiling. By cooking the vegetables in just a small amount of liquid, you concentrate the flavour of the juices, while retaining the sweetness and character of the vegetables. If you wish you can add in some aromatics, or herbs at the end, and naturally include either a little olive oil or butter when cooking.

## Stir-frying
Stir-fries are a brilliant means of making use of endless tasty odds and ends, not least any lost and lonely vegetables in the basket or salad drawer. Stir-fries are very much a supper for small numbers; an average-sized frying pan or wok will only be able to cope with enough for one person, but given the speed of cooking this is easily scaled up to two.

## Grilling
Ridged griddles have transformed the potential for how we cook many of our fallback veggies. Delicate vegetables such as courgettes, mushrooms, spring onions and tomatoes can be cooked from raw, while harder ones such as asparagus, long-stem broccoli and sweetcorn benefit from being lightly boiled first. As a rule of thumb, if you would happily eat the vegetable raw, grill them uncooked, however if you would normally cook them, they will probably need blanching before griddling.

## Roasting
Year on year we seem to discover more vegetables that are great roasted, latterly cauliflower and broccoli. So think beyond the Italianate classics such as peppers, courgettes and aubergine (as well as potatoes and parsnips), and if in doubt, give it a whirl. The majority of veggies enjoy a lively heat of around 190°C fan/210°C electric/gas 6½ (a few even higher). Drizzle with a lick of olive oil and scatter over a handful of aromatics such as whole unpeeled garlic cloves, thyme and rosemary sprigs and bay leaves. Season with salt and pepper, naturally, and if you wish splash over a few drops of balsamic vinegar at the end.

# Essential Veg: Boiled & Braised

## Glazed Carrots

Serves **6** / Start to Finish **30 m**

Hard to think of a better way of making a star out of this humble root, these braised carrots are meltingly tender and sweet, so totally different to boiled carrots. You will never turn back.

large carrots – 800g, trimmed, peeled, halved if large and thickly sliced

chicken or vegetable stock, or water – 125ml

unsalted butter – 40g, diced

Maldon sea salt – 1 level teaspoon

caster sugar – 1 level teaspoon

flat-leaf parsley – 2 tablespoons, finely chopped (optional)

**Assemble the ingredients in a saucepan**
Place the **carrots** in a medium-sized saucepan with the **stock** (or **water**), **butter**, **salt** and **sugar**.

**Cook the carrots and dish up**
Bring the liquid to a simmer, and then cover and cook over a low heat for 8 minutes. Give the carrots a stir, turn the heat up and cook them uncovered until all the liquid evaporates and they are glossy and coated, approx. 8 minutes, stirring occasionally. Stir in the **parsley** (if using) and serve.

### Variation

**Glazed Carrots with Feta:** Stir 100g coarsely crumbled feta into the carrots immediately before serving. Cover and leave to stand for a few minutes to allow the cheese to soften.

## Cauliflower Mash with Watercress & Hazelnut Pesto

Serves **6** / Start to Finish **40 m**

Mash doesn't have to mean potatoes, although this treatment of streaking the lily-white purée with pesto is also great with mashed spuds.

**For the mash**

cauliflower florets – 1kg

soured cream – 100g

sea salt, black pepper

freshly grated nutmeg

**For the pesto**

watercress – 30g, plus a few leaves to serve

extra virgin olive oil – 4 tablespoons

roasted chopped hazelnuts – 15g

Parmesan – 15g, freshly grated

**Make the cauliflower mash**
Bring a large pan of salted water to the boil, add the **cauliflower** and cook for about 15 minutes until tender. Drain into a colander, leave to steam-dry for a few minutes and then whizz to a purée in a food processor with the **soured cream**, **salt**, **pepper** and **nutmeg**. You may need to do this in batches.

**Whizz up the pesto**
While the cauliflower is cooking, whizz the **watercress**, **olive oil**, **nuts** and a little salt in a food processor to a textured purée. Add the **Parmesan** and briefly whizz again. The recipe can be prepared to this point in advance.

**Combine the mash and pesto**
If necessary, reheat the mash and transfer it to a serving dish. Spoon the pesto on top and fold over a few times until streaked with green. Scatter over a few watercress leaves if you wish.

# White Wine & Butter Leeks

Serves **4** / Start to Finish **40 m**

A Jane Grigson classic that can't be bettered when it comes to a simple dish of leeks to serve with a roast, chop or pie. The wine fuses with the butter into a decadent sauce that coats the vegetable, its acidity challenging that slightly bland sweetness. The texture? Heaven, pure silk.

leeks – 700g, washed *
unsalted butter – 50g
dry white wine – 150ml
sea salt, black pepper

**Prepare the leeks**
Trim the root off each **leek** and cut off the dark green shoots. Remove the outer layer of leaves and rinse the surface. Cut the leeks into slices 5mm thick and rinse well in a sieve.

**Braise the leeks**
Place **all the ingredients** in a medium-sized saucepan. Bring the liquid to the boil, cover the pan with a lid, and cook over a low heat for 25–30 minutes. Remove the lid. The leeks should be coated in a buttery sauce. If there is any liquid remaining, turn up the heat and continue to cook until it has all evaporated.

# Perfect Peas

Serves **4** / Start to Finish **10 m**

Braising fresh peas renders them buttery and perfectly seasoned, where boiling tends to drain their character. Cook them this way whether you want an aside, or to include them in another dish such as a frittata.

unsalted butter – 25g
Maldon sea salt – ½ teaspoon
caster sugar – ½ teaspoon
water – 3 tablespoons
shelled fresh peas – 350–400g

**Cook and serve**
Place the **butter**, **salt**, **sugar** and **water** in a medium-sized saucepan. Bring this to a simmer over a high heat, and once the butter has melted add the **peas**. Cook, tossing or stirring constantly, for 2–3 minutes. They will turn a beautiful luscious green. Drain into a sieve and serve immediately.

**Variation**
**Minted peas:** Braise the peas with a couple of sprigs of fresh mint.

The knack

\* **Washing the leeks:** Many leeks are so clean it is hard to believe they have ever seen a field. But for those with soil clinging, having trimmed them, slit the top and fan the leaves under the tap to get rid of any soil. No amount of rusticity allows for grit.

## Braised Cabbage with Cumin

Serves **4–6** / Start to Finish **30 m**

Braising and stir-frying cabbage are my preferred routes for Savoy and white cabbages. They also roast beautifully.

Savoy cabbage – 1

cumin seeds – ⅓ teaspoon

extra virgin olive oil – 2 tablespoons

dried chilli flakes – small pinch

sea salt

water – 3 tablespoons

**Prepare the cabbage and cumin**
Trim the base and remove the outer leaves from the **cabbage**. Cut into quarters, remove the core, and then finely slice the leaves. Give the **cumin** seeds a light pounding using a pestle and mortar to break them up.

**Fry the cabbage**
Heat the **olive oil** in a large saucepan over a medium heat, add the cumin and **chilli** and give it a stir. Add the cabbage, season with **salt** and stir-fry for a couple of minutes until glossy.

**Steam the cabbage**
Add the **water**, clamp on a lid and cook over a low heat for 15 minutes, or until the toughest parts are tender, stirring halfway through.

**Variation**

**Braised White Cabbage with Nutmeg:** Melt 30g unsalted butter in a large saucepan over a medium-low heat, add the finely sliced cabbage, season with sea salt, black pepper and a generous grating of nutmeg and fry for 5–10 minutes until relaxed and lightly coloured, stirring frequently.

## Cavolo Nero with Garlic, Ginger & Chilli

Serves **6** / Start to Finish **25 m**

Other spring greens (and also kale) will be equally lovely cooked this way.

cavolo nero – approx. 500–600g, stalks cut out and leaves thickly sliced

sesame oil – 2 tablespoons

groundnut oil – 1 tablespoon

garlic – 1 tablespoon, finely chopped

fresh root ginger – 1 tablespoon, finely chopped

medium-hot red chilli – 1 tablespoon, finely chopped

lemon juice – 2 tablespoons

sea salt

spring onions – 6, trimmed and thickly sliced

**Cook the cavolo**
Bring a large pan two-thirds full with salted water to the boil. Add the **cavolo nero** and cook for 3 minutes, pushing it down now and again. Drain into a colander, press out the excess water using a wooden spoon and return to the pan.

**Prepare the dressing**
Heat 1 tablespoon **sesame oil** and the **groundnut oil** in a non-stick frying pan over a medium heat. Add the **garlic**, **ginger** and **chilli** and cook briefly until the garlic is just starting to colour. Remove from the heat, stir in the **lemon juice** and a little **salt** and pour over the cavolo nero, tossing to coat.

**Fry the spring onions and dish up**
Heat the remaining tablespoon **sesame oil** in the frying pan over a medium heat and fry the **spring onions** until softened and lightly coloured. Spoon over the cabbage in a serving dish.

# Buttered Spinach

Serves **6** / Start to Finish **20 m**

Spinach loves to be spoilt with copious amounts of butter; like scrambled eggs it seems to get better with every knob it absorbs, and you can add up to double this amount if the health regime allows. Buttered spinach is especially good with chicken or fish – grilled, roasted or laced with olive oil, lemon, herbs and spices. It also makes a sublime supper in the company of a poached egg.

spinach leaves – 900g, picked over

unsalted butter – 50g

sea salt, black pepper

freshly grated nutmeg

**Wash and steam the spinach in a covered pan**
Wash the **spinach** thoroughly in a sink of cold water. Shake the leaves dry and place them in a large saucepan, cramming it down to get it all in. Cover with a tightly fitting lid and cook over a medium heat for 10–15 minutes or until the spinach has completely wilted, pressing it down halfway through.

**Drain the spinach**
Drain into a sieve and press out as much liquid as possible using a potato masher. Be thorough about this; it is a constant source of amazement just how much water this vegetable contains.

**Melt the butter and reheat the spinach**
Melt the **butter** in the saucepan with some **seasoning** and **nutmeg** over a medium-low heat. Once the butter is seething, add the cooked spinach and stir to coat. Heat through and serve. The spinach can be reheated but will lose its lovely bright green sheen.

# Sesame Spinach

Serves **4** / Start to Finish **20 m**

Despite its Oriental profile, this mélange of flavours is surprisingly adept at swinging both sides of the East/West divide – perfect with shredded ham hock (see page 126), roast pork belly (page 120) or roast chicken (page 82).

spinach leaves – 500g, picked over

toasted sesame seeds (see page 278) –
a sprinkling, to serve

**For the dressing**

sesame oil – 1 tablespoon

light or dark soy sauce – 1 ½ tablespoons

lemon juice – 2 teaspoons

ginger juice – 1 teaspoon *

caster sugar – 1 teaspoon

**Cook the spinach**
Bring a large pan of water to the boil. Add the **spinach**, bring back to the boil and cook for 1 minute. Drain into a sieve and press out as much water as possible using a potato masher, then return the spinach to the saucepan.

**Make the dressing and toss**
Whisk together **all the ingredients for the dressing** and toss with the spinach. Transfer to a serving bowl. Serve hot or at room temperature, scattered with **sesame seeds**.

**The knack**
* **Ginger juice:** To make ginger juice, cut a 2cm knob of root ginger into pieces and press through a garlic press to extract the juice.

# Green Beans in a Tomato & Chilli Sauce

Serves **4** / Start to Finish **40 m**

This is surprisingly accommodating towards slightly mealy green beans, the ones that are a little plumper than you might want were you eating them plain with a lick of butter.

extra virgin olive oil – 2 tablespoons

shallots – 4, peeled and finely chopped

garlic cloves – 2, peeled and finely chopped

medium-hot red chilli – 1 teaspoon, finely chopped

cherry tomatoes – 300g, halved

sea salt, black pepper

dry white wine – 50ml

green beans – 400g, stalk ends trimmed, halved if long

flat-leaf parsley – coarsely chopped, to serve (optional)

**Prepare the sauce**
Heat the **olive oil** in a medium-large saucepan over a medium heat and fry the **shallot** for about 5 minutes, stirring frequently, until softened and lightly coloured. Add the **garlic** and **chilli** just before the end. Add the **tomatoes, season** and continue to cook for a minute or two until these start to soften. Add the **wine** and bring to the boil.

**Add the beans and cook**
Add the **beans** and stir to coat them. Bring to a simmer, and then cover and cook over a low heat for 15–30 minutes depending on their size until just tender, stirring halfway through. Turn the heat up to medium-high and cook, uncovered, until the beans are coated in a rich sauce. Serve hot or cold, scattered with **parsley** if you wish.

# French Beans with Crispy Lardons

Serves **4** / Start to Finish **20 m**

This is one step up from serving French beans very simply with a knob of butter, a dish I am forever turning to in order to glam up roast chicken or pan-fried fish.

unsmoked lardons – 100g

shallots – 2, peeled and finely chopped

dry white wine – 5 tablespoons

unsalted butter – 25g

black pepper

fine French beans – 500g, stalk ends trimmed

**Prepare the sauce**
Bring a large pan of salted water to the boil. Meanwhile heat the **lardons** in a small non-stick frying pan over a medium heat until the fat renders, and then continue to cook for 6–8 minutes until crisp and golden, stirring occasionally, and adding the **shallots** a few minutes before the end. Pour in the **wine** and simmer until almost evaporated, then whisk in the **butter** and season with **black pepper**.

**Boil the beans and mix with the sauce**
Add the **beans** to the boiling water and cook for 3–4 minutes or until just tender; drain into a sieve and return them to the pan. Spoon the contents of the frying pan over the beans and toss to combine.

# Lentils with Fennel & Watercress

Serves **6** / Start to Finish **1 h 10 m**

It does seem a shame not to hand this one to vegetarians, it is so very good served with young goat's curd on top, but there again it makes a perfect aside to any meat dish – in particular, the ham hock on page 126.

extra virgin olive oil – 6 tablespoons

garlic cloves – 4, peeled, halved and sliced

medium onion – 1, peeled and finely chopped

leeks – 3, trimmed and finely sliced

fennel bulbs – 3, base trimmed, stalks and outer sheath removed, finely diced

Puy lentils – 500g

water – 1.7 litres

thyme sprigs – 6, tied with string

bay leaves – 2

sea salt, black pepper

flat-leaf parsley – 50g, roughly chopped

watercress – 2 bunches (approx. 150g), roughly chopped

**Fry the vegetables and lentils**
Heat 3 tablespoons **olive oil** in a large saucepan over a medium heat and fry the **garlic, onion, leeks** and **fennel** until glossy and relaxed. Add the **lentils** and stir-fry for a minute or two to coat them in the oil and flavourings.

**Braise the lentils and dish up** *
Pour in the **water**. Add the **thyme** and **bay leaves**, bring to a simmer and cook for 50 minutes, adding a little more water if the lentils appear dry. By the end they should be a coherent mass rather than separate, but definitely not mushy. Just before serving, **season** generously and stir in the remaining olive oil along with the **parsley** and **watercress**.

*Serving suggestion*
— Serve with a dollop of young goat's curd (approx. 250g).

The knack

* **Avoid salting the water when cooking lentils** or it will toughen them. Instead you should season them when dressing.

# Stir-fry Supper

Serves **1** / Start to Finish **10 m**

The answer to so many suppers, when you're feeling pushed and haven't planned, and haven't shopped, and a quick scout around the kitchen renders a lone red pepper, half a punnet of mushrooms, and a head of broccoli that you really should use up. Not to mention those scraps from the Sunday roast.

groundnut oil – 1 tablespoon

sesame oil – 1 teaspoon

Stir-fry Essential – 1 teaspoon *

stir-fry vegetables of your choice, (see below) – 250g (prepared weight) **

Add-ons of your choice – (optional, see below)

coriander – coarsely chopped, to serve

dark soy sauce, to serve

**Vegetable contenders:**

beansprouts

broccoli – cut into tiny florets

button mushrooms – finely sliced

cabbage (white or green) – cut into fine slices 3–4cm long

carrots – peeled and finely sliced

cauliflower – cut into tiny florets

courgettes – finely sliced

mangetouts – cut into long thin strips

pak choi – trimmed and thinly sliced

peppers (red and/or yellow) – cut into 3–4cm wide strips and finely sliced (core and seeds discarded)

spring onions – finely sliced

**Add-ons (optional) – per stir-fry**

150g leftover roast chicken, guinea fowl or duck – shredded

150g leftover roast pork or beef – cut into thin strips 2–3cm long, or 1cm dice

75g ham – cut into thin strips 2–3cm long

100g raw or cooked shelled king prawns

150g straight-to-wok noodles

### Preheat the wok or frying pan

If you have a wok (see page 14), all to the good, but if you don't then you want your largest frying pan for the task, 24cm or bigger. Heat the pan over a high heat for several minutes.

### Stir-fry the vegetables

Add the **groundnut** and **sesame oil**, and then the **Stir-fry Essential**, spreading it over the base. Immediately add all the **veggies** (and **prawns** if using them raw), and stir-fry for 3–4 minutes, turning them over every 10–15 seconds. After 2 minutes, add any **cooked meat** and **noodles** (if using).

### Dish up

Serve scattered with plenty of fresh **coriander**, accompanied by a bottle of **dark soy sauce**.

### The knack

* **Stir-fry Essential (Serves 6, allow 1 teaspoon per stir-fry):** Finely chop 20g peeled garlic cloves, 20g peeled fresh root ginger and 20g fresh medium-hot red chillies (seeds removed) in a food processor, scraping down the sides as necessary. Spoon into a small bowl, cover the surface with a layer of vegetable oil and chill in the fridge for up to 3–4 days.

** **Selecting and preparing the vegetables:** Avoid supermarket mixes; they are almost always browning at the edges and past their best. The majority of veggies can be used here, providing they are cut finely enough, but they do need to be prepared within about one day of using them. The quickest route to slicing many vegetables is to use a food-processing attachment. For the best results, think about combining at least 3–4 different varieties (see vegetable contenders, left, for ideas).

# Homemade Pot Noodle

Serves **4** / Start to Finish **20 m**

Even when the cupboard is in a Mother Hubbard state, the chances are we can still amass the necessary for a stir-fry. This version is also delicious with leftover roast chicken, shredded and stirred in.

medium egg noodles – 175g

shelled fresh peas – 200g

mangetouts – 150g, ends trimmed and cut into long thin strips

groundnut oil – 1 tablespoon

garlic cloves – 3, peeled and finely chopped

fresh root ginger – 1 teaspoon, finely grated

medium-hot red chilli – 1, core and seeds removed, finely chopped

spring onions – 6, thinly sliced

sea salt, black pepper

fresh flat-leaf parsley or coriander – 3 tablespoons, finely chopped

light soy sauce, to serve

### Cook the noodles and blanch the vegetables

Bring two medium-sized pans of salted water to the boil. Add the **noodles** to one, give them a poke to break them up and boil as directed on the packet; drain into a sieve and rinse briefly under cold running water. Add the **peas** to the other pan and boil for 2 minutes, adding the **mangetouts** after 1 minute; drain into a sieve and rinse briefly under the cold tap.

### Heat the oil in a wok or large frying pan

Heat the **groundnut oil** in a wok or large non-stick frying pan over a medium-high heat for several minutes. It is essential that your pan is hot enough before you add the veggies, otherwise they will end up stewing.

### Add the aromatics and stir-fry the vegetables

Add the **garlic, ginger** and **chilli** and stir-fry momentarily until sizzling and fragrant. Put in the drained cooked noodles and fry for about 1 minute, turning them occasionally. Add the cooked mangetouts and peas along with the **spring onions** and stir-fry for a further 2 minutes, lightly seasoning with **salt and pepper**. Remove the pan from the heat and stir in the **parsley or coriander**. Serve with **light soy sauce**.

# Essential Veg: Roasted

## Roast Aubergines

Serves **6** / Start to Finish **45 m**

This way of roasting aubergine slices in the oven is so much easier than charring them whole by hovering over an open flame or grill. Meltingly tender and addictively chewy and caramelised on the outside, these make a great healthy snack, served either hot or cold.

aubergines – 3 (approx. 700g), cut into 1cm slices (ends discarded) *
extra virgin olive oil, for brushing
sea salt, black pepper

**Brush the aubergine slices with oil**
Preheat the oven to 190°C fan/210°C electric/ gas 6½. Lay the **aubergine** slices out on a couple of baking sheets and brush with **olive oil** on both sides. **Season** the top.

**Roast the aubergine**
Roast for 20 minutes, and then turn and cook for a further 15–25 minutes until golden – the lower sheet may need longer than the top. Loosen with a spatula and serve hot or cold.

*Serving suggestions*
— Serve in a salad with chopped tomato, shallot and parsley, dressed with extra virgin olive oil.
— Use thick roast slices as the base for a little salad, including chopped tomato, shallot and feta, or some Quinoa Tabbouleh (see page 272).

**The knack**
* **Slicing the aubergine:** Thinly sliced aubergine makes for the crispiest, golden slices. You can slice them up to 3cm thick, in which case they need about 25 minutes cooking after turning.

## Roast Beetroots

Serves **6** / Start to Finish **55 m**

Roasting beetroot in this fashion has taken over from boiling. Just a little balsamic or lemon juice is all that is needed to balance their sweetness.

small beetroots – 700g
rosemary sprigs – 4
extra virgin olive oil – 4 tablespoons, plus a little extra to serve
lemon – juice of 1
garlic cloves – 3, peeled and crushed to a paste
sea salt, black pepper

**Prepare the beetroots**
Preheat the oven to 220°C fan/240°C electric/ gas 9. Trim the shoots of the **beetroots** to within 1cm of the top, leaving the whiskery tail intact, and give them a good scrub. Place them in a large bowl. Pull off half the **rosemary needles** and scatter these and the twigs over the beetroots. Toss with 4 tablespoons **olive oil**, the **lemon juice, garlic** and some **seasoning**.

**Roast the beetroots and dish up**
Tip into a roasting pan and roast for 30–40 minutes until the skins are golden and puffy and the insides tender, turning them halfway through. Leave to stand for about 10 minutes. To serve, trim the top and bottom off the beetroots, and cut into wedges or slices. Place in a serving bowl and drizzle over the roasting juices and a little more oil. Serve hot or cold.

*Serving suggestions*
— Scatter over some crumbled feta and coarsely chopped flat-leaf parsley.
— Serve with smoked fish (e.g. mackerel, salmon or eel), and accompany with horseradish sauce (see page 113).

# Roast Onions

Serves **6** / Start to Finish **45 m**

A wardrobe essential. Layer these with burgers in buns, toss them slightly warm into salads, scatter them over soups (great in lieu of croûtons), or wherever you want a tasty little frill to finish a dish. Over a beef stew? Lovely. Equally over veggie mash.

red onions – 900g, peeled, halved and thinly sliced

extra virgin olive or vegetable oil, for coating

red wine vinegar or lemon juice – 1 teaspoon

sea salt

**Arrange the sliced onions on two baking sheets**
Preheat the oven to 170°C fan/190°C electric/ gas 5. Spread out the **onions** in a thin layer over two baking sheets, separating the slices as much as possible with your fingertips.

**Roast the onions**
Drizzle over a little **olive oil** and toss to coat them. Roast for about 35 minutes, stirring halfway through to ensure they caramelise evenly. Place the caramelised onions in a bowl, and toss with a teaspoon of **vinegar or lemon juice** and some **salt**. Serve hot or warm.

# Roast Parsnips

Serves **4** / Start to Finish **1 h 10 m**

There would be an outcry in our house if these didn't appear on the Christmas table – whatever other trimmings we might forego, these are sacrosanct. The recipe comes courtesy of an old family friend, Jo Higgo. The Parmesan toasts to delectably crispy little shards that cling to the parsnips, and together they make a great combination. Don't save them for December, anytime you're roasting will do.

parsnips – 600g, trimmed, peeled, halved lengthways and cut into 2 shorter lengths

unsalted butter – 50g, melted

Parmesan – 30g, freshly grated

black pepper

**Parboil the parsnips**
Preheat the oven to 180°C fan/200°C electric/ gas 6 and bring a large pan of salted water to the boil. Add the **parsnips** to the boiling water and cook for 8 minutes; drain into a colander and set aside for a few minutes to steam-dry.

**Roast the parsnips**
Place the parsnips in a roasting pan, drizzle over the **butter** and shake from side to side to coat. Sprinkle over the **Parmesan** and season with **black pepper**. Roast for 40–45 minutes until the cheese is golden and crisp, loosening them with a spatula and basting halfway through. Serve straight away.

# Essential Veg: Roasted

## Roast Peppers

Serves **6** / Start to Finish **1 h 20 m**

The cocktail hour, a summer lunch, barbecue or picnic, these peppers are multi-tasking. Especially once you pad them out with other little eats – salami, olives, slivers of Parmesan, pickled chillies, goat's cheese and so on.

red, yellow or orange peppers – 6 *
thyme sprigs – 8–10
bay leaves – 2
extra virgin olive oil – 4 tablespoons
sea salt, black pepper
garlic cloves – 5, peeled and thinly sliced
balsamic vinegar – 1 teaspoon

**Prepare the peppers**
Preheat the oven to 190°C fan/210°C electric/ gas 6½. Cut out the core from each **pepper**, and then quarter them, discarding any seeds inside. Arrange in a crowded single layer in a roasting pan. Tuck in the **herbs**, drizzle over the **olive oil** and season with **salt and pepper**.

**Roast the peppers and cool**
Roast for 20 minutes, and then stir in the **garlic** and continue roasting for a further 30–40 minutes, stirring halfway through. By the end, the peppers should be succulent and evenly singed at the edges. Drizzle over the **vinegar**, gently stir in and set aside to cool.

The knack

* **Which peppers?** Plump bell peppers roast into particularly luscious strips, but Mediterranean Romano peppers offer a certain delicacy too. Avoid green peppers, however, which are merely unripe yellow or red peppers.

## Roast Squash

Serves **4** / Start to Finish **55 m**

Roast butternut has the edge on pumpkin, it's all those sugars that lead to tantalisingly golden caramelised edges, and the flesh within melts to an exquisite tenderness. A pan of these in the oven and you are one step away from a bowl of pasta, which is just as good eaten cold as a salad.

butternut squash flesh – 1kg (approx. 1.5kg whole)
garlic cloves – 6, unpeeled and kept whole
medium-hot red chillies – 3
bay leaves – 3
thyme sprigs – 5
extra virgin olive oil – 4 tablespoons
sea salt

**Prepare the squash**
Trim the top and base of the **squash** and halve it where the bulb meets the trunk. Cut off the skin. Quarter the bulb and remove the seeds, and then slice into wedges 1–1.5cm thick. Halve the trunk lengthways and slice this too. Alternatively, cut into 3–4cm dice.

**Roast the squash**
Preheat the oven to 200°C fan/220°C electric/gas 7. Arrange the squash in a large roasting pan, and tuck in the **garlic cloves**, **chillies** and **herbs**. Drizzle with **olive oil** and scatter over some **salt**. Roast for 45–55 minutes until golden and caramelised, turning halfway through to ensure the butternut colours evenly. Serve hot or cold.

*Serving suggestions*
— Stir some cooked pasta shells into the hot butternut and serve scattered with Parmesan.
— Fold some crumbled feta into the hot butternut and serve as a veggie main, accompanied by a green salad.

# Roast Roots with Garlic & Thyme

Serves **4** / Start to Finish **1 h 20 m**

This healthy wintery mélange will take the place of spuds, parsnips and the like.

celeriac – 500g, skin cut off and sliced into wedges 1–2cm thick

beetroot – 400g, tops and tails trimmed, scrubbed and cut into wedges

carrots – 400g, scrubbed, halved lengthways and cut into two shorter lengths

garlic – 1 head, broken into cloves

thyme – a handful of sprigs (approx. 10)

extra virgin olive oil – 4 tablespoons

sea salt, black pepper

**Prepare the vegetables for the oven**
Preheat the oven to 190°C fan/210°C electric/gas 6½. Arrange the **vegetables, garlic** and **thyme** in a large roasting pan that will hold them in a crowded single layer. Drizzle over the **olive oil,** season with **salt and pepper** and toss to coat.

**Roast the vegetables**
Roast for 70–75 minutes until golden, turning with a spatula halfway through. Serve hot or at room temperature.

*Serving suggestions*
— For a meat-free supper, dress them up with olives, feta and cooked spelt (see page 280) or quinoa (see page 272).
— Combine with peppery leaves and serve as a wintery salad.

# Griddled Corn with Lime & Chilli Butter

Serves **6** / Start to finish **25 m**

These griddled corn cobettes come at the recommendation of our lovely food stylist, Nicole Herft, true to her Australian roots, and are ideal for those outdoor summer barbies. They make a great aside to any spicy line-up such as the Tex Mex Fajitas on page 136, but it could be the Peking-style duck on page 88 or the Hip Ham Hock on page 126 or some other leisurely feast.

sweetcorn cobettes (½ cobs) – 6

salted butter – 50g

lime zest – ½ teaspoon, finely grated

medium-hot red chilli – 1 level tablespoon, finely chopped

fresh coriander – 2 tablespoons, finely chopped

**Boil and griddle the corn**
Bring a large pan of water to the boil, add the **corn** and cook for 5–8 minutes until tender, then drain into a colander and leave for a few minutes to steam-dry. Heat a griddle over a high heat and grill the corn for a few minutes on either side until a few of the kernels blacken.

**Make the flavoured butter**
Gently melt the **butter** in the corn pan, and then stir in **all the remaining ingredients**. Add the grilled corn back to the pan and stir to coat with the butter. Transfer to a serving plate and drizzle over the remainder.

# Essential Veg: Griddled

## Griddled Broccoli

Serves **4** / Start to Finish **30 m**

I buy tender stem broccoli on pretty much every visit to the supermarket. It's delicious boiled and cooled for dunking into taramasalata and guacamole, and healthier than a piece of bread. You can also build it into a salad. This way of grilling it is one step on from boiling, and has the edge in luxury.

tender stem broccoli – 400g, trimmed
extra virgin olive oil – 2 tablespoons
sea salt, black pepper

**Blanch the broccoli**
Bring a large pan of salted water to the boil, add the **broccoli** and cook for 3 minutes; drain into a colander and leave for a few minutes to steam-dry.

**Grill the broccoli**
Heat a ridged griddle over a medium heat. Toss the broccoli in a large bowl with the **olive oil** and some **seasoning**, and grill in two or three batches for 2–3 minutes on each side until golden, turning it using tongs. Leave to cool. Serve hot or cold.

*Serving suggestion*
— Mix some halved and sliced dates into the cold broccoli, with some lamb's lettuce. If you wish you can drizzle over a herb purée made by whizzing 10g each of coriander and basil with 3 tablespoons extra virgin olive oil, a squeeze of lemon and a little salt in a food processor.

## Griddled Courgettes

Serves **6** / Start to Finish **30 m**

Courgettes are on the austere side eaten raw, whereas grilling them releases their sweetness and relaxes their texture. Like roast peppers, these are a great all-rounder, whether you want to serve them as an appetiser, build them into a salad, or as an aside to grilled meat or fish.

courgettes – 4, ends trimmed or removed and cut into long thin strips
extra virgin olive oil
sea salt, black pepper

**Grill the courgette slices in batches**
Heat a ridged griddle over a medium-high heat. Brush the **courgette** slices with **olive oil** on one side and season with **salt and pepper**. Arrange in a single layer on the hot griddle, oiled-side down. Grill for 3–5 minutes until striped with gold, and then brush the top side with oil and turn and grill on this side too. Set aside on a plate while you grill the rest. Serve hot or at room temperature.

*Serving suggestions*
— Mix some toasted pine nuts or olives into the cold grilled courgettes.
— Combine them cold in a salad with chopped tomatoes and finely chopped shallot or sliced spring onion.

# Mini Halloumi-stuffed Peppers

Serves **6** / Start to Finish **1 h 10 m**

These multi-tasking stuffed peppers will keep any vegetarians happy at a Tex Mex gathering, and any spare will do as an aside for others. They are also great for those in-betweeny drinks, where you want more than a bowl of crisps without going the full way of dinner. Add some salami, olives and skinny artisanal bread sticks or wafer-thin bread into the line-up.

mini peppers – 600g

halloumi – 250g

feta – 100g, finely crumbled

extra virgin olive oil –
2 tablespoons, plus extra to drizzle

pickled chillies (e.g. Fragata) – 30g,
thinly sliced

mint leaves – 2 tablespoons, coarsely
chopped

lime wedges, to serve

### Deseed the peppers
Slice the top off the **peppers**, and then nick out the seeds from the hollow by running a sharp knife around the rim to detach them. Give the lids a gentle tap on the worksurface to dislodge any loose seeds. Keep the peppers and lids paired as you go.

### Make the filling and stuff the peppers *
Coarsely grate the **halloumi**, chopping any stubborn ends that remain, and place in a large bowl. Add the **feta, olive oil, chillies** and **mint** and stir to combine. Stuff the peppers with this mixture, pressing it down well using your thumb. Replace the lids and arrange the stuffed peppers in a roasting pan with the lid propped against the side in order to hold it in place. (The peppers can be prepared to this stage several hours in advance, in which case cover and chill them.)

### Roast the peppers
Preheat the oven to 240°C fan/260°C electric/gas 9. Drizzle a little oil over the peppers and roast for 20–30 minutes or until patched with gold. Serve straight away while the cheese is gooey, accompanied by **lime wedges.**

The knack

* **Leftover filling?** It is hard to give an exact quantity of filling for the peppers, which may differ in volume. Any leftover mixture can be sprinkled into a salad or inside an omelette.

# Gratin of Chicory with Roquefort & Figs

Serves **6** / Start to Finish **20 m**

I was first introduced to this dish by a friend, Alex Beard, and it has become one of those recipes that I turn to again and again as the solution to a starter in relaxed company, since it takes no time to throw together and can be popped into the oven while a roast is resting.

Belgian chicory heads – 9
(preferably a mixture of red and white)

extra virgin olive oil – 4 tablespoons

Roquefort – 225g, diced

dried figs – 9, stalks trimmed and thinly sliced

**Combine the ingredients**
Preheat the oven to 220°C fan/240°C electric/gas 9. Trim the base of the **chicory heads**, discarding any damaged outer leaves. Separate out the remainder and toss them in a bowl with the **olive oil** and gently mix in the **Roquefort** and **figs**.

**Roast in the oven**
Tip into a large roasting pan and roast for 10–12 minutes until the chicory is golden on top, and the cheese is melted and gooey.

*Serving suggestion*
— Accompany with Parma ham.

# Cauliflower Cheese with Tomatoes

Serves **6** / Start to Finish **30 m**

This is an update on a retro fave, altogether sprightlier with its herbs, tomatoes and Lancashire cheese. Despite the apparent indulgence of the white sauce, it is not an unhealthy dish. As ever, a bottle of Worcestershire sauce on the table is essential. Dish it up with a salad of lamb's lettuce or pea shoots, and it makes a great meat-free supper.

cauliflower florets – 700g (approx. 1 large or 2 small)

unsalted butter – 50g

plain flour – 45g

whole milk – 500ml

bay leaf – 1

Dijon mustard – 1 tablespoon

sea salt, black pepper

Lancashire cheese – 150g, crumbled

flat-leaf parsley, basil and chives – 2 tablespoons of each, finely chopped

Parmesan – 50g, freshly grated

small cherry tomatoes on the vine – 250g

vegetable oil – 1 tablespoon

you will need a 20 x 30cm gratin dish (or an ovenproof dish of an equivalent size)

**Boil the cauliflower**
Bring a large pan of salted water to the boil, add the **cauliflower** and simmer for 10 minutes until tender; drain into a colander.

**Make the white sauce**
Meanwhile melt the **butter** in a medium-sized, non-stick saucepan over a medium heat. Add the **flour** and cook the roux for about 1 minute until floury in appearance and seething nicely. Remove the pan from the heat and gradually work in the **milk** using a wooden spoon, just a little at a time to begin with. Return the sauce to the heat and bring to the boil, stirring frequently as it thickens. Add the bay leaf and simmer over a low heat for 10 minutes, stirring occasionally. Remove the **bay leaf**, add the **Dijon mustard** and give the sauce a whisk to ensure it is completely smooth and silky. Season to taste with a touch of **salt and pepper**.

**Finish the gratin under the grill** *
Towards the end of this time, preheat the grill to high and place the gratin dish underneath to warm through. Stir the cauliflower into the sauce and gently reheat, then mix in the **Lancashire cheese** and **herbs** and tip into the hot dish. Scatter over the **Parmesan**, lay the **tomatoes** on top, and drizzle over the **vegetable oil**. Set under the grill until the tomatoes are softened and starting to colour, and the gratin is golden. Serve straight away.

**The knack**
* **Grilling**: It is very difficult to bake cauliflower cheese without overcooking the vegetable, so I prefer this method where the cooked vegetable is folded into the sauce and finished under the grill.

# Salads

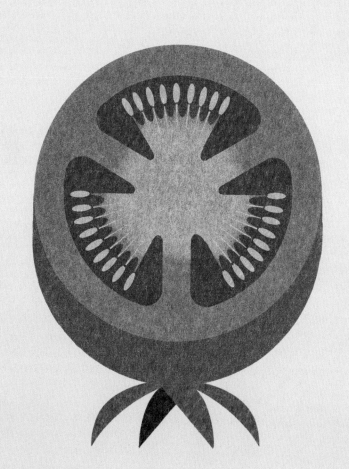

# 10

# Essential Dressings

## Barely There Vinaigrette

Serves **4–6** / Start to Finish **5 m**

One part vinegar or lemon juice to four parts oil is pleasantly sharp without being aggressive. Balsamic vinegar is especially good with slightly punchy leaves such as rocket and watercress, and equally good for dressing steamed and lightly boiled vegetables, and raw crudités.

balsamic vinegar, lemon juice or red wine vinegar – 1 tablespoon

sea salt, black pepper

extra virgin olive oil – 4 tablespoons

**How to make barely there vinaigrette**
Whisk the **vinegar** (or **lemon juice**) with a little **salt and pepper** in a small bowl, and then add the **olive oil** so they remain separate. Shake or whisk immediately before dressing the salad.

**Variations**
**With walnut or hazelnut oil:** Combine one part lemon juice to 3 parts nut oil for a really feisty nut dressing. Alternatively, mix it half and half with groundnut oil, or even less to avoid overwhelming the salad.

**With rapeseed oil:** Replace the olive oil with rapeseed for a mild, nutty savour that is more discreet than walnut or hazelnut.

## Real French Dressing

Serves **4–6** / Start to Finish **5 m**

Given to me by a chef in France, after many years of whisking up what I believed to be the ultimate dressing, this was a turning point. It wasn't simply that Louis promised he would eat salad with every meal if I smothered it with this dressing, although that did help, it was the method, which is subtly different from the way I would usually make a vinaigrette (see opposite). Today I am more likely to whisk this up than any other dressing, not least for the sheer ease.

Dijon mustard (e.g. Maille) – 1 rounded teaspoon *

sea salt, black pepper

groundnut oil – 3 tablespoons

red wine or cider vinegar – 1 teaspoon

water – 2 teaspoons

**How to make French dressing**
Whisk the **mustard** with a little **seasoning** in a medium-sized bowl, scrunching the salt if it is flaky. Whisk in the **groundnut oil**, a tablespoon at a time, until the dressing becomes thick and mayonnaise-like. Stir in the **vinegar** and then about 2 teaspoons **water** to thin the vinaigrette to the consistency of single cream.

**The knack**
* **The secret to a creamy dressing** lies with Dijon mustard, which emulsifies with the oil as you slowly whisk it in.

# House-style Vinaigrette

Serves **6** / Start to Finish **5 m**

At some point in everyone's cooking career they turn sorcerer's apprentice, and by adding a little bit of what you fancy you come up with your own family recipe. This is ours.

red wine vinegar – 1 tablespoon

grainy mustard – ½ teaspoon

Dijon mustard – ½ teaspoon

garlic clove – ½, peeled and crushed to a paste

caster sugar – 1 teaspoon

sea salt, black pepper

extra virgin olive oil – 2 tablespoons

groundnut oil – 5 tablespoons

**How to make house-style vinaigrette** *
Whisk together the **vinegar, mustards, garlic, sugar** and **seasoning** in a bowl. Gradually whisk in the **oils** until you have a light emulsified dressing.

The knack

\* **Which order to add the ingredients?** Here you whisk the vinegar with the flavourings and seasoning, which will only ever dissolve in a water-based liquid. Then you slowly whisk in the oil until you have a creamy emulsion.

# Caesar Dressing

Serves **6–8** / Start to Finish **10 m**

This is an iconic dressing that we eat endlessly in our house – voluptuous and rich, it is the consistency of single cream. Caesar dressing doesn't have to be used hand in hand with Parmesan, although this is what constitutes a classic Caesar salad and they are so very good together. If using the dressing on its own, I would use rapeseed oil or olive oil with half groundnut so that it is less assertive.

medium organic eggs – 2

garlic clove – ½, peeled and coarsely chopped

lemon juice – 2 tablespoons

Worcestershire sauce – 2 teaspoons

extra virgin olive oil – 150ml

sea salt, black pepper

**How to make Caesar dressing**
Bring a small pan of water to the boil, carefully lower in the **eggs** and cook for just 1 minute. Drain the hot water very carefully, refill the pan with cold and leave the eggs to cool for a couple of minutes.

Crack the eggs open, working over the blender as they will still be raw, and scoop out the insides using a teaspoon, including the thin layer of cooked white lining the shell. Add **all the remaining ingredients** and whizz briefly to a pale and creamy emulsion; don't overdo it. Pour the dressing into a bowl, cover and chill until required. It will keep well for a couple of days.

*Serving suggestion*
— For a basic Caesar salad, drizzle the dressing over 4 sliced crisp Romaine lettuce hearts and sprinkle with 70g freshly grated Parmesan. For a heartier salad, build in slivers of avocado, cold roast chicken, crispy bacon and sliced radishes.

# Mayonnaise

Serves **6** / Makes approx. **225g** / Start to Finish **10 m**

However tempting it is to reach into the fridge for a jar of Hellman's, the real thing is sublime. Homemade mayonnaise elevates the humblest of offerings – chargrilled burgers, lightly cooked asparagus and chicken sarnies, as well as cold crab, shell-on prawns and roast salmon if you want to raise the bar. For the savvy cook it is a time-saver for a special occasion – you can get away with making something much simpler than otherwise.

medium organic egg yolk – 1, at room temperature
Dijon mustard – 1 teaspoon *
fine sea salt – pinch
groundnut oil – approx. 220ml **
lemon juice – squeeze

## Variations

**Lower-fat Mayonnaise:** Add an additional pinch of salt at the beginning, and an additional squeeze of lemon at the end. Fold 125g fromage frais into the mayonnaise at the last moment.

**Watercress Mayonnaise:** A great aside to steak (see page 156), roast beef and fish. Heat 50g crème fraîche in a small saucepan with 50g coarsely chopped watercress. Once it starts to simmer, cover and cook for 2 minutes, and then purée in the mini bowl of a food processor. Set aside to cool, and then combine with the mayonnaise.

**Cheat's Mayonnaise:** Bottled mayonnaise is delicious in its own right, a convenience for slathering onto sarnies and burgers. But, for something a little more *soigné*, I like to blend it half and half with soured cream, which softens the effect. If you wish, you can stir in some herbs, finely grated lemon zest or mustard for added character.

**Aioli:** see page 168.

### Whisk the egg yolk with the mustard by hand ***
Place the **egg yolk** in a medium-sized bowl with the **mustard** and **salt** and whisk to blend them, ideally using a magic whisk (see page 16).

### Whisk in the oil
Add just a dribble of **oil** and whisk it in, and then another, making sure it is incorporated before adding the next. Continue adding the oil, just a dribble at a time, until you can see the sauce thickening and you are confident the mayonnaise is 'taking'.

You can now start to add the oil in bolder streams, whisking with each addition. By the end the mayonnaise should be so thick it clings to the whisk and sits in mounds in the bowl. Season it with a squeeze of **lemon juice**. (If by any misfortune the mayonnaise splits, simply whisk another egg yolk with 1 teaspoon Dijon mustard in a separate bowl and then gradually whisk in the curdled mayonnaise. With the addition of an extra yolk the consistency will be that much looser, however you can always whisk in extra oil until you reach the thickness you want.)

### Store the mayonnaise
Cover and chill until required. (If you wish you can thin the mayonnaise with a few drops of water to give a looser consistency, depending on what you are using it for.) It should keep well for a couple of days in the fridge.

The knack

* **The magic ingredient:** The secret is to include some Dijon mustard with the egg yolk at the beginning. As well as guaranteeing your mayonnaise will 'take' or thicken, as opposed to turning to vinaigrette, it provides a lovely savour.

** **Why groundnut?** Extra virgin olive oil is, for my taste, much too strong for a mayonnaise and I prefer groundnut oil. OK, you can add a splash of extra virgin just to give it that flavour – but only to taste, and at the very end.

*** **Why by hand?** Despite the many high-tech contraptions in our kitchens today, there is nothing quite like a small magic whisk for this sauce. I learnt this the hard way many years back when I was working as a lowly Commis Chef in Rowley Leigh's kitchen at Kensington Place, when I was instructed to make some mayonnaise *by hand*, he told me, as I headed in the direction of the food processor. But hey, then he turned his back, and I really couldn't see the point of wasting all that energy on something that could be done in seconds by a robot. I seem to recall he re-entered the kitchen just as my mayonnaise started to split, and such was my mortification that I have been making it by hand ever since.

# Essential Side Salads

## Green Salad

Serves **4** / Start to Finish **10 m**

Is there anything a green salad doesn't finish off to perfection? It is the great all-round aside, for roasts, grilled meat, pies and pasta. But it does have to be fresh, crisp and prepared with love. Equally so, a homemade dressing will make a star turn.

Aim for two or three different varieties of leaf:

**Something sweet** – Romaine, Little Gems, lamb's lettuce, pea shoots, baby spinach, round lettuce, oak-leaf

**Something peppery** – rocket, watercress

**Something bitter** – frisée, escarole, Belgian chicory, dandelion

#### Prepare the lettuce
Pull off and discard any tough or leathery outer leaves. Cut off the base of each lettuce and separate out the leaves. Tear or slice the leaves as wished, leaving baby ones whole. Give them a good wash in a sink of very cold water and spin in a salad dryer. Store loosely wrapped in plastic in the bottom of the fridge.

#### Toss the salad
Place the leaves in a roomy bowl and toss with just enough dressing to coat them (see pages 258–9 for recipes). You may find it easiest to dive in there with both hands, something that is ever satisfying.

## Classic Tomato Salad

Serves **4** / Start to Finish **20 m**

There are endless ways of jazzing up a classic tomato salad: add some torn buffalo mozzarella, slivers of avocado or chopped shallot. Or mix in a couple of tablespoons of coarsely chopped flat-leaf parsley, mint or basil.

Aim for a selection of two or three different varieties of tomato:

**Cherry or baby plum** – the smallest and sweetest of all

**Cocktail** – a personal favourite that is in-between a cherry and a classic round

**Plum** – lovely when they are in season and at their best

**Beefsteak** – big misshapen tomatoes in a variety of colours, which look as though they can't contain themselves, are what we are after

#### Slice or quarter the tomatoes
Cherry tomatoes excepted, cut out the core, then halve, quarter or slice the tomatoes as seems appropriate. There is a lot to be said for the safety of a serrated knife, which will grip the fruit, as opposed to a razor sharp chef's one. The jelly that surrounds the seeds harbours lots of lovely tasty acids and volatile flavours, so be sure to include these.

#### Bleed the tomatoes
Place the sliced or quartered tomatoes in a bowl, sprinkle them with salt (and a little sugar if needed) and set aside for 15–30 minutes. Effectively you are drawing out the juices and, hey presto, you have a ready-made dressing.

#### Dress the tomatoes
Arrange the tomatoes on a large shallow plate, with any juices given out, and drizzle over some olive oil.

# Mayonnaise Potato Salad

Serves **4** / Start to Finish **1 h 10 m**

A great basic, and parsley works wonders to bring it alive. Yummy with roast chicken, shell-on cooked prawns and lightly boiled eggs. It also transports well, so bear it in mind for picnics and alfresco lunches.

small waxy potatoes such as Charlotte – 750g, peeled or scrubbed

**For the dressing**

soured cream – 100g *

mayonnaise – 100g

sea salt

shallot – 1 tablespoon, finely chopped

small capers (e.g. Nonpareille) – 2 tablespoons, rinsed

flat-leaf parsley – 2 tablespoons, finely chopped, plus extra to serve

cayenne pepper (optional)

**Cook the potatoes**
Bring a large pan of salted water to the boil, add the **potatoes** and cook until tender when pierced with a knife; drain into a colander and set aside to cool. Cut into 2cm dice and place in a serving bowl.

**Make the dressing and mix with the potatoes**
Blend the **soured cream** and **mayonnaise** in a bowl with a pinch of **salt**. Stir in the **shallot**, **capers** and **parsley**. Spoon the dressing over the potatoes and toss to combine. Dust with **cayenne pepper** if you wish and scatter over some more parsley.

**The knack**
* **Soured cream:** A little soured cream mixed with bottled mayonnaise softens the edges.

# French Bean Salad with a Mustard Dressing

Serves **4** / Start to Finish **35 m**

A salad of lightly cooked French beans is effortlessly chic. They are particularly good dressed with vinaigrette, and my vote goes for a classic French dressing, mixed with a little shallot and parsley to highlight that gentle sweetness. This is one of my great suppertime fallbacks as it goes well with every meat I can think of, including cold cuts and salami.

fine French beans – 400g, stalk ends trimmed *

French dressing – 1 batch (see page 258)

medium shallot – 1, peeled and finely chopped

flat-leaf parsley – 2 heaped tablespoons, finely chopped

**Cook the beans**
Bring a large pan of salted water to the boil, add the **French beans** and cook for 3–4 minutes until just tender. Drain into a colander, refresh under the cold tap and leave to cool.

**Dress the beans**
Dress with the **French dressing** in a large bowl, and then mix in the **shallot** and **parsley**.

**Variations**
Add finely chopped chives in lieu of the shallot and parsley.
Throw in some crispy lardons.

**The knack**
* **Which beans?** The French excel at 'skinny' when it comes to beans. Think thin and avoid the slightly plumper ones, which can be mealy and tough.

# Essential Side Salads

## Speedy Pickled Cucumber

Serves **4** / Start to Finish **40 m**

This speedy pickled cucumber is great to serve
as a little aside – whether with prawn or seafood
cocktail, egg mayonnaise, pâté or cold cuts.

cucumber – 1, ends discarded, peeled and thinly
sliced

sea salt

water – 50ml

white wine vinegar – 50ml

caster sugar – 50g

**Salt the cucumber**
Place the **cucumber slices** in a large bowl,
season with **salt** and set aside for 30 minutes.
Tip into a colander, rinse well under cold
running water and return to the bowl.

**Prepare the pickling solution**
Bring the **water** and **vinegar** to the boil with
the **sugar** in a small saucepan, pour over the
cucumber and set aside to cool. Drain the
cooled cucumber in a sieve, discarding the
soaking liquor, and dry between sheets of
double thickness kitchen paper.

**Variation**
**Cucumber & Avocado Salad:** Dress the pickled
cucumber with 1 tablespoon extra virgin olive oil.
Mix in 1 heaped teaspoon finely chopped medium-
hot red chilli, 1 avocado (cut into long strips), and
1 tablespoon coarsely chopped flat-leaf parsley.

## Korean Smacked Cucumber

Serves **4** / Start to Finish **45 m**

Giving the cucumber a sharp smack is meant to
assist in taking up the flavours of the dressing.
We rather like the sheer barminess of the
procedure, whether or not this is the case.

cucumbers – 2, ends discarded

sea salt

toasted sesame seeds (see page 278) – 1 heaped
tablespoon

coarsely chopped coriander, to serve

**For the dressing**

light soy sauce – 1 tablespoon

cider vinegar – 1 tablespoon

chilli sauce (e.g. Vietnamese or Thai) –
1 tablespoon

sesame oil – 1 tablespoon

garlic clove – 1, peeled and crushed to a paste

caster sugar – 1 level tablespoon

**Prepare the cucumbers and make the dressing**
Give the **cucumbers** a hard smack on either side
using a rolling pin. Halve lengthways and cut
into slices 3–4mm thick. Toss the cucumber
in a large bowl with a little more **salt** than you
might want to season it, and set aside for 30
minutes. Meanwhile blend **all the ingredients
for the dressing** in a small bowl. Drain the
cucumber into a colander, rinse under the cold
tap and shake dry. Drain between sheets of
double thickness kitchen paper and place in a
serving bowl. (You can prepare the salad to this
point a couple of hours in advance.)

**Dress the salad**
To serve, pour over the dressing and toss to coat.
Pour off all but a little of the dressing, mix in the
**sesame seeds** and scatter with **coriander**.

# Essential Side Salads

## Everyday Couscous Salad

Serves **6** / Start to Finish **35 m**

The best couscous salads resemble a carb-rich tabbouleh (see page 272), with lots of fresh herbs, spring onions, lemon and olive oil.

couscous – 200g

boiling water – 200ml

coriander – 6 tablespoons, coarsely chopped

mint – 6 tablespoons, coarsely chopped

spring onions – 2, trimmed and finely sliced

lemon juice – 1 tablespoon

sea salt

extra virgin olive oil – 4 tablespoons

**Prepare the couscous**
Place the **couscous** in a large mixing bowl, trickle over half the **boiling water** and set aside for 10 minutes to swell. Fluff up the couscous with a fork, pour over the remaining 100ml boiling water and set aside to cool.

**Combine with the rest of the ingredients**
Mix the **herbs** and **spring onions** into the cold couscous. Whisk the **lemon juice** with some **salt** in a small bowl, and then add the **olive oil**. (You can prepare the salad to this point in advance.) Pour the dressing over the salad at the last moment and toss to serve.

**Variation**
**Party Couscous:** Make up the couscous as above, flavouring the boiled water with a pinch of saffron threads. At the end, stir in the seeds of 1 medium pomegranate, 75g shelled roasted or unroasted pistachios and the grated zest of 1 lemon. Drizzle with a little pomegranate syrup at the last moment.

## Celeriac Remoulade

Serves **6** / Start to Finish **40 m**

I am more likely to turn to celeriac remoulade than any other type of coleslaw. It is a world apart from those made with cabbage and manages to cater to every occasion – from a lunchtime snack with roast ham to an elegant starter with grilled prawns or Parma ham. We eat mounds of it in this house, not least through time spent in Normandy where it is one of the great chill-cabinet convenience foods. There is no need to make your own mayo, it actually benefits from the punch of a jar of Hellman's.

celeriac bulb – 1 (approx. 800g)

Maldon sea salt – 1 tablespoon

mayonnaise – 150g

soured cream – 50g

cider vinegar – 1 tablespoon

Dijon mustard – 1 teaspoon

flat-leaf parsley – 4 tablespoons, coarsely chopped, plus a little extra to serve

**Prepare the celeriac**
Cut the skin off the **celeriac** and coarsely grate the flesh – I use the grating attachment on a food processor. Toss with the **sea salt** in a large bowl and set aside for 20 minutes. Place the celeriac in batches in a clean tea towel and wring out as much liquid as possible, which should rid it of any browning juices. Return it to the bowl and tease the lumps with your fingers to unravel the strands.

**Mix with the remoulade and parsley**
Combine the **mayonnaise, soured cream, vinegar** and **mustard** in a medium-sized bowl, add to the grated celeriac and blend using a wooden spoon, then mix in the **parsley**. Transfer to a clean bowl, and scatter with extra parsley.

# Tuscan Tomato & Bread Salad

Serves **4** / Start to Finish **1 h**

Based very simply on good tomatoes, bread and olive oil, this salad reminds me of summer holidays in Tuscany and Umbria. After a trip to the market in the morning, it makes for the perfect lunch.

mixed tomatoes of your choice – 700g, halved, quartered or diced *

Maldon sea salt, black pepper

caster sugar – 1 teaspoon

extra virgin olive oil – 6 tablespoons, plus extra to serve

red wine vinegar – 1 tablespoon

small ciabatta – 1 x approx. 270g loaf (preferably 1–2 days old), crusts removed and torn into 2–3cm chunks **

pitted green or black olives – 100g

flat-leaf parsley – 6 tablespoons, coarsely chopped

### Bleed the tomatoes
Place the prepared **tomatoes** in a bowl, toss with a level teaspoon of **salt** and the **sugar** and set aside for 30 minutes. Drain the tomatoes into a sieve, collecting the juice in a bowl below. Add the **olive oil** and **vinegar** to the bowl with the juices.

### Soak the bread with the dressing
Place the chunks of **bread** in a large serving bowl, drizzle over the dressing a little at a time so it soaks in evenly, and set aside until it has been absorbed.

### Combine the bread and tomatoes and set aside
Toss the tomatoes with the bread and **olives**, cover the bowl with clingfilm and set aside for 30–60 minutes for the bread to soften further. Gently mix in the **parsley** at the last moment and splash over some more olive oil.

**Variation**

**Gazpacho Salad:** Add some diced cucumber, finely sliced red onions, capers and basil.

The knack

* **Mixology:** Take advantage of the many types of tomato on offer – tiny pert cherries in gold and red, slightly larger ones on the vine, plum, beefsteak, and so on – the choice is yours.

** **Which bread?** The bread needs to be a tad dry, stale is the wrong word as it implies a negative when what we want is a loaf of white bread with a sturdy crumb that is a day or two old – still good for toasting, but that little bit drier than you might want for slathering with butter and Marmite. Unsalted Tuscan bread is like this by default – dry even on day one, it seems to last forever.

# Potato Salad with Caramelised Onions, Broad Beans & Macadamia Nuts

Serves **6** / Start to Finish **1 h 10 m**

A more modern take on a classic potato salad, full of relaxed and hearty exuberance. It looks great piled high on an oversized plate, and will survive out of doors for several hours, making it perfect for picnics. It's worth making a good amount too, as any leftovers can be usefully employed in a frittata.

small new potatoes such as Charlotte or Jersey Royal – 1.2kg, scrubbed but not peeled

extra virgin olive oil – 6 tablespoons

dry vermouth or white wine – 2 tablespoons

sea salt, black pepper

shelled fresh broad beans – 300g (approx. 1kg unpodded) *

medium red onions – 4, peeled, halved and thinly sliced

chives or spring onion tops – 5 tablespoons, snipped

macadamia nuts – 100g

**Cook and dress the potatoes**
Preheat the oven to 180°C fan/200°C electric/gas 6 and bring a large pan of salted water to the boil. Halve any large **potatoes**, so they are all roughly the same size, add to the pan and boil for 20–25 minutes until tender; drain into a colander and set aside for a few minutes to steam-dry. Transfer the potatoes to a large bowl and toss with 4 tablespoons **olive oil**, the **vermouth or wine** and some **seasoning**. Set aside to cool.

**Cook and skin the broad beans**
Meanwhile bring a medium-sized pan of unsalted water to the boil. Add the **broad beans** and cook for 7–8 minutes until tender; drain into a sieve, briefly pass under the cold tap, and set aside to cool. Unless they are real babies, slip the kernels out of their skins.

**Roast the onions**
While the potatoes are cooking, toss the **onions** in a bowl with 2 tablespoons oil and spread them out in a single layer on a couple of baking sheets. Roast for 20–25 minutes until golden, giving them a stir halfway through to ensure they colour evenly. Set aside to cool.

**Assemble the salad**
Toss the roasted onions, broad beans, **chives** and **nuts** into the potatoes and transfer to a serving plate or bowl. (The salad can be prepared a couple of hours in advance, in which case cover and set aside in a cool place.)

**The knack**
\* **Broad beans:** Shelling broad beans doesn't take more than about 10 minutes, but if this seems like a task too many, then baby frozen ones can be relied upon to be small and tender.

# Quinoa Tabbouleh with Feta

Serves **4–6** / Start to Finish **45 m**

Tabbouleh is all about herbs. Try to buy them in nice big bunches, but use just the tender young leaves. The cooling fragrance of this salad is especially welcome during the summer months, which is when tomatoes are at their best. Use any type that promises to be really sweet and juicy.

quinoa – 200g

lemon juice – 3 tablespoons

water – 2 tablespoons

sea salt, black pepper

extra virgin olive oil – 8 tablespoons

young mint leaves – 15g, coarsely chopped

young flat-leaf parsley leaves – 75g, coarsely chopped

cherry tomatoes – 250g, halved or quartered depending on their size

spring onions – 6, trimmed and thinly sliced

feta – 200g, cut into 1cm dice

**Toast and cook the quinoa**
Bring a medium-sized pan of salted water to the boil. Heat a large non-stick frying pan over a medium heat, scatter the **quinoa** over the base and toast for a few minutes, stirring frequently, until it gives off a lovely warming aroma and starts popping. Transfer to a bowl and set aside to cool for a few minutes. Tip the toasted quinoa into the pan of boiling water and simmer for 15–20 minutes until tender. Drain into a sieve, return it to the saucepan, and then cover with a lid and set aside to cool.

**Make the dressing**
Whisk the **lemon juice** with the **water** and some **seasoning** in a small bowl, and then whisk in the **olive oil**.

**Combine the ingredients**
Combine the **herbs** in a large bowl with the **tomatoes**, **onions** and quinoa. (If you wish you can prepare the salad to this point up to a couple of hours in advance.) Shortly before serving, pour the dressing over the quinoa, toss to combine and then gently mix in the **feta**.

# Layered Pasta Shell Salad

Serves **4** / Start to Finish **1 h 15 m**

A pasta salad can and should be just as fresh and succulent as a hot pasta dish. The method suggested here is one that can be adapted for any pasta salad, whatever the ingredients.

medium red onions – 2, peeled, halved and thinly sliced

thyme leaves – 1 teaspoon

extra virgin olive oil – 7 tablespoons, plus extra for drizzling

sea salt, black pepper

pasta shells – 150g

baby plum tomatoes – 400g, halved

flat-leaf parsley – 7 tablespoons, coarsely chopped

pitted green and black olives – 125g

balsamic vinegar – 1 tablespoon

**Roast the onions**
Preheat the oven to 200°C fan/220°C electric/gas 7. Arrange the **onion** slices in a crowded single layer in a roasting pan, scatter over the **thyme**, drizzle over a little **olive oil** and **season**. Roast in the oven for 20–25 minutes until lightly golden, and then leave to cool.

**Cook the pasta**
Meanwhile bring a large pan of salted water to the boil, add the **pasta**, give it a stir and cook for 10–12 minutes until just tender, or as indicated on the packet. Drain it into a sieve, run cold water through it, and then return it to the pan. Toss with 1 tablespoon olive oil, which should stop the pasta from sticking together.

**Assemble the salad**
Place the **tomatoes** in the bottom of a large, deep salad bowl and season with salt and pepper. Scatter the **parsley** over, then the pasta, then the onions and finally the **olives**. (The salad can be prepared to this stage in advance, in which case cover with clingfilm and set aside in a cool place.) To make the dressing, whisk the **balsamic vinegar** with 6 tablespoons olive oil in a small bowl. Pour the dressing over the salad at the last moment and toss to coat.

# Salade Niçoise

Serves **4** / Start to Finish **40 m**

A summer weekend lunch with oodles of potential if you go to town with the tuna, tomatoes, eggs and olive oil. Accompany it with a sturdy loaf of sourdough, and use this to seamlessly move on to a course of goat's or sheep's cheese, and then some summer fruits – peaches, raspberries and apricots. Serve with a chilled rosé (a Bandol, for instance) for a little midsummer magic.

medium eggs – 4

extra virgin olive oil – 6 tablespoons

lemon juice – 1 ½ tablespoons

sea salt, black pepper

small capers (e.g. Nonpareille) – 2 tablespoons, rinsed

tuna in spring water – 2 x 200g jars or tins, drained *

salted anchovy fillets – 4, halved lengthways

ripe plum or speciality tomatoes – 3, cores cut out and cut into wedges

pitted green or black olives – 70g

rocket leaves – 70–80g

**Variation**

**Salmon Niçoise:** *Replace the tuna with fresh salmon.*

Heat a large, non-stick frying pan over a medium-high heat. Season 500g skinned salmon fillets and fry for 3–5 minutes on each side, until golden and crusty on the outside and just cooked through; there should be a slight give when you press them. (If necessary, pour off the oil halfway through.) Transfer the cooked salmon to a plate and set aside to cool before breaking into pieces.

### Boil the eggs
Bring a medium-sized pan of water to the boil, carefully lower in the **eggs** and boil for 7–8 minutes to leave them slightly wet in the centre; drain and cool in cold water.

### Make the dressing and add the tuna
Whisk the **olive oil**, **lemon juice**, some **seasoning** and the **capers** in a large deep salad bowl, with room to spare for tossing once you have layered all the ingredients. Dry the **tuna** between sheets of double thickness kitchen paper, and break into chunks or coarsely flake. Add to the dressing, and turn gently to coat.

### Finish layering the salad
Lay the **anchovy fillets** on top, then the **tomatoes** and scatter over the **olives**. Finally pile the **rocket** on top. (The salad can be prepared up to a couple of hours in advance, providing you don't toss the leaves, in which case cover with clingfilm and set aside in a cool place.)

### Dish up
To serve, shell and quarter the eggs. Gently turn the salad over a couple of times, and arrange the eggs on top.

**The knack**

\* **Which tuna?** I prefer tuna in spring water to oil, which tends to vary in quality – better to add your own olive oil. In particular, look out for French and Spanish brands.

# Puy Lentil, Chicory & Pomegranate Salad

Serves **6** / Start to Finish **1 h 10 m**

Everything in this salad is geared towards offsetting the earthy nature of lentils – crisp succulent leaves and juicy pomegranate seeds, with a sprightly nut dressing.

Puy lentils – 300g

walnut or hazelnut oil – 5 tablespoons

lemon juice – 5 tablespoons

orange – finely grated zest of 1

sea salt, black pepper

Belgian red chicory – 2 heads, base trimmed and outer leaves discarded

spring onions – 4, trimmed and cut into 1cm slices on the diagonal

flat-leaf parsley – 6 tablespoons, coarsely chopped

pomegranate – 1, seeds only (see page 150)

**Cook and dress the lentils \***
Bring a large pan of water to the boil, add the **lentils** and simmer for about 20 minutes or until tender. Drain into a sieve, briefly rinse under the cold tap and shake free of water. Tip into a serving dish and toss with the **oil**, **lemon juice, orange zest** and plenty of **seasoning**. Leave to cool.

**Toss the salad**
Shortly before serving, halve the **chicory** heads lengthways, finely slice them into thin strips and halve. Mix into the lentils along with the **spring onions**, 4 tablespoons **parsley** and half the **pomegranate** seeds. Spoon into a serving dish and scatter over the remaining parsley and pomegranate.

**The knack**
**\* Avoid salting the water when cooking lentils** or it will toughen them. Instead you should season them when dressing.

# Ratatouille

Serves **6** / Start to Finish **2 h 30 m**

For a number of years when our eldest son Rothko, who is autistic, was growing up, he wouldn't eat anything except ratatouille smothered in melted cheese. I do admire his good taste, even if it did prove a challenge at motorway service stations at three in the morning. And then one day he discovered sausages and moved on, although he has never lost his love of this dish. And neither have I.

Ratatouille is sublime with roast guinea fowl or chicken, roast lamb, grilled or roast white fish like sea bream and any barbecue – and it's a great one for entertaining, given you can make it the day beforehand. Ratatouille also makes an ideal starter, padded out with lots of little grazing goodies such as olives, fine shavings of Parmesan, salami or air-dried ham, caper berries, and rocket dressed with lemon juice and olive oil.

beefsteak tomatoes – 1kg, halved

aubergines – approx. 500g, stalk ends trimmed, halved lengthways (or quartered if large) and thickly sliced

extra virgin olive oil – 8 tablespoons, plus extra for brushing

red peppers – 4, thinly sliced lengthways (core and seeds discarded)

courgettes – approx. 500g, ends trimmed, thickly sliced

sea salt, black pepper

medium red onions – 3, peeled, halved and sliced

garlic cloves – 4, peeled and thinly sliced

flat-leaf parsley – handful, coarsely chopped

**Assemble the veggies and brush the aubergines with oil ***
Preheat the oven to 200°C fan/220°C electric/gas 7. You will need three good-sized roasting pans that will fit in the oven together. Arrange the **tomatoes** in a tight-fitting single layer in one. Brush the **aubergine** pieces with **oil** on both sides and arrange them with the **peppers** and **courgettes** in another couple of roasting pans in a crowded layer; they will shrink as they cook. Drizzle 2 tablespoons oil over the tomatoes, and about 6 tablespoons oil over the other veggies and **season** everything.

**Roast the vegetables and set aside to cool ****
Roast all three trays of vegetables for 1–1 ¼ hours, stirring the **onions** and **garlic** into the peppers and courgettes after 30 minutes. Gently stir or turn again 15 minutes later, concealing any well-coloured vegetables below the surface. Continue to roast until all the veggies are well-coloured, and then remove them from the oven and set aside to cool.

**Skin the tomatoes and combine everything**
Remove the skin from the tomatoes, nick out the hard core, and then coarsely chop the flesh using a knife and fork. Combine all the vegetables, including the chopped tomatoes, in a large serving dish and gently fold in the chopped **parsley**.

The knack

* **Brushing the aubergine slices with oil** might seem fiddly, but if you simply drizzle it over, any uncoated bits will become tough and dry.

** **Roasting method:** Ratatouille's Achille's heel is its tendency to be watery. Here the veg are roasted in the oven to drive off the moisture and concentrate their flavour. Stand well back when opening the oven door, to avoid the cloud of steam.

# Bang Bang Chicken Salad

Serves **6** / Start to Finish **1 h**

Another iconic salad – the dressing can be slathered over any salad of crisp veggies, but is especially good with chicken. Cutting the vegetables into thin strips gives this salad an ethereal air, but don't be put off if you're in a rush and can't be doing with that – just slice the vegetables any way you want.

## For the dressing

smooth peanut butter – 200g
sesame oil – 4 tablespoons
vegetable oil – 3 tablespoons
sweet chilli sauce – 2 tablespoons
lime juice – 2 tablespoons
cayenne pepper – ½ teaspoon
sea salt

## For the salad

cucumber – 1, peeled, quartered lengthways and deseeded, and then cut into thin strips 5–8cm long
medium carrots – 4, trimmed, peeled and cut into thin strips 5–8cm long
sprouting seeds or beansprouts – 100g
spring onions – 4, trimmed and cut into thin strips about 5cm long
lime juice – generous squeeze
cooked chicken – 450–500g, (i.e. 1 x 1.6kg roast chicken), shredded
toasted sesame seeds – 1 tablespoon *

### Make the dressing

Gently warm the **peanut butter** in a bowl set over a pan with a little simmering water in it, stirring occasionally until it melts. Stir in the **oils**, then the **chilli sauce**, **lime juice** and **cayenne pepper** and taste for **seasoning**. Leave to cool to room temperature.

### Combine the vegetables in a bowl

Combine all the **vegetables** in a bowl. (You can prepare everything to this point in advance, in which case cover and set aside.)

### Dress the salad **

Just before eating, toss the vegetables with a squeeze of **lime juice** and a little salt, and arrange in a pile on six serving plates. Pile the shredded **chicken** on top and drizzle the dressing over the chicken and vegetables. Finally scatter with the toasted **sesame seeds**.

---

## The knack

\* To toast sesame seeds: Heat a dry frying pan over a medium heat, scatter the sesame seeds over the base and stir constantly until pale golden brown. Transfer to a bowl and set aside to cool.

\*\* If the dressing gets too cold it will start to firm up again, in which case it can be gently rewarmed in a bowl over simmering water until it thins to the right consistency. You can treat any leftover dressing this way too.

# Roast Pepper, Spelt & Pistachio Salad

Serves **6** / Start to Finish **1 h 20 m**

This style of salad is something like a risotto in reverse – a big pan of colourful caramelised vegetables with lots of sweet roasting juices is the starting point for dressing up the spelt. Lovely summer into autumn fare.

long red Romano peppers – 7, halved lengthways and cut into wide strips (core and seeds discarded)

medium-hot red chilli – 1, cut into long thin strips (core and seeds discarded)

extra virgin olive oil – 7 tablespoons

sea salt

medium red onions – 3, peeled, halved and thickly sliced

garlic cloves – 4, peeled and sliced

balsamic vinegar – 2 tablespoons

pearled spelt – 200g

basil leaves – a handful, torn

shelled pistachio nuts – 30g

**Roast the peppers**
Preheat the oven to 200°C fan/220°C electric/gas 7. Arrange the **peppers** and **chilli** strips in a crowded single layer in a roasting pan. Drizzle over 4 tablespoons **olive oil** and season with **salt**. Roast for 40–50 minutes, stirring in the **onions** after 20 minutes, and the **garlic** after 30 minutes. By the end, everything should be nicely golden at the edges. Remove from the oven, drizzle over the **vinegar** and the remaining 3 tablespoons olive oil and set aside to cool.

**Cook the spelt** *
Meanwhile bring a large pan of salted water to the boil, add the **spelt** and simmer for 15–20 minutes until just tender. Drain into a sieve, and then return to the pan. Cover with a lid and set aside to cool.

**Combine the ingredients**
Mix the spelt into the peppers and onions, and then carefully stir in the **basil** and **pistachios**. (If making the salad in advance, add the basil close to the time of serving.)

**The knack**
* **Cooking the spelt:** You can use this method whenever you want to cook pearled spelt, either for serving hot or cold. Lovely with any salad based on roasted veg – red onions and butternut squash are particularly good (see pages 245–6).

# Puddings

II

# Essential Sweet Sauces

## Easy Chocolate Sauce

Serves **4** / Start to Finish **3 h**

Reliant on a good hot chocolate powder, this sauce is as economical as it is quick to make.

| | |
|---|---|
| hot chocolate powder (e.g. Green and Black's) – 50g | |
| whole milk – 50ml | |
| whipping cream – 50ml | |

**Prepare the sauce**
Bring **all the ingredients** to the boil in a small non-stick saucepan, whisking until smooth.

**Leave to cool and then chill**
Transfer to a small bowl, cover the surface with clingfilm, leave to cool and then chill when it will firm up to the consistency of double cream.

*Serving suggestions*
— Make a sundae with caramel ice-cream, whipped cream and crushed Oreos.
— Ladle over chocolate or vanilla ice-cream, and scatter with marshmallows and toasted flaked almonds for a Rocky Road.
— Fill meringue nests with chocolate ice-cream and drizzle with the sauce.
— Pour over toasted waffles.
— Wrap a chocolate loaf cake in foil, reheat for 25 minutes at 170°C fan/190°C electric/ gas 5 and serve drizzled with the chocolate sauce. Accompany with double cream.

## Milk Chocolate Sauce

Serves **4–6** / Start to Finish **3 h**

This luxurious sauce is silky and rich, laced with real chocolate.

| | |
|---|---|
| cornflour – 1 level teaspoon | |
| whole milk – 100ml | |
| whipping cream – 100ml | |
| vanilla extract – 1 teaspoon | |
| cocoa powder – 1 heaped teaspoon | |
| milk chocolate – 100g, broken into pieces | |

**Prepare the sauce base**
Blend the **cornflour** with a little of the **milk** in a small bowl, and then combine this with the remaining milk in a small non-stick saucepan. Stir in the **cream**, **vanilla** and **cocoa** and bring to the boil, whisking constantly until smooth and slightly thickened.

**Add the milk chocolate and whisk**
Remove the pan from the heat and add the **chocolate**. Leave for a few minutes for this to melt, and then whisk to a smooth sauce. Pour into a small bowl, cover the surface with clingfilm, leave to cool and then chill for several hours. It will keep well for several days. Stir before serving.

*Serving suggestions*
— see Easy Chocolate Sauce, left.

# Thin Vanilla Custard

Serves **6** / Start to Finish **1 h 15 m**

This custard is more formally known as *crème anglaise*. It is the consistency of pouring cream, thickened with egg yolks, and is very definitely French in its tasteful austerity. It adds finesse to any crumble or pie.

whole milk – 300ml
medium organic egg yolks – 6
golden caster sugar – 75g
vanilla bean paste or extract – 1 teaspoon
whipping cream – 150ml

**Prepare the custard and leave to cool**
Pour the **milk** into a small saucepan and bring to the boil. Whisk the **egg yolks** and **sugar** in a medium-sized bowl until creamy, and then whisk in the hot milk. Return the mixture to the pan and heat gently until you have a thin pouring custard that coats the back of the spoon. Take care not to overheat, as it will curdle if it is boiled. Pour straight away through a sieve into a large bowl. Stir in the **vanilla**, cover the surface with clingfilm and set aside to cool to room temperature.

**Whip the cream and fold in, then chill**
Whip the **cream** in a medium-sized bowl until soft peaks form using an electric whisk, and then whisk into the vanilla custard. Cover the custard and chill until required, giving it a good stir before serving. Serve hot or cold. To reheat, stir over a low heat without boiling.

# Raspberry Sauce

Serves **6** / Start to Finish **5 m**

The tart sting of raspberry makes for an especially intense sauce, so this is a good one if your raspberries fail to live up to expectations.

raspberries – 450g
icing sugar – 75g
lemon juice – 1 tablespoon

**Liquidise and then strain ***
Place the **raspberries, icing sugar** and **lemon juice** in a blender and whizz to a purée. Pass through a sieve into a bowl, and then cover and chill until required.

*Serving suggestions*
— Great for a peach melba with halved ripe peaches and vanilla ice-cream.
— Make an Eton Mess with crushed meringues, strawberries and raspberries.

**The knack**

**\* How to strain purée through a sieve:** Half fill a medium-hole sieve with the purée and, using the back of a ladle, swirl it in a circular motion around the inside of the sieve until you are left with the fibrous pulp containing the seeds, which can be discarded.

# Petits Pots au Chocolat

Serves **6** / Start to Finish **3 h 45 m**

If a chocolate mousse is dark and pitted with bubbles, *petits pots* are creamy and more in line with very rich, very thick custard. I cannot think of a silkier texture.

double cream – 225ml

whole milk – 180ml

medium organic egg yolks – 4

milk chocolate – 90g, broken into pieces

dark chocolate (approx. 50 per cent cocoa solids) – 150g, broken into pieces

vanilla extract – ½ teaspoon

you will need 6 x 150ml ramekins or other little pots, or coffee cups of a similar size

**Variations**

**Cinnamon Chocolate Pots:** Add approx. ⅓ teaspoon ground cinnamon with the vanilla.

**Make the custard**

Bring the **cream** and **milk** to the boil in a small non-stick saucepan. Meanwhile whisk the egg yolks in a medium-sized bowl until smooth. Pour the hot cream over the **egg yolks**, whisking constantly – the mixture should thicken instantly into a thin custard. Pass through a sieve into a clean bowl, cover the surface with clingfilm and set aside to cool to room temperature.

**Melt the chocolate and combine with the custard**

Gently melt the **milk and dark chocolates** in a large bowl set over a pan with a little simmering water in it. Whisk in the cooled custard in two goes and stir in the **vanilla**. Divide the chocolate mixture between six ramekins, cover and chill for several hours or overnight.

*Serving suggestion*

— Spread a heaped teaspoon of crème fraîche over the top of each little pot and decorate with a chocolate almond or coffee bean. Chill for a few hours.

# Chocolate Mousse

Serves **6** / Start to Finish **3 h 15 m**

Impossible to go wrong with chocolate mousse for pud, whatever the occasion, it touches a particular soft spot. And despite the many ways of making it, none is as delightful as the original combination of eggs and chocolate, and none as easy.

dark chocolate (approx. 50 per cent cocoa solids) – 250g, broken into pieces *

medium organic eggs – 6, separated

strong black coffee – 2 tablespoons

cocoa, for dusting

### Variations

**Boozy Chocolate Mousse:** Instead of the coffee, flavour the mousse with 1–2 tablespoons Cointreau, Calvados or Tia Maria.

**Orange Chocolate Mousse:** Instead of the coffee, flavour the mousse with 1–2 tablespoons orange juice.

**Melt the chocolate and combine with the egg yolks**
Gently melt the **chocolate** in a large bowl set over a pan with a little simmering water in it. Carefully remove the bowl and allow the melted chocolate to cool to room temperature. Stir in the **egg yolks,** followed by the **coffee.**

**Whisk the egg whites and combine with the chocolate mixture**
In another large bowl, whisk the **egg whites** until stiff peaks form using an electric whisk. Add a couple of tablespoons of the beaten egg white to the chocolate mixture and stir in. Add the remaining egg whites in two goes, folding them in as lightly as possible to avoid knocking out the air.

**Transfer the mousse to a bowl and chill**
Transfer the mousse to a serving bowl, smoothing the surface, cover with clingfilm and chill for several hours or overnight until firm. Dust with **cocoa** just before serving.

*Serving suggestion*
— Accompany with some delicate dessert biscuits.

**Chocolate Mousse**

The knack

* **Which chocolate?** Easy to get right, easy to get wrong. You need chocolate with about 50 per cent cocoa solids here; 70 per cent would be ruinous, as it will cause the yolks to seize into a claggy mass. Cocoa butter is the other desirable to look out for in the small print.

# Chocolate Fondant Puddings

Serves **6** / Start to Finish **30 m**

Fondant puddings are about as decadent (and alluring) as chocolate gets – half dense fudgy cake and half rich warm sauce.

softened unsalted butter – 75g, diced, plus extra for greasing

dark chocolate (70 per cent cocoa solids) – 300g, broken up

light muscovado sugar – 75g, plus extra for dusting

medium organic eggs – 5

plain flour – 40g, sifted

dark rum – 1 tablespoon (optional)

you will need 6 x 150ml ramekins or small coffee cups of a similar size

**Prepare the ramekins and melt the chocolate**
Preheat the oven to 180°C fan/200°C electric/gas 6, and grease the ramekins with a little **butter**. Gently melt the **chocolate** in a bowl set over a pan with a little simmering water in it. Carefully remove the bowl and allow the melted chocolate to cool to room temperature, if necessary.

**Prepare the batter**
Place the **butter, sugar, eggs** and **flour** in the bowl of a food processor and whizz to a smooth batter. Add the melted chocolate and whizz again. Finally add the **rum** (if using).

**Fill the ramekins and bake** *
Divide the mixture between the six ramekins and dust the tops with a little more sugar, using a tea strainer. Arrange the filled ramekins on a baking sheet and bake in the oven for 9 minutes until just starting to rise. There should be a thin rim of cooked cake on the outside, and a sticky river of molten goo inside. Serve straight away.

*Serving suggestion*
— Serve with crème fraîche, double cream or Vanilla Ice-cream (see page 303).

The knack

* **Preparing the puds in advance?** If you are planning a supper or dinner party, you can prepare the cake mixture a day in advance. Make up the cake mixture as above, pour into the ramekins, cover with clingfilm and chill in the fridge until needed. Increase the baking time to 11–15 minutes.

# Blackberry & Apple Crumble

Serves **6** / Start to Finish **1 h**

This recipe is particularly close to home as I write, having just come in from a wet and windy walk across the fields (at the end of our summer holiday in Normandy) with enough deep purple blackberries for a pie or crumble. The elder branches were positively dripping with berries too, so a mixture it will be.

## For the fruit

Bramley and eating apples – approx. 400g of each, peeled, quartered, cored and sliced

demerara sugar – 75g

blackberries – 375g

## For the crumble

plain flour – 150g

ground almonds – 150g *

demerara sugar – 150g **

unsalted butter – 150g, chilled and diced ***

you will need a shallow 2 litre baking dish

## Variations

Replace the apples and blackberries with 800g of the following:

**Pears:** These benefit from being tossed with 1 tablespoon sugar to draw off some of the juices, and also 1 tablespoon lemon juice to stop them discolouring.

**Plums:** These acquire a rich lushness when baked with deep crimson juices. Toss with 50g sugar and 2 tablespoons plain flour.

### Prepare the fruit

Preheat the oven to 180°C fan/200°C electric/gas 6. Combine the **apples** with the **sugar** in a bowl, and then gently mix in 300g of the **blackberries**. Tip the fruit into the baking dish.

### Make the crumble topping

Whizz **all the ingredients for the crumble** in a food processor until the fine crumbs are just starting to cling together in biscuity nibs. Be careful not to overdo this, otherwise you will end up with dough.

### Assemble the crumble

Evenly sprinkle the crumble over the fruit and then scatter the remaining blackberries on top.

### Bake

Bake in the oven for 30–40 minutes until the topping is lightly golden and the fruit is bubbling at the edges. Serve hot, 15–20 minutes out of the oven, or at room temperature.

*Serving suggestion*
— Accompany with thick cream, Vanilla Ice-cream (see page 303) or custard (see page 285).

### The knack

\* **Ground almonds:** Cutting the flour with ground almonds is the secret to a crisp and fragrant crumble. Equally you could grind some hazelnuts in an electric coffee grinder, or pistachios, and add those instead.

\*\* **Demerara sugar** makes for a crunchy finish. If you want a more delicate crumb, go for golden caster; light muscovado sugar makes for a fine brown sugar crumble topping.

\*\*\* **Always use chilled butter** for the crumble topping, rather than softened, or you will end up with biscuit dough.

**Blackberry & Apple Crumble**

# Apple Pie

Serves **4** / Start to Finish **1 h** (+ making the pastry)

Even though I am more likely to make a crumble than a pie as a spontaneous gesture, the whole ritual of making and baking a pie, and the sugar and spice nostalgia that accompanies it, encapsulates so much of what I hold dear about traditional cooking. You would be deprived not to have grown up with the occasional treat of a warm apple pie and cream for tea on a blustery day.

This isn't necessarily something to be served at the end of a hearty dinner, apple pie demands a starring role of its own. I find it most welcome during the in-between hours of breakfast, lunch and dinner, when it is a real indulgence.

sweet shortcrust pastry – 1 batch (see page 22)

plain flour – 1 tablespoon, plus extra for dusting

Bramley apples – 900g (3 good-sized), peeled, cored and sliced

light brown sugar – 125g

ground cinnamon – ½ teaspoon

lemon – finely grated zest of 1, plus juice of ½

unsalted butter – 25g

milk, for brushing

caster sugar, for dusting

you will need a 1.5 litre pie dish

### Variation

**Apple and Raisin Pie:** Soak 50g raisins in 2 tablespoons dark rum for several hours or overnight and combine with the fruit.

### Roll out the pastry

Preheat the oven to 170°C fan/190°C electric/gas 5. Allow the **pastry** to come up to room temperature for a few minutes, and then knead it until pliable. On a lightly **floured** surface, roll out two-thirds of the pastry to form a circle slightly larger than your dish. Transfer the pastry to the dish, easing it gently into the sides, and trim off the excess. Don't worry if the pastry tears and you end up partly pressing it into the dish.

### Prepare the filling

Put the **apples** in a bowl, sprinkle over 1 tablespoon **flour** and toss together. Add the **brown sugar, cinnamon, lemon zest and juice** and toss again. Tip the apples into the pie dish, arranging them evenly, and dot with the **butter**.

### Finish preparing the pie

Gather together the pastry trimmings with the remaining pastry and shape into a ball. Roll out slightly larger than your pie dish, and carefully lay over the top of the fruit. I find it easiest to wrap the pastry around the rolling pin and lift it up, as it's quite short and delicate. Press the layers of pastry together around the rim, and trim neatly, leaving 1cm for shrinkage. Crimp the edges using the tip of your finger or else the tip of a knife. If you wish, you can roll out the pastry trimmings and use them to decorate the pie with cut-out leaves or an apple, brushing the base with **milk** before laying in place. Cut several diagonal slits in the surface of the pie to allow the steam to escape and dust all over with **caster sugar**.

### Bake

Bake in the oven for 40 minutes until golden. (The pie can be reheated for 20 minutes at 160°C fan/180°C electric/gas 4.)

### Serving suggestion

— Accompany with thick cream, Vanilla Ice-cream (see page 303) or custard (see page 285).

# Sticky Toffee Pudding

Serves **6–8** / Start to Finish **45 m**

Our taste for sponge puddings may have waned, but our love of this one lives on. And being baked, rather than steamed, it is altogether friendlier – a gorgeously indulgent traybake, sticky with dates and smothered in a rich molasses sauce. If you're going to go the whole hog with this type of pudding, then why not do it in style with a river of cream?

### For the sponge

unsalted butter – 75g, diced, plus extra for greasing

pitted dates – 150g, chopped

water – 250ml

bicarbonate of soda – 2 teaspoons

light muscovado sugar – 125g

medium eggs – 2

golden syrup – 2 tablespoons

vanilla extract – 1 teaspoon

plain flour – 200g, sifted

### For the caramel sauce *

dark muscovado sugar – 100g

unsalted butter – 100g

double cream – 150ml

you will need a 27 x 18cm traybake style tin

### Prepare the tin and simmer the date mixture

Preheat the oven to 170°C fan/190°C electric/gas 5 and grease the tin with a little **butter**. Bring the **dates** and **water** to the boil in a small saucepan and simmer over a low heat for 5 minutes. Remove from the heat and stir in the **bicarbonate of soda**, which will froth up.

### Make the sponge and add the dates

Cream the **butter** and **sugar** together in a food processor, add the **eggs** one at a time, and then the **golden syrup**, **vanilla** and **flour**. Transfer the mixture to a large bowl and beat in the date mixture, half at a time.

### Bake the sponge

Pour the mixture into the prepared tin and bake for 25 minutes until the top is set and the cake is risen and shrinking from the sides.

### Make the sauce and dish up

Meanwhile heat the **sugar**, **butter** and **cream** in a small saucepan, whisking until smooth. Smooth half the sauce over the top of the hot cake and cut it into squares. Accompany with the remaining sauce for those who like lots.

*Serving suggestion*
— Accompany with thick cream or crème fraîche.

---

### The knack

* **Quick caramel sauce:** This is a clever little sauce to have up your sleeve for ice-cream, sundaes, or any other cake or sponge that is served hot. For salt caramel sauce, add a little fine sea salt to the finished sauce.

# Five-hour Rice Pud

Serves **6–8** / Start to Finish **5 h**

The sight of burly tattooed Norman men delicately eating a bowl of *teurgoule* with a teaspoon, seated alone at a table in a truckers' stopover, is what attracted me to this particular pudding. Whichever other culture thinks they have a call on rice pudding, I have never encountered the same hallowed appreciation associated with slow-cooked rice pudding as in Normandy.

Large earthernware bowls on dairy stalls at market, where it is ladled cold into tubs, are equally enigmatic. As slow-cooking goes, this one belongs in the hall of fame – a thick bank of rice pudding at the base, a creamy head of sauce on top and a thick golden skin.

short-grain rice (e.g. pudding rice or risotto rice) – 125g

golden caster sugar – 125g

orange – finely grated zest of 1

whole milk – 1.5 litres

ground cinnamon, for dusting

you will need a deep 1.8 litre ovenproof dish, such as a 20cm soufflé dish

**Variation**

**Vanilla Rice Pudding:** Omit the orange zest and replace with 1½ teaspoons vanilla extract.

**Combine the ingredients**

Preheat the oven to 120°C fan/140°C electric/gas 1. Combine the **rice, sugar** and **orange zest** in the ovenproof dish, working them with a wooden spoon to make sure the zest is evenly distributed. Slowly add the **milk**. Lightly dust the surface with **cinnamon**.

**Bake the pudding**

Bake in the oven for 5 hours until the surface is covered with a thick deep-brown skin, and the milk beneath has thickened into a thin, buff-coloured cream. Either serve hot, when it will be loose and creamy, at room temperature, or chilled, when the rice will firm up and the milk will thicken. It can also be rewarmed.

# Best Ever Cheesecake with Mango Purée

Serves **8** / Start to Finish **12 h**

Put a good New York Cheesecake on a café menu and the world will beat a path to its door. There is something about the deep creamy vanilla curd and thin pastry that implants itself in our memory. And as we graze our way around the world on cappuccinos and cakes, there is always going to be 'The One' by which we will judge all others. This is my family's version.

### For the base

plain flour – 85g, sifted

ground almonds – 40g

golden caster sugar – 50g

unsalted butter – 85g, melted

### For the filling

full-fat cream cheese – 850g

golden caster sugar – 270g

medium eggs – 2,
plus 1 extra egg yolk

whipping cream – 420ml

plain flour – 50g, sifted

vanilla extract – 1½ teaspoons

freshly grated nutmeg

### For the mango purée

ripe mangoes – 900g, approx. 3 medium or 2 large

lemon juice – squeeze

passion fruit – 4, halved

pomegranate – 1, seeds only

kiwi fruit – 2, skin cut off, halved and sliced

you will need a 24cm cake tin with a removable base, 7cm deep

**Make the base**
Preheat the oven to 150°C fan/170°C electric/gas 3. Mix **all the ingredients for the base** together in a bowl. Using your fingers, press the mixture onto the bottom of the tin in an even layer and bake for 20–25 minutes until pale gold. Set aside to cool.

**Make the filling**
Increase the oven to 170°C fan/190°C electric/gas 5. To make the filling, blend the **cream cheese** and **sugar** in a food processor. Add the **eggs, extra yolk** and **cream** and process briefly, then incorporate the **flour** and the **vanilla extract**. Carefully pour the mixture over the cooked base and liberally dust the surface with freshly grated **nutmeg**.

**Bake the cheesecake**
Bake in the oven for 1 hour until puffy around the edges and just set – it should wobble slightly if you move it from side to side.

**Mature the cheesecake overnight**
Leave the cheesecake to cool, and then run a knife around the collar. Loosely cover the whole thing with foil* and set aside in the fridge overnight. **

**Make the purée**
Cut the skin off the **mangoes**, slice the flesh off the stone and purée in a blender. Pass through a medium-hole sieve using the back of a ladle into a medium-sized bowl and season to taste with a squeeze or two of **lemon juice**.

**Dish up**
Serve each slice with a tablespoon of mango purée spooned over, the seeds of half a **passion fruit**, a few **pomegranate seeds** and some **kiwi slices**.

---

### The knack

\* **Why foil?** During the ripening process, the cheesecake needs to be able to breathe. So instead of wrapping it up tightly in clingfilm, just loosely blanket it with foil, which will protect it from staling without cutting off its air supply.

\*\* **Why can't you eat it straight away?** A baked cheesecake needs time to ripen, at least overnight. The good news is it will then keep for many days, getting better with every one.

# Tira-mi-su

Serves **6** / Start to Finish **2 h 30 m**

Italian cousin to a trifle, a mélange of cake, booze and creamy mascarpone. This one never dates – it made it through the 80s and hasn't looked back. Tira-mi-su is always a good choice for a bring-along-a-pud, as it can be made well in advance and is guaranteed a welcome.

golden caster sugar – 50g

medium organic eggs – 3, separated

vanilla extract – 1 teaspoon

mascarpone – 500g

strong black coffee – 150ml, cooled

Kahlua or Tia Maria – 75ml

sponge fingers – 200–250g

cocoa powder, for dusting

you will need a shallow 2 litre serving dish

### Prepare the mousse
Whisk the **sugar, egg yolks** and **vanilla** together in a large bowl to blend. Using a wooden spoon, beat in the **mascarpone** until smooth. In a separate large bowl, whisk the **egg whites** until stiff peaks form using an electric whisk, and then fold them into the mascarpone mixture. Smear 1–2 large spoonfuls of the mascarpone mousse over the base of the serving dish.

### Assemble the tira-mi-su
Combine the **coffee** with the **Kahlua or Tia Maria** in a shallow bowl. Dip the **sponge fingers**, a few at a time, into the coffee mixture until the sponge just starts to yield between your fingers, but is not totally sodden (otherwise the pudding will be soggy). Cover the bottom of the serving dish with a single layer of the sponge fingers, and smooth half the mascarpone mousse on top. Repeat with the remaining ingredients so you have two layers of each. Smooth the surface with a palette knife.

### Chill and dish up
Cover and chill for at least 2 hours, preferably overnight. Shortly before serving, dust the surface of the tira-mi-su with **cocoa powder** using a tea strainer or fine-mesh sieve.

# Strawberries & Cream Pavlova

Serves **6** / Start to Finish **3 h**

Strawberries, whipped cream and meringue, it doesn't matter whether you settle for the crowning glory that is a pavlova or an uppercrust Eton Mess.

### For the pavlova
large egg whites – 6, at room temperature
white caster sugar – 350g
cornflour – 1 tablespoon
white wine vinegar – 1 teaspoon

### For the sauce
strawberries – 800g, hulled
icing sugar – 40g
raspberry eau-de-vie or kirsch – 2 tablespoons (optional)
lemon juice – squeeze
double cream – 300ml
passion fruit – 3, halved

### Variation
**Chocolate Pavlova:** Make up the meringue as above, sifting over 25g cocoa powder with the cornflour. For chocolate cream, gently melt 100g milk chocolate in a bowl set over a pan with a little simmering water in it, and then cool to room temperature. Whip the cream as above, drizzle over the melted chocolate and fold over a couple of times until it appears marbled. Spoon the cream into the centre of the pavlova and scatter over some chocolate curls or shavings. (You can assemble it up to an hour in advance.)

**Make the meringue ***
Preheat the oven to 200°C fan/220°C electric/gas 7. Place the **egg whites** in a large bowl and whisk with an electric whisk until they form stiff peaks. Add the **caster sugar** a few tablespoons at a time, whisking well with each addition and allowing the meringue to thicken before adding more. Gradually whisk in the **cornflour**, and then the **vinegar**, by which time you should have a very stiff, glossy meringue.

**Bake the meringue**
Cut out a circle of baking paper about 23cm in diameter and place this on a baking sheet. Spoon the meringue onto the circle, taking it almost to the edge of the paper, and swirl the top with the spoon to form peaks. Place the pavlova in the oven, reduce the temperature to 110°C fan/130°C electric/gas ¼ and bake for 1½ hours until crusty but moussey within. Remove the pavlova from the oven, and set aside to cool.

**Make the sauce**
Place one-third of the **strawberries**, the **icing sugar**, **eau-de-vie or kirsch** (if using) and **lemon juice** in a blender and purée. Pass through a sieve into a bowl, taste and add more sugar or lemon juice as necessary. Halve or quarter the remaining strawberries if large and mix with the sauce.

**Assemble the pavlova**
Shortly before serving, carefully tip the pavlova onto its side, gently pull off the baking paper and place the meringue on a large serving plate or cake board. Pour the **cream** into a mixing bowl and whip to fluffy peaks, taking care to stop before the cream turns buttery. Spoon the cream into the centre of the pavlova, and then spoon the berries and sauce over the cream – don't worry if they trickle down the sides. Using a teaspoon, drizzle the passion fruit seeds over the top. Serve straight away.

### The knack
* **Make sure the bowl and whisk are completely dry** before adding the egg whites – even a drop of water will prevent them from thickening. Equally, the smallest amount of yolk will spoil your meringue, so carefully spoon this out should any get in.

# Vanilla Panna Cotta with Raspberries

Serves **4** / Start to Finish **½ day**

The full-on indulgence of panna cotta made with pure cream is a little OTT for my own taste, I am much more likely to eat this healthier version made using Greek yogurt. In keeping it is lily white and just as silky, and you can still drizzle it with a little liqueur.

gelatine leaves (e.g. Dr Oetker) – 2, cut into broad strips

Greek yogurt (e.g. Total) – 450g

white caster sugar – 75g

vanilla bean paste – 1 teaspoon

Cointreau or Grand Marnier – 4 tablespoons (optional)

raspberries – 125g

you will need 4 x 150ml ramekins

### Prepare the gelatine
Place the **gelatine** strips in a medium-sized bowl, cover with cold water and set aside to soak for 5 minutes; drain. Pour a few tablespoons boiling water over the gelatine and stir to dissolve.

### Make the yogurt base
Place the **yogurt** and **sugar** in a small saucepan and heat gently until the sugar dissolves, stirring constantly and taking care not to boil the yogurt. Remove the pan from the heat and stir in the **vanilla bean paste**.

### Set the panna cottas
Stir 3 tablespoons of the hot, sweetened yogurt into the gelatine, one spoonful at a time, and then stir this back in with the rest of the yogurt. Divide the mixture between four ramekins, cover the surface with clingfilm and chill in the fridge for several hours or overnight until set. (They will keep well for several days.)

### Dish up
To serve, run a knife around the edge of each cream to loosen it, and then turn it out onto a plate. Pour 1 tablespoon **Cointreau or Grand Marnier** over each cream (if using) and sprinkle over a small handful of **raspberries**.

# Blackberry Sorbet

Serves **6** / Makes approx. **900ml** / Start to Finish **1 h 20 m**

Blackberries, like blackcurrants which we so very rarely see, make for a fantastically daring deep-purple sorbet.

golden caster sugar – 150g

water – 150ml

blackberries – 900g, chilled, plus extra to serve

small edible white flower petals such as primrose, viola or rose, to decorate (optional)

**Make the sugar syrup several hours in advance**
Place the **sugar** and **water** in a small pan and bring to the boil over a medium-low heat, stirring to dissolve. Simmer gently for 3 minutes. Pour into a bowl or jug and set aside to cool to room temperature.

**Make up the sorbet solution and freeze**
Purée the **blackberries** in a blender and press through a sieve into a large bowl. Stir in the cooled sugar syrup, and then freeze according to the instructions for your ice-cream maker. Either serve the sorbet soft or as a slush straight from the machine, or freeze it in a covered container (see storage tips, opposite). To serve, scoop into small bowls and scatter over a few blackberries. Decorate with **flower petals** if you wish.

# Vanilla Ice-cream

Serves **6** / Makes approx. **900ml** / Start to Finish **2 h 30 m**

The best ice-cream consists roughly of half custard and half whipped cream, with the scales tipped in favour of the latter. Use this formula whenever you want a classic ice-cream, bearing in mind when tasting the mixture that it needs to be sweeter than normal custard.

Ice-cream is home for vanilla, and you will rarely find anything, even among the top-end ices, that will be able to compete with your own made using a whole vanilla pod.

whole milk – 300ml
medium organic egg yolks – 6
white caster sugar – 150g
vanilla pod – 1
double cream – 350ml

**Variations**

**Strawberry Ice-cream:** Omit the vanilla and liquidise the custard base with 225g strawberries and 25g caster sugar. Pass through a sieve and then combine with the cream.

**Cinnamon Ice-cream:** Follow the method above, substituting a 7cm cinnamon stick for the vanilla pod. Remove the stick prior to liquidising.

**Boozy Ice-cream:** Alcohol such as rum, whisky, brandy or fruit eaux-de-vie are lovely for flavouring ices. Stir no more than 2 tablespoons into the finished custard – any more will prevent the ice-cream from freezing.

**Make the vanilla custard**
Pour the **milk** into a small saucepan and bring to the boil. Whisk the **egg yolks** and **sugar** in a bowl until creamy, and then whisk in the hot milk. Return the mixture to the pan and heat gently over a low heat until you have a thin pouring custard that coats the back of the spoon. Keep stirring all the time and take care not to overheat the mixture or the custard will curdle. Once the custard has thickened, pour it straight away into a bowl. Slit the **vanilla pod** lengthways, cut it up and add it to the custard. Cover the surface with clingfilm and set aside to cool and infuse.

**Liquidise and chill the custard**
Liquidise the custard (vanilla pod and all) in a blender, and then pass through a sieve into a bowl. Cover the surface with clingfilm and chill in the fridge for several hours.

**Enrich the base with whipped cream and freeze \***
Whip the **cream** in a large bowl using an electric whisk until it forms soft, fluffy peaks. Whisk into the chilled custard and freeze according to the instructions for your ice-cream maker.

*Serving and storage tips*
Ice-cream is always fab served straight from the machine when it will be thick and sticky rather than scoopable. If freezing for more than a couple of hours, transfer the ice-cream to a covered container. Remove from the freezer 15–30 minutes in advance if freezing longer than a couple of hours.

The knack

\* **No-churn method:** Although you can make ice-cream without a machine by whizzing the semi-frozen mixture in a food processor, there will always be some residual ice crystals, and without incorporating any air the end product tends to heaviness. If you don't have an ice-cream machine I would opt for a 'no-churn' ice instead, such as the Oreo Ice-cream on page 304.

# No-Churn Oreo Ice-cream

Serves **6** / Makes approx. **1.1 litres** / Start to Finish **½ day**

The guilt of dishing up a retro pud that relies on a tin of condensed milk for instant results knows no bounds. And yet there is a time and place, rather too frequently in fact. This cheat is a friend for life, and will also do wonders for the confidence of the beginner. By far the easiest of ice-cream recipes.

whipping cream – 600ml

condensed milk – 250g

vanilla bean paste or extract –
1 teaspoon

Oreos – 6, cut into 1–2cm dice

**Whisk the ice-cream base** *
Place the **cream**, **condensed milk** and **vanilla** in a large bowl and whisk until it forms soft, fluffy peaks, using an electric whisk.

**Fold in the Oreos and freeze**
Fold in the **Oreos**, discarding any crumbs. Transfer to a container, seal and freeze for a good half day. (If freezing overnight, remove from the fridge 20–30 minutes in advance to allow the ice-cream to soften.)

The knack

* **Whisking the cream:** It can take some minutes for cream to start to thicken – and, if you're not careful, splatter the kitchen with tiny droplets. The trick is to use a really roomy bowl – one of those old-fashioned mixing bowls is ideal.

# Essential Fruit

## Fruit Sharing Plates

The idea of fruit salad seems horribly dated, but the call for a plate of fruit at the end of supper or lunch (or for breakfast or tea) is as strong as ever. These sharing plates make lovely grazing.

**Kiwi and pomegranate**
Skin kiwis, slice and arrange on a plate. Halve a pomegranate and press down on the skin over a bowl to extract the seeds, picking out any white pith, and scatter over.

**Pineapple and mango**
Skin the pineapple, slice into rounds, cut out the hard core and quarter the slices. Skin the mango, slice off the stone and cut into 2–3cm pieces. Arrange together on a plate.

**Orange bonanza**
Slice the skin and outer pith off a selection of oranges, clementines and satsumas using a small serrated knife. Cut across into rounds, picking out any pips, and discard any tough end slices. Pomegranate seeds are lovely scattered over, as well as hulled and halved strawberries.

**Strawberries, raspberries and blueberries**
Hull and halve or quarter strawberries if large. Arrange on a plate with an equal amount of raspberries and blueberries.

**Melon and fig**
Skin and deseed melon, and cut into thin slivers. Trim the fig stalks, halve or quarter and arrange together on a plate.

**Peaches and nectarines**
Slice into crescents on the stone, then twist to remove and arrange on a plate. Lovely with raspberries or strawberries.

*Serving suggestion*
— Drizzle over a few drops of rosewater or a tablespoon of Cointreau or fruit eau-de-vie.

## Strawberry Shots

Serves **4** / Start to Finish **3 h**

A hit of pure strawberry in jelly form, it's hard to know whether to embrace its childish fruit charm with a tube of squirty cream and some hundreds and thousands or take the restrained route of a good vanilla ice-cream. And for that reason alone this is a great one for a mixed age-group because no-one ever really grows out of jelly.

| |
| --- |
| gelatine leaves (e.g. Dr. Oetker) – 4, cut into broad strips |
| strawberries – 900g |
| golden caster sugar – 100g |
| lemon – juice of 1 |
| whipped cream, to serve (optional) |

| |
| --- |
| you will need 4 x 150ml glasses |

**Soak the gelatine**
Place the **gelatine** strips in a large bowl, cover with cold water and set aside to soak for 5 minutes; drain well.

**Make the strawberry purée**
Reserving 2 small **strawberries** for decoration, hull the remainder and cut up if large. Liquidise these with the **sugar** and **lemon juice**, and then pass the purée through a sieve into a small saucepan. Bring the strawberry purée briefly to the boil, and then pour into a measuring jug. You should have about 600ml liquid; if not, make up the amount with boiling water.

**Make and set the jelly**
Pour 3–4 tablespoons of the hot strawberry juice over the soaked gelatine and stir to dissolve, then stir in the remainder. Divide the jelly between four ramekins or little glasses and set aside to cool. Cover and chill overnight. Serve decorated with a halved strawberry in the middle, with a spoonful of **cream** if you wish.

# Salt Caramel Brownie Bites

Makes approx. **35–50** bites / Start to Finish **2 h**

Made with ground almonds rather than flour, so no loss for gluten-free seekers, these are especially dense. Serve them small and chilled with coffee, or a little larger and warm with a scoop of vanilla ice-cream (see page 303).

## For the brownies

unsalted butter – 150g diced, plus extra for greasing

cocoa powder – 75g

baking powder – 1 teaspoon

ground almonds – 150g

demerara sugar – 100g

dark chocolate (approx. 70 per cent cocoa solids) – 200g, broken into pieces

vanilla extract – 1 teaspoon

medium eggs – 4

icing sugar – 150g, sifted

## For the frosting

dark chocolate (approx. 70 per cent cocoa solids) – 50g, broken into pieces

dulce de leche or Nestlé 'caramel' – 50g

fine sea salt – pinch

water – 4–5 teaspoons

pistachios – 10g, finely chopped

you will need a 23cm square brownie tin

### Prepare the tin
Preheat the oven to 150°C fan/170°C electric/gas 3½. **Butter** the tin, and line the base and sides with baking paper, marking the corners and cutting out a square from each one so the sides sit flat.

### Prepare the dry ingredients
Sift the **cocoa** and **baking powder** into a large bowl, and stir in the **ground almonds** and **demerara sugar**.

### Melt the chocolate and whisk the eggs
Gently melt the **chocolate** and **butter** together in a large bowl set over a pan with a little simmering water in it, then stir in the **vanilla**. At the same time whisk the **eggs** and **icing sugar** in a large bowl using an electric whisk for 4–5 minutes until very pale and moussey, and several times the volume.

### Combine the mixtures and bake
Lightly fold the chocolate mixture into the eggs in two goes, taking care not to overwork it. Now fold in the dry ingredients in two goes. Transfer the mixture to the prepared tin, smoothing the surface, and bake for 30–35 minutes (i.e. longer than you might normally cook a brownie) until a skewer inserted into the centre emerges with a sticky crumb or two, but without being at all wet. Leave to cool.

### Make the frosting and drizzle over the top
Gently melt the **chocolate** with the **dulce de leche** and **salt** in a bowl set over a pan with a little simmering water in it. Stir in the **water** and beat with a wooden spoon until glossy, and a thick trickling consistency. Drizzle in spirals over the brownie and scatter with the **pistachios**. Loosely cover and chill for at least half a day, preferably overnight.

To serve, remove from the tin, peel off the paper and cut into 3–4cm squares. The brownies will keep well, covered with clingfilm and chilled, for several days.

# Chocolate Birthday Cake

Makes **1 x 20cm** cake / Start to Finish **4 h**

Allowed just one cake for those special occasions, my vote goes to Devil's Food Cake. One of the greatest chocolate cakes of all, with its layers of gooey fudge icing and delicate sponge. Tall and dramatic, decorate it with lots of equally tall thin candles and whatever chocolate frills capture your imagination.

## For the cake
cocoa powder – 75g
boiling water – 200ml
bicarbonate of soda – ¾ teaspoon
unsalted butter or oil, for greasing
medium eggs – 4
light muscovado sugar – 370g
groundnut oil – 180ml
self-raising flour – 200g, sifted
chocolate frills, to decorate
(optional)

## For the fudge icing
milk chocolate – 250g, broken into pieces
unsalted butter – 40g, diced
cocoa powder – 60g, sifted
whole milk – 120ml
runny honey – 2 tablespoons

you will need 2 round cake tins with removable bases, 20cm in diameter and approx. 5cm deep

### Make the cocoa solution and prepare the tins
Whisk the **cocoa** with the **boiling water** in a medium-sized bowl using a small whisk, and then whisk in the **bicarbonate of soda**. Set aside to cool for 20 minutes. Preheat the oven to 160°C fan/180°C electric/gas 4. **Butter** or **oil** the cake tins and line with baking paper.

### Prepare the sponges
Whisk together the **eggs**, **sugar** and **oil** in a large bowl until smooth – you can use an electric whisk if any stubborn lumps remain. Stir in the **flour**, and then the cocoa solution. Pour one-third of the mixture into one tin and two-thirds into the other tin – you can weigh them for accuracy. Make sure the mixture is evenly spread and give each tin a sharp tap on the worksurface to bring up any air bubbles. Bake the small cake for 30 minutes and the deeper one for 45–50 minutes, or until risen and firm and a skewer inserted into the centre comes out clean. Run a knife around the edge of the cakes and leave to cool.

### Make the icing *
Gently melt the **chocolate** and **butter** in a large bowl set over a pan with a little simmering water in it, stirring until smooth. Meanwhile combine the **cocoa**, **milk** and **honey** in a small saucepan and heat almost to boiling point, giving it a whisk using a magic whisk. Pass the hot cocoa milk through a sieve into the bowl with the melted chocolate in it and whisk to a thick, glossy icing.

### Decorate the cake
Remove the larger cake from the base, peel off the paper and slice into two equal layers using a bread knife. Place the lower half on a cake stand or plate, and spread with a quarter of the icing. Remove the paper from the smaller cake, lay this on top of the base and spread with another quarter of the icing. Lay the top layer in place, cut-side down, and smooth the remaining icing over the surface, taking it up to the sides and leaving it to drip down. Decorate with **chocolate frills** if you wish. Set aside for a couple of hours for the icing to set. The cake will keep well in a covered container for several days.

### The knack
* **The fudge icing sets quickly** so use straight away. If for any reason it starts to appear oily, simply rewhisk over simmering water with 1–2 teaspoons water.

# What to Eat When?

# Barbecuing Advice

Many of the recipes in the book can also be cooked on a barbecue (see list, below). The limit for grilling over fierce coals without burning is about 20 minutes, so quick-cooking cuts (off the bone) promise the best results. More often than not, you will be grilling over hot coals, which doesn't allow time for the inside to cook through without charring the exterior. Cuts that are delicate enough to cook through quickly, or that benefit from being eaten medium-rare are ideal. You can always take a rolling pin to them to reduce their thickness. When cooking bangers, I find slitting and opening them out is a good ruse.

## BARBECUING TIPS
### Kettle barbecues
These come with a lid, which not only reduces flare-ups, but also creates an oven so the food cooks through on the inside at the same time as charring on the outside. The lid also acts as an insurance against that untimely shower of rain or gust of wind.

### Barbecue coal
Buy untreated briquettes for best results. Build a pyramid of these on the barbecue grid, with a few firelighters around the bottom. Once they are dusted in white ash, you can spread them out.

### Firelighters
Make sure that they are intended for barbecues to avoid tainting the food.

### Preheating time
Always give your coals longer than the packet suggests. For example, if the instructions say 20 minutes, give them 40. Make sure that you wait until the coals are properly coated in a fine dusting of grey ash, moving them around if necessary, before you start grilling. And beware that leftover half-full bag from last year on the first barbecue of the season. It is guaranteed to be damp.

### Safety
Failing a lid, keep a water spray to hand to put out any flames. A really long spatula will save on feeling the heat as you tend the grill.

### Cooking tips
By pressing down on the food you will encourage those lovely golden stripes that we so covet. Otherwise, just think of a barbecue in terms of a very hot outdoor griddle, and the cooking times will be much the same. If you are grilling your food in batches, you can always keep it warm in a low oven (60°C fan).

## Barbecuing Ideas

# Stockists

**www.zwilling.co.uk**
My swear-by source for pots and pans. I cannot imagine life without Staub's cast iron, their oval *cocotte*, their baking and roasting dishes (the oval ones stack), and their griddles. All of these will last a lifetime, as will Zwilling's saucepans. The Twin Classic is a great entry-level brand, but if you want to push the boat out then Demeyere saucepans are exemplary.

**www.nisbets.co.uk**
This online trade supplier has a massive range of professional quality cookware. Their own-brand non-stick Vogue is the best value, as well as the most durable – a 24cm frying pan and a 16–18cm saucepan are must-haves. Also great for REX potato peelers, tea-towels, wooden spoons, everything basically.

**www.lakeland.co.uk**
Brilliant for user-friendly kitchenware that is always up with the latest trends and innovations. Their own-brand non-stick pans and bakeware are excellent.

**www.inthehaus.co.uk**
A set of good knives is another essential investment. I have only ever used Wusthof's Classic riveted knives, which are as timelessly beautiful as they are functional. I carry these around with me if I am likely to be cooking in an unfamiliar kitchen.

**www.typhoonhousewares.com**
For a great range of woks with lids, including ones with wooden handles.

**www.masoncash.co.uk**
I have stacks of these pudding bowls in different sizes that I use for everything from measuring and mixing to storage too.

**www.leparfait.co.uk**
These classic clip-top jars are indispensable for storing all manner of things from granola and chutney to teabags.

**www.thermapen.co.uk**
The best digital meat thermometer for measuring the internal temperature of meat.

**www.salterhousewares.com**
For digital timers.

**www.brabantia.com**
For electronic scales, kitchen bins and lasting cookware solutions. Their lightweight steel mixing bowls with rubber bases are brilliant.

**www.divertimenti.co.uk**
For iconic cooking and tableware, including Peugeot peppermills and Pillivuyt white china gratin dishes and ramekins. A good place to go when you can't find something anywhere else.

**www.magimix.uk**
Their food processor, blender and Nespresso machine are all permanent fixtures on my kitchen counter.

**www.seasonedpioneers.co.uk**
I buy all my spices from this online specialist that roasts, grinds and blends in-house. Fab range of mixes as well as the less usual spices.

**www.amazon.co.uk**
Stockists of the Rosle Food Mill, which makes for the silkiest mashed potato.

**www.weber.com**
Stockists of kettle barbecues in different sizes. The bijoux travelling size is good for 2–4 people, while larger barbecues are great for parties.

# Buying Tips

### Cast iron v. Stainless Steel

Cast iron cooks with an even, nurturing heat, which spreads slowly throughout the material. The perfect choice for casseroles and *cocottes*, griddles and roasting dishes, where stainless steel (a rapid conductor of heat) would burn.

However, cast iron makes for a very heavy saucepan that takes an age to heat up; equally it takes an age to cool down, should you need to adjust the temperature on the hob. So the ideal here is a cutting-edge stainless-steel pan that has been manufactured with multiple layers, including an aluminium core (an excellent conductor of heat). Bottom of the range pans lack an aluminium core, resulting in hot spots that burn the food; the same applies to lightweight enamel saucepans. If you want to buy into retro enamel cookware, pie dishes are the items to go for.

The more you use cast iron the better it gets, acquiring non-stick properties as it becomes seasoned with life. Try not to bung it in the dishwasher, which will only strip this patina off. And if you do, rub a little vegetable oil over it afterwards, to reseal the surface and prevent it from rusting.

### Non-stick

Non-stick is one of the last areas of kitchen equipment that remains to be cracked. The black plastic coating invariably wears off, scratches or discolours with time, shedding its non-stick property. Top of the range non-stick pans can be an expensive choice, so my suggestion would be to buy cheaper non-stick pans more frequently; mine rarely last longer than a year with regular use. Nisbets' Vogue pans come highly recommended (see left). The newer ranges of ceramic non-stick pans are a joy, although these too become less efficient with time, but they do have the added advantage of being environment friendly and better for our health. And they can be used as a standard pan even once their non-stick properties diminish.

As with cast iron, I would avoid the dishwasher for any non-stick pans, even if the packaging states that they are dishwasher friendly.

### Table Friendly

All of the cast ironware I have recommended will do you proud on the table and double as a serving dish, whatever the occasion. If it is a family supper, then I extend that to the wok, the saucepans and frying pan. I love the relaxed informality of dishing food up from the pan it cooked in. It also means less washing up, and keeps the food hot until you are ready for a second helping. So it's win-win.

# Index

*For Louis*

## Acknowledgements

This book has been instilled with a sense of passion from the word go on the part of everyone involved, and it has been a real pleasure to be part of the hugely talented team, who have worked to bring it together. Firstly, thank you Kyle, for your experience and judgement and seeing the potential in the book in the first place. It is ever comforting to know you are there in the background. To Catherine Ward, your attention to detail and ability to see order among chaos is second to none. I will miss our ten-daily email exchange.

To Matt Cox, our designer, quite simply, you are brilliant. You considered every single, tiny detail, and every suggestion was in perfect keeping with the material. To the lovely Nassima Rothacker, our photographer, for infusing the pictures with your style, and always wearing a smile (even during power cuts). And Katrina Alexander her assistant, for her 'keep calm and have another cup of tea' resolution to such problems. To the food stylist Nicole Herft, your assured command meant we could all relax, and I want to eat everything you cook. Thanks also to Rukmini Iyer. And to Polly Webb-Wilson, for her stylish ability in selecting the perfect background and the pan to go with it.

Helping the book take shape as it progressed, enormous thanks go to the teenage panel of tasters and testers: Louis Bell, Alice, Anna and Ben Ward, Jac, Cellan, Llŷr and Ifan Cox, Toby Clyde, Charlie Clifford and Hugo Rimmer. Also Finn and Milo Endres, and my sounding boards the Hinton sisters, Chloe and Lucy, and Jasmine Endres.

To my agent Lizzy Kremer, as ever, thank you for your wisdom and friendship. And many thanks to Angela Mason, Associate Editor of *YOU Magazine* in the *Mail on Sunday*, for her support over many years.

And for being there throughout, my husband Jonnie, and sons Louis and Rothko, with love.

First published in Great Britain in 2015 by Kyle Books, an imprint of Kyle Cathie Limited, 192–198 Vauxhall Bridge Road, London SW1V 1DX

general.enquiries@kylebooks.com
www.kylebooks.com

10 9 8 7 6 5 4 3 2 1

ISBN: 978 0 85783 242 9

A CIP catalogue record for this title is available from the British Library.

Editor: Catherine Ward
Editorial Assistant: Claire Rogers
Design: Matt Cox at Newman+Eastwood
Photography: Nassima Rothacker
Food styling: Nicole Herft & Rukmini Iyer
Props styling: Polly Webb-Wilson

Production: Nic Jones & Gemma John

Colour reproduction by ALTA London

Printed and bound in China by C&C Offset Printing Co., Ltd.